D0918060

The Secret
War Diaries
of
Abraham Lincoln

Including His Recurring Dreams

Volume Four of Four Volumes

January 1, 1864 to April 15, 1865

By Paul R. Dunn

*Cover Photos: The Abraham Lincoln Presidential Library & Museum
Springfield, Illinois.
ISBN: 978-0-9991567-5-9*

Copyright @ 2020 by Paul R. Dunn

*All rights reserved. No part of this book may be used or reproduced in any manner
whatsoever without the written permission from the publisher except in the case of
brief direct quotations embodied in critical articles or reviews. For information address: Paul R. Dunn*
*125 Lake Shore Drive, Pinehurst, North Carolina, 28374. Paulandbj@nc.rr.com
Printed in the United States of America.*

Dedication

To my children: Claudia, David, Susan, Eileen, Kevin, Jeannette, Matthew, Patrick, Timothy and Beth. They are a constant source of pride and pleasure.

GIVEN MEMORIAL LIBRARY
.50 Cherokee Rd PO Box 159
Pinehurst, NC 28370
910-295-6022

Introduction to Volume IV

The Secret War Diaries of Abraham Lincoln - Including His Recurring Dreams

This is the final book of a four-volume work. It begins on New Year's Day, 1864, and continues to April 15, 1865, the day following the assassination of the president. It provides fictional diary entries; President Lincoln never kept a diary. Each entry, usually written at night, is based upon documented chronological records. Author's notes inform the reader of historic events and the people referred to on the date's entry.

The dreams of Lincoln that are described are fictional but are based upon actual happenings in his life. There are some days in which no entries are made due to the exigencies of the period. Generally, Lincoln makes no entries on Sundays or when he is traveling from Washington. Except for illnesses, Lincoln worked seven days a week, every week throughout the Civil War. He even held Cabinet meetings or attended to public business on Easter and Christmas.

The purpose of the war diaries is to give the reader insights into the inner workings of the president's mind. They present the day by day doings of Lincoln, and endeavor to show how the 16th president of the United States might have reacted to the people and challenging events swirling around him and his family during the Civil War. Almost every battle on land and sea is described. His re-election campaign and victory at the polls is also covered.

Volume IV reveals a tired president determined to win the war while simultaneously making plans for the ultimate reunion of the nation and reconstruction. His goal was to act "with malice towards none; with charity for all, with firmness in the right as God gives us to see the right."

Paul R. Dunn

The White House – Friday, January 1, 1864

Today Mother and I hosted the annual New Year's Day reception at the White House. The crowd was larger than usual, and a genuine spirit of optimism was in the air. A year ago, ultimate victory was much in doubt; today the feelings of those I spoke to is of the inevitable triumph of our arms over those in secession. I met with the diplomatic corps at a little after 10 A.M. Mary appeared at 11:30 to join me in welcoming the officers of the Army and Navy. The public reception began at noon. It was a well-behaved and well-dressed gathering. Mother particularly enjoyed speaking with the French ambassador in his own tongue. I received four Negroes who stood in line to visit the White House. They thanked me for my policies related to the enlistment of colored soldiers and sailors and expressed the wish that when hostilities end their race will be granted the right to vote.

Author's notes:

Lincoln had written to General James S. Wadsworth in early January of 1864, "How to better the condition of the colored race has long been a study which has attracted my serious and careful attention; hence I think I am clear and decided what course I shall pursue in the premises, regarding it a religious duty, as the nation's guardian of these people, who have heroically vindicated their manhood on the battle-field, where in assisting to save the life of the Republic, they have demonstrated in blood their right to the ballot, which is but the humane protection of the flag they have so fearlessly defended. The restoration of the Rebel States must rest upon the principle of civil and political equality of both races, and it must be sealed by general amnesty."

General Wadsworth was shot through the head on the second day of the Wilderness Battle in early May of 1864. George Washington Templeton Strong wrote in his diary, "We have lost a brave and useful man, but this is just the death Wadsworth would have ordered of the destinies had they consulted him on the subject."

The White House – Saturday, January 2, 1864

Last night I dreamed that I was back in New Salem in 1831. I was 22 years old. At the time I must have weighed about 214 pounds and reached six foot four in height. I had wrestled several of the town's stronger men and been the winner. After I had defeated the best of the lot, a very competitive man by the name of Jack Armstrong, I soon found that I had few challengers. Jack and his wife, Hannah, were especially kind to me, and we became lifelong friends. I have always attributed my unusual strength to the fact that my arms are longer than the average man of my weight. Because they are longer, I was always able to have a greater swing and thus acquire more force and momentum than the arms of the ordinary man. I could usually throw a weight farther and lift a heavier weight than others. I once threw a cannon ball at least 20 feet farther than anyone who tried to match me. Some of that strength must be attributed to the great number of trees I felled as a boy. I can still hold an axe straight away from my body in one hand longer than most people. Lately I have dreamed about my New Salem days more often. Those were among the happiest times of my life.

This evening I visited the theatre. Mother and I occupied the box of Colonel James D. Greene. She plans to go with Tad to Philadelphia on the 5th of the month. She will be staying at the Continental Hotel there.

Author's notes:

On May 7, 1833, Lincoln was commissioned postmaster of New Salem, the first office he ever held under the federal government. The mail arrived once a week. He made his headquarters in Samuel Hill's store. Hill had been the postmaster before Lincoln. Lincoln derived income from the post office and from land surveys.

The White House – Monday, January 4, 1864

After dinner last evening, John T. Hall of Albany, New York, visited with me to discuss the inevitable appointment of a Supreme Court justice once the aged Justice Robert Brooke Taney dies in office. Taney has been on the bench forever. He was appointed by Andrew Jackson in 1836. Some thought he might resign when the Civil War began because he is a slave holder, but he elected to stay where he is. At that time Associate Justice Archibald Campbell did resign to join the Confederacy. Taney believed that the Southern states had the right to secede. Last year he was in the minority when he dissented and held in the Prize Cases that I had overstepped my authority by ordering a blockade without the express consent of Congress. In Ex Parte Merryman he held that I could not suspend the writ of Habeas Corpus.

I directed Hay to go to Point Lookout, Maryland, with blank forms to provide to General Butler for the purpose of recording the discharge of prisoners who take the oath of December 8, 1863. These are men who offer to enlist in our services. They will be discharged and allowed to return to their homes within our military lines.

Author's notes:

Justice Taney sympathized with the seceding Southern states but did not resign from the Supreme Court. He strongly disagreed with President Lincoln's more broad interpretation of executive power. His Dred Scott ruling is widely considered to be one of the worst Supreme Court rulings ever made. Taney died on October 12, 1864. He was succeeded by Salmon P. Chase.

The White House – Tuesday, January 5, 1864

So far this week I have suspended the execution of 10 men. They will better serve their country alive than dead. I also wrote to Henry Blow thanking him for the picture of me made by the artist John Schaerp, which he had recently delivered to the White House. It is a very good likeness. I was named an honorary officer of the Ladies Great National Sanitary Fair soon to be held in Washington, D.C. The fairs are raising lots of money, which goes to help our wounded soldiers and sailors.

I was pleased to learn from the War Department that in October, November and December 45,529 men voluntarily enlisted in the Army and that the daily number of enlistments is increasing. The paying of bonuses is working better than expected. The people of the country prefer bonuses as incentives to a draft system.

Author's notes:

The Civil War sanitary fairs represented one of the most successful democratic, humanitarian and philanthropic efforts in American history. The fairs raised millions of dollars for the medical and humanitarian care of Union military and naval personnel. It provided a way for civilians to contribute time, energy and money to show their support for the Union cause. The U.S. Sanitary Commission, the agency for whom the benefits were held, improved civilian morale and provided medical care for a predominantly volunteer Army and Navy.

The White House – Wednesday, January 6, 1864

I sent congratulations to Dom Luiz I, king of Portugal, on the birth of Prince Carlos Fernando. A letter was also sent giving greetings to Christian IX, king of Denmark, upon the demise of King Frederick VII and of his succession to the throne. King Frederick was a good friend of the United States. Secretary Seward and our State Department representatives have maintained excellent relations with these, as well as the major powers of Europe. None have seen fit to recognize the Confederacy. Let us hope that continues to be the case. The federal victories at Gettysburg and Vicksburg sent strong signals to European nations that the United States is winning this dreadful war, and that support for the Confederacy will only act to prolong the conflict.

Mr. A. Kidder of Chicago kindly sent me 50 engraved copies of the Emancipation Proclamation. I have not decided what to do with them. Perhaps I will give them to some members of Congress and to all of my Cabinet members. It is a handsome printing. I think I may order more copies so I can give one to every member of the House and the Senate.

Author's notes:

In the 38th Congress there were 52 senators, 184 members of the House of Representatives and 10 non-voting delegates.

The White House – Thursday, January 7, 1864

I stayed at the telegraph office in the War Department until the wee hours of the morning seeking news from various fronts. Last night there were three operators on duty at the time, Thomas Eckert, Charles Tinker and Albert Chandler. The fastest operator is Albert Chandler, a 23-year-old, who hails from Randolph, Vermont. I admire his skill at recording and decoding the messages based upon dots and dashes arriving at breakneck speed. The fastest operator in the entire system is S.H. Beckwith, one of General Grant's operators.

The operators' methods are to write out the received message in longhand, using a piece of carbon paper. The originals are dispatched to the appropriate offices and the carbon filed in a drawer in the order they arrive. I usually read the messages from the top down, in reverse chronological order. The office is in the War Department's former library, just a block from the White House. Lately, I have been accompanied by an armed guard when I visit because there have been threats made of assassinating me. I used to always come alone, but now I have company on my walks to and from the office.

Because of the telegraph I can now send to the appropriate commanding officer notices to halt executions rather than rely upon slow mail delivery. Because replies acknowledging compliance can be sent back to me within just minutes, in most cases, I can rest assured that a man condemned to death has been saved from it. I believe that I send more messages dealing with the appeal of military court-martial decisions than any other specific topic by far. Because the enemy can easily tap into the wires and intercept our messages, they must be sent and received in code. This slows the system down, but the code requirement is necessary to assure secure delivery.

Author's notes:

Albert Brown Chandler kept a journal during the Civil War. A collection of his wartime experiences (minus a particularly valuable 1863 volume, which has been lost) sold at auction in 2012 for $15,000. Chandler became a prosperous telegraph executive who amassed a sizeable fortune. He donated the Chandler Music Hall, a location known for its superior acoustics to his hometown of Randolph, Vermont.

Chandler learned to operate a telegraph as a teenager. He became an operator for Western Union in 1858 in Bellaire, Ohio. He began work for the U.S Military Telegraph Corps in 1863. He developed ciphers for transmitting secret communications and served as a telegrapher for President Lincoln and Secretary of War Stanton. After the war he returned to Western Union, where he oversaw the completing of new cables for operating trans-Atlantic telegraph service, and for service between the United States and Cuba. In 1875 he became general manager of the Atlantic and Pacific Telegraph Company. In 1885 he joined the Postal Telegraph Company, Western Union's chief competitor. In the 1896 National Electrical Exposition in New York City, he transmitted the first around-the-world telegram. It traveled 16,000 miles on cable owned by Postal Telegraph Company and was received and transcribed by Thomas A. Edison four minutes after it had been sent.

The White House – Saturday, January 9, 1864

Yesterday Secretaries Seward and Welles presented members of the National Academy of Science to me. The organization was signed into being last year. It it to investigate, examine and experiment, and report upon any subject of science or art whenever called upon to do so by any department of the government. Joseph Henry of the Academy has proposed to the Navy the formation of an advisory agency for the testing of new weapons. I have suggested to Welles that we implement the plans soon as possible. Welles plans to ask the Academy to study wind and current charts and to consider ways that the bottoms of new iron-hulled ships can be protected from corrosion and other damage from saltwater. Salmon Chase has already asked for a study on the uniformity of weights, measures and coins related to domestic and international commerce.

Mother's reception at the White House was well-attended today. It ran from 1 to 3 P.M. Several wives of Cabinet members attended. She wore a new blue gown made for her in Philadelphia. I wrote a letter to 83-year-old Mrs. Esther Stockton of Pittsburgh, the widow of Reverend Joseph Stockton, thanking her for knitting some 300 hundred pairs of stocking for our troops. Mother showed the stockings to her guests and suggested that they might wish to emulate the good works of Mrs. Stockton.

At 4 P.M. Secretary of the Navy Gideon Welles and I interviewed Captain William Lavender, a sea captain from New York. He has developed a contrivance for discovering and removing underwater obstructions. He is an interesting man and an inventor who believes his device can save lives. Welles will ask the Navy Yard staff to take a good look at it.

Author's notes:

Fifty years after the Academy of Science's work came to an end, the Navy Department was still investigating various types of ship's paints in order to come up with the most protective composition.

The White House – Monday, January 11, 1864

Yesterday, after returning home from church, I consulted with Navy Secretary Gideon Welles, Postmaster Francis P. Blair Sr. and former Governor William Dennison of Ohio regarding the upcoming presidential election campaign. Blair noted that there has not been an incumbent candidate re-elected since Andrew Jackson beat Henry Clay in 1862. This will be the first time in American history that the country will vote while a civil war is being waged. It did hold an election during the War of 1812. It will be important to the nation that men in military and naval service are provided practical means to have access to the ballot. Kansas, Nevada and West Virginia will be voting for the first time during this election cycle. My fear is that any significant military defeats this year may significantly affect the election results. Welles pointed out that there is a war weariness in the land. As Dennison noted, the election will be a test of our war policies and war management. I fully agree.

I directed General Hitchcock to offer Confederate General Isaac Trimble, now a prisoner of war in Fort McHenry, in exchange for Major Harry White, now a prisoner in Richmond.

Author's notes:

When all the votes were counted, Abraham Lincoln received 212 electoral votes and George B. McClellan received 21 votes. Lincoln won by over 400,000 popular votes. Several states allowed citizens serving as soldiers in the field to cast ballots, a first in United States history. Soldiers gave Lincoln 70 percent of the vote. None of the states loyal to the Confederacy participated.

The White House – Tuesday, January 12, 1864

Mother and I attended a lecture at the First Presbyterian Church given by noted temperance orator John Bartholomew Gough. Gough is a powerful speaker who has addressed thousands of audiences on behalf of temperance reform. He has spoken in Great Britain, including talks given at Oxford. His oratory was not acquired but is natural and compelling. He admits to having no elocutionary training. After his lecture Mary and I met with him and invited him to come to the White House for her next reception.

I established the western base of the Sierra Nevada Mountains relative to the construction of the Central Pacific Railroad. Under the Act approved July 1, 1862, the railroad will receive sixteen $1,000 U.S. bonds per mile and treble this number of bonds per mile for the portion most mountainous and difficult of construction, to wit: one hundred and fifty miles westward from the eastern base of the Rocky Mountains, and 150 miles eastward from the western base of the Sierra Nevada Mountains, said point to be fixed by me.

I advised the Senate that no Kansas troops were being "invariably put to death by Confederate troops when captured by them," as wrongly claimed by Senator James H. Lane in a resolution of December 16, 1863.

Author's notes:

The president devoted salary warrants, August through October and December1863 to purchase $8,000 in Treasury notes.

John Bartholomew Gough was born in Sandgate, Kent, England, on August 22,1817. He died at his work, being stricken with apoplexy on the lecture platform in the First Presbyterian Church of Frankford, Philadelphia, where he died two days later February 18, 1886.

The White House – Thursday, January 14, 1864

I ordered Major Theodore Laidley to test the Absterdam projectile as soon as possible and report his findings to the secretary of war. I feel this weapon shows great promise, but nothing will ever happen unless the wheels start turning much faster than they have to date. Government inertia when it comes to weapon-testing is infamous. I trust Laidley will get results and be the exception to the rule. John Hay has been appointed assistant adjutant general and ordered to Florida to aid General Gilmore in reconstructing local government there. I have written to General Banks to proceed with all possible dispatch to construct a free state government in Louisiana. I signed the act authorizing the payment of enlistment bonuses to March 1, 1864.

Author's notes:

For seven weeks in 1863 Hay traveled with Hunter's Army as it made its way down the South Carolina and Florida coastline. He held the honorary rank of colonel and wrote glowing letters to Nicolay describing the warm weather and beautiful sunsets. He visited freedmen's schools that were staffed principally by white abolitionists from the North. On April 27, 1864, he recorded, "Miss Harris and Miss Smith, white abolitionists from Massachusetts and New Hampshire, respectively are "in charge of the light mulatto girls and white children. All singing together. The words to one popular song were:

Say my brother ain't you ready

Get ready to go home

For I hear the word of promise

At de breaking of the day

I'll take de wings of de morning

And fly away to Jesus

I'll take de wing of de morning

And sound de jubilee.

By the end of his Southern tour he became an ardent supporter of the cause of black enlistments in the Army. He realized that freed slaves were highly motivated to fight. Hay returned to Washington in June. The following year he again visited Florida, this time as a major in the Army. He reported to General Quincy Gilmore, commander of the Department of the South. His job was to secure the allegiance of vanquished Confederates in Florida.

The White House – Friday, January 15, 1864

I sent two requested autographed photographs to Bishop Charles P. McIlvaine, who had kindly sent Mother and me a warm New Year's greetings. I have invited him to come to Mary's next reception at the White House. I expressed my appreciation for the number of Catholic chaplains now in the Army. He informed me that a great many have been killed while serving with the men. I thanked him for their sacrifices.

I met with Kentucky Congressman Brutus J. Clay and Mrs. Jane Haggard, who asked that her 19-year-old son, Edward Haggard, now confined in a prisoner of war camp at Camp Douglas, be discharged. I ordered that he take the oath and be released, and that the same be done for William H. Moore, another Rebel prisoner being held at the camp.

I showed Mary and Tad a collection of beautiful photographs sent to me by Edward and Henry T. Anthony. They came to me yesterday courtesy of House Speaker Schuyler Colfax. The Anthony brothers are manufacturers of photographs and stereoscopes of scenes from New York of bridges, lakes and scenic landscapes, including New York's Central Park.

Author's notes:

During the Civil War, 117 Union chaplains and 41 Confederate chaplains were killed in battle.

The White House – Saturday, January 16, 1864

Secretary Seward came by after lunch and brought with him Waldemar R. de Raasloff, the Danish minister to the United States, who speaks English with almost no accent. His family have been in the diplomatic service of his country for several generations. He was complimentary in his views of the Emancipation Proclamation and said that it is being described in flattering terms in Europe right now. He believes that because the Confederacy is committed to slavery it will never gain recognition among the great powers in Europe. He presented me with a large wheel of Danish cheese, which I look forward to sampling tonight.

Mrs. Lincoln and I attended a lecture by Anna Elizabeth Dickinson. Later Miss Dickinson came to a reception at the White House, where she was warmly received by our guests. Dickinson has given lectures to large audiences all over the country. She has toured the country in support of aid for the Sanitary Commission. She speaks about abolition, reconstruction, women's rights and temperance. She now visits hospitals and camps speaking to our troops. In New England she has spoken of Army hospital life to large audiences. Mother was thrilled to meet her and hear what she had to say.

Author's notes:

In 1863 U.S. Senate elections, Anna Dickinson campaigned for several pro-Union Republican candidates in New York, Pennsylvania, New Hampshire and Connecticut to audiences that included people who did not support the war. She spoke in support of radical Republicans' anti-slavery platform and for the preservation of the Union. She was called the Civil War's "Joan of Arc" for her promotion of the Union. When she spoke at Cooper Institute more than 5,000 people attended. In 1864 she addressed the U.S. House of Representatives, the first woman to do so. Lincoln and military leaders were in attendance. Mark Twain, in a April 5, 1867, letter to the San Francisco Alta California wrote, "She talks fast, uses no notes whatever, never hesitates for a word, always gets the right word in the right place and has the most perfect confidence in herself."

The White House – Monday, January 18, 1864

I wired Governor Thomas Bramlette of Kentucky that General Grant was fully aware of orders I had issued directly to General Foster in moving troops from Kentucky to Knoxville, Tennessee. I informed him that the troops are in strict law only to be removed by my order; but General Grant's judgment would be the highest incentive to me to make such an order. I instructed the Judge advocate general that A.Z. Boyer, sentenced to be hung as a spy, is pardoned and to be discharged from the Army after he takes the oath. I also ordered that Charles Thomas Hagan, a prisoner at Camp Chase may also be given the oath and discharged. This was done at the specific request of Hon. Aaron Harding of Kentucky.

I met with two ladies whose sons have been in prison for resisting the draft in Pennsylvania. I was shown a list of all the men so held by Hay. I told the ladies that I believed both men had suffered long enough and that they and all the other men on the list should be freed. I said let's turn out the whole flock. The older woman ran up to me and kneeled before me. I ordered her to get up but said, "Thank God" and go. She was in tears. She said, Good-bye, Mr. Lincoln, I shall never see you again till we meet in heaven. She held my hand in hers and I was very deeply moved. I said to her, "I am afraid with all my troubles I shall never get to the resting place you speak of; but if I do, I am sure I will find you. That you wish me to get there is, I believe the best wish you could make for me." I then wished her and her friend good-bye. They had traveled all the way from Harrisburg to see me.

Author's notes:

On this date Lincoln interviewed Private John P.M. Thornton, Company E, 61st New York Volunteers and granted him a pardon if he returned to his regiment.

The White House – Tuesday, January 19, 1864

I telegraphed son Robert, informing him that there is still a good deal of smallpox in Washington, and that he may wish to delay his visit. He had planned to come down from Harvard with some friends for a brief stay. Mother is anxious to see him but fears greatly for his well-being. The Cabinet again discussed the annoying issue of the admission of cotton into Union lines. Before dinner I discussed with former congressman and now consul general to British North American Provinces Joshua R. Giddings his strong wish that his son, Major Grotius R. Giddings, be named a brigadier general. My sense is that a move up to colonel is more appropriate. Joshua has been a stalwart supporter of mine since he was one of the founders of the Republican Party. I like and trust him. He is not looking well, and I hope he will soon be feeling better.

Author's notes:

Most Americans were not inoculated against smallpox in the 19th century. The origin of the disease is unknown. Earliest evidence of the disease dates to the third century in Egyptian mummies. Edward Jenner discovered in 1798 that vaccination could prevent smallpox. The last naturally occurring case was diagnosed in 1977, and the World Health Organization certified the global eradication of the disease in 1980.

The White House – Thursday, January 21, 1864

Yesterday I sent a report from the secretary of state to the Senate reporting on the actions of American citizens, who in Santiago, Chile aided people to evacuate a deadly fire that broke out in the Church of Compañia, a large cathedral in that city. Over 2,500 persons reportedly lost their lives in this tragedy, according to information provided by Thomas H. Nelson, our minister to Chile.

This evening Mother and I hosted a state dinner for members of the Cabinet and the justices of the Supreme Court. Chief Justice Taney sat next to Mary. He seemed to be enjoying himself. He looks frail but she told me that his mind seems as sharp as ever. He has been on the bench since March of 1836. He is a tough old bird as my father might say. His unfortunate decision in the Dred Scott case back in 1857, which denied to Congress or any territorial government the power to exclude slavery, on that grounds that such exclusion would violate the slave owner's right to process under the Fifth Amendment, did much to bring about the Civil War. It inflamed the abolitionists when he ruled for the majority that no slave or descendant of a slave had any rights which the white man was bound to respect. His opinion had an incendiary effect on the tinderbox nation of that day. It repudiated the Missouri Compromise as an overreach of congressional power. It disallowed the prohibition of slavery by any territorial legislature popularly elected or not. I spoke out against his decision in my House Divided speech on June 16, 1858. We disagree totally, but tonight I shook his hand, giving him the respect due the chief justice of the land.

Author's notes:

Chief Justice Roger Taney died on October 12, 1864. Lincoln appointed Secretary of the Treasury Salmon Chase to be chief justice of the Supreme Court on December 15, 1864.

The White House – Friday, January 22, 1864

House Speak Schuyler Colfax of Indiana and Samuel Sinclair of the New York Tribune spent time with me this morning discussing the possibility of having a prominent painter do a rendering of the first reading of the Emancipation Proclamation. The painter's name is Francis Bicknell Carpenter. He has painted portraits of Millard Fillmore, who is a fellow upstate New Yorker, and also of Franklin Pierce, John Tyler, Henry Ward Beecher, Horace Greely, Ezra Cornell, James Russell Lowell and John C. Fremont. Frederick Lane, a wealthy friend of Colfax has offered to pay for the commission, which will take several months to execute. According to Colfax, Carpenter will pose me and all the Cabinet members for the scene. I will ask the Cabinet members if they are willing to cooperate and if so, I'll write to Carpenter and invite him to come to Washington.

Author's notes:

Francis Bicknell Carpenter met with Lincoln on February 6, 1864 and spent six months at the White House painting the president and his cabinet. The State Dining Room was given to the artist for a studio. He began with many sketches of the president and photographs of the president and Cabinet taken by Mathew Brady. On July 12, 1864, Lincoln led his Cabinet into the State Dining Room to view the completed work. William Stoddard, Lincoln's private secretary campaigned for Congress to purchase the painting, but it did not appropriate the money. The painting remained in the artist's possession until 1877, when he arranged for Elizabeth Thompson to purchase it for $25,000 and donate it to Congress. A joint session of Congress was held in 1878 on Lincoln's birthday, to serve as a reception for the painting with the artist present.

The White House – Saturday, January 23, 1864

Several staff officers and General Halleck reviewed with the Cabinet this morning the battle fought in Jefferson County, Tennessee, at a place called Dandridge, on the 16th and 17th of the month. In this action involving the Army of the Ohio, under General Samuel Sturgis and General John G. Parke, and Confederate Department of East Tennessee forces under General James Longstreet, we were not successful. Union cavalry could not dislodge Confederate troops and were compelled to withdraw on the 16th. On the 17th the battle began at 4 P.M. and continued until after dark. Our men retreated to New Market and Strawberry Plains during the night. Due to a lack of cannons, ammunition and shoes the enemy broke off and fell back to Dandridge while our forces left the area. I concluded one thing: The fact that our foe is sending men into battle in the bitter cold of winter without shoes or socks tells me he is in bad shape.

I wrote to Alpheus Lewis, Esq., a cotton trader regarding cases where owners of plantations in Arkansas might recognize the freedom of slaves and hire them to cultivate the land. I told him that I would recognize freedom of slaves and hire them to farm the land where possible. I would treat them precisely as I would treat the same number of free white people in the same relation and condition. Whether black or white they deserve government protection. I told him that the U.S. government favors to advance freedom, restore peace and prosperity, and such hiring and employment of the freed people would be regarded by me with rather special favor.

Mrs. Lincoln's reception this afternoon was attended by an immense throng of citizens and sojourners. She does these events with great style and warmth. I am very proud of her.

Author's notes:

On this date President Lincoln transmitted to the Senate papers relative to modification of a treaty with China. He attended a performance of Tom Taylor's "The Ticket of Leave Man," in aid of the Ladies Soldier's Relief Association. The renomination of Lincoln was unanimously recommended by the Union Central Committee of New York.

The White House – Monday, January 25, 1864

Senator Orville Browning, Senator Charles Sumner, Congressman George Ashmun, Generals George Ramsay and Robert Schenck (resigned), Congressmen James Garfield of Ohio, Samuel Hooper of Massachusetts and their wives attended a dinner party last night at the White House. The conversation and the food were excellent. Mother sat next to the Garfields. She told me that she believes he has a bright future in politics. She has a good sense about such things. Our son Robert is home from Harvard college and joined us for dinner. Mother has not wanted him to serve in the Army, but I have asked General Grant to accept him as an assistant adjutant with the rank of captain. He has agreed and Robert will be serving on Grant's staff beginning next month. I think the experience will serve him and the country well.

Author's notes:

Robert Lincoln was present at Appomattox when Lee surrendered to Grant. He resigned his commission on June 12, 1865, and returned to civilian life. Following his father's assassination, in April 1865, Robert Lincoln moved with his mother and Tad Lincoln to Chicago, where he completed his law studies at the Old University of Chicago Law School (now Northwestern University Pritzker School of Law). He was admitted to the bar on February 25, 1867, and certified to practice law in Chicago on February 26, 1867.

The White House – Tuesday, January 26, 1864

This morning Tad asked me if John Brown was a Republican. I told Tad that in my speech in February 1860 at Cooper Union in Manhattan I had said that John Brown was an "Enthusiast but not a Republican." I said that John Brown was a "fanatic who brooded over the oppression of a people he fancies himself commissioned by Heaven to liberate them." Most Southerners believed that John Brown was a portent of things to come. They believed most Northerners approved of his foul and murderous methods. Fervent abolitionists did approve of Brown's vile methods, but as many or more who knew of his murders abhorred them.

Hay and Nicolay estimate that about 8,000 people passed through the White House for a public reception earlier this evening. I believe it is important that the people's house be available to the average citizen; Mother and I are merely tenants living here at their expense.

Author's notes:

Herman Melville's poem published after Lincoln's death, titled "The Portent" from his book of poetry, "Battle Pieces," described John Brown's body swinging from the gallows as foreshadowing doom for the South: "Hanging from the beam/Slowly swaying (such the law)/Gaunt the shadow on your green/Shenandoah!"

The White House – Thursday, January 28, 1864

I reread Washington's Farewell Address today. I consider it an almost sacred document. I was pleased when the House of Representatives decided that it deserves to be read on the first president's birthdate each year. I will suggest to the nation that on his soon-to-be-celebrated birthday of February 22nd that it be occasioned by remembering his unique greatness and by citizens reading his farewell message. It is filled with wisdom, which was not heeded when the South elected to secede from the Union. Washington had warned of this possibility and urged restraint in the dealings between the states over important differences like slavery. Jefferson reported that Washington, a fellow Virginian, insisted that if a civil war broke out in the United States that he had made up his mind "to remove and be of the Northern portion." Washington would never have gone the way of General Robert E. Lee, the son of one of his generals, Henry "Light Horse" Harry Lee. The son joined the South in rebellion. Henry Lee, upon Washington's death in 1799, while serving in the U.S. Congress, delivered his famous eulogy describing George Washington as "first in war, first in peace, first in the hearts of his countrymen."

Author's notes:

When King George III was told by the American-born painter Benjamin West that George Washington planned to retire to his farm after the war, King George said, "If he does that, he will be the greatest man in the world."

The White House – Friday, January 29, 1864

I sent to the Senate today a report notifying the senators that Secretary Seward, on January 21, 1864, has requested to Great Britain that U.S. troops be authorized to pursue Sioux Indians that have fled from the United States into Canada. These are hostile tribes who are now believed to be in the Hudson Bay Territories of Canada. The alternative option is that U.S. troops be used by Canada to restrain the hostile tribes from raiding across the border from Canada back into the United States. Stanton has given Lord Lyons, the British minister in the United States, the proposal to be forwarded by him to London.

General Halleck has provided to the Cabinet a summary of a military action which took place at Athens, Alabama, on January 26th. What makes this battle interesting is that 100 Union soldiers of the 9th Illinois Mounted Infantry Regiment repulsed a cavalry attack by over 600 Rebels on horseback. It is unusual to read of 100 of our boys resisting six times their number and then forcing the enemy to retreat in a two-hour battle in which we fought with no fortifications to protect the men.

I requested General Daniel E. Sickles immediately take a trip for me to Arkansas.

Author's notes:

General Sickles replied, "I can walk without crutches by use of an artificial leg and am anxious for duty. My first wish is to resume command of my Corps – next to that, the command of Washington – but shall be entirely satisfied to undertake any duty which you think I can be most useful to the government, whether in the field or in Washington, Arkansas or elsewhere." Sickles made the trip to Arkansas for Lincoln.

The White House – Saturday, January 30, 1864

Mrs. Lincoln held her usual Saturday afternoon reception today, which was well-attended. I have authorized Bell & Brothers Photographers, 480 Pennsylvania Avenue of this city to make and sell my photograph to benefit the Sanitary Fair.

Secretary Stanton, General Halleck and staff reviewed with me the results of recent battles waged in Sevier County, Tennessee, near the town of Fair Garden, on the 27th and 28th of the month. Cavalry units of the Army of the Ohio under Generals Samuel Sturgis and Colonel Edward McCook defeated Confederate cavalry under General William Martin. Our forces had about 100 casualties and the enemy an estimated 150 or more. According to Halleck, when Sturgis attacked the Rebels on the 38th he found that they were in a strongly fortified position with three infantry regiments on hand to reinforce them. Thus, Sturgis suffered severe casualties in the battle that lasted to dark, when our forces retired from the area. Hay and I prepared the order for the drafting of 500,000 men into the military services to serve for three years.

Author's notes:

The Order for Draft of 500,000 Men reads:
Ordered: February 1st, 1864. That a draft for five hundred thousand men to serve for three years or during the war, be made on the 10th day of March next, for the military service of the United States, crediting and deducting therefrom, so many as may have been enlisted or drafted into the service prior to the first day of March, and not heretofore credited. ABRAHAM LINCOLN

The White House – Monday, February 1, 1864

I directed Secretary Stanton to have a steam or sail transport sent to Ile à Vache, on the coast of San Domingo, to bring back to the United States such of the Negro colonists living there who have indicated that they now wish to return to this country. The transport is to have enough victuals and water and is to have a surgeon on board with a guard of 20 men and a few non-commissioned officers of the Invalid Corps. The colonists are to be brought to Washington and to be taken to camps for colored persons around the city. Only those who wish to return are to be brought from the island and their effects will be taken with them. Although I have for a long time strongly favored the establishment of Negro colonies by former slaves and freed black men and women, my sense of the matter is that this concept has not been and probably will not become popular with many Negroes. They prefer America to foreign lands.

Author's notes:

The ship Maria L. Day was chartered by the Army in the port of New York City and ordered to sail for a voyage to pick up the colonists in Santo Domingo by way of the Windward Passage.

The White House – Tuesday, February 2, 1864

Secretary Seward came by with a letter of sympathy for me to sign and send to Kamehameha V, the new Queen of the Hawaiian Islands, who ascended to the throne upon the death of her brother. I have often thought it would be a marvelous adventure to sail to Hawaii, which has been described as a tropical paradise.

Admiral John Dahlgren's son, Colonel Ulric Dahlgren came by early this morning for a discussion of Army matters. As we spoke, I was being shaved. Ulric entered the service in the Navy and then soon transferred to the Army. He saw action at Bull Run, Fredericksburg, Chancellorsville, Brandy Station and Gettysburg. Wounded on July 6th while on the way to Hagerstown, his foot had to be amputated. He is a remarkably gifted young man. A chip off the old block.

Author's notes:

Colonel Ulric Dahlgren was killed in action on March 2, 1864, near Stevensville, King and Queen County, Virginia while under the command of Brigadier General Hugh Judson Kilpatrick. He was participating in the "Kilpatrick Raid," upon the Confederate capital of Richmond, Virginia. Papers found on his corpse shortly after his death contained orders for the assassination of Confederate President Jefferson Davis. The publication of the papers sparked a controversy in the South and may also have contributed to John Wilkes Booth's decision to assassinate President Lincoln a year later.

The White House – Thursday, February 4, 1864

Yesterday I came home late and was too tired to write in my diary. I visited the Army Arsenal to observe trials of the Absterdam projectile, which were conducted under the supervision of Major Theodore Laidley. It is the Army's viewpoint that more testing will be required before shells can be ordered for use by the Army. I approved the use of government property in Springfield, Illinois, for the construction of a soldiers' home. No government funds are to be used for the purpose. Governor Yates brought this to my attention. The Sanitary Commission has donated $2,000 for the purpose. It is needed and the sooner it can be built the better. The lot is located at Sixth and Monroe Streets. A frame building with lounge and sleeping rooms for furloughed soldiers will be erected.

Today I sent to Edward Everett the manuscript of my remarks at Gettysburg Cemetery for delivery to the Ladies Committee of New York Metropolitan Sanitary Fair.

Author's notes:

The manuscript is in the Everett Papers at the Massachusetts Historical Society. The manuscript address which Lincoln enclosed on February 4th, known as "the Everett Copy," was probably prepared in November 1863, shortly after the ceremony at Gettysburg.

The White House – Friday, February 5, 1864

I received a visit from my close friend Associate Justice David Davis, who brought some young lawyers with him. I told them that it has always been my belief that every man has his peculiar ambitions. I myself at their ages had no other so great as that of being truly esteemed of my fellow men, by doing acts and saying words worthy of their esteem. I felt that way as a young man and continue to feel that way today. When I was their age, I was very uncertain if I would succeed in life by gratifying that ambition. Politics is a difficult road to follow. I told them that whatever I have accomplished in life I attribute greatly to those things I learned from my beloved mother, Nancy Hanks. She was smart, keen with a powerful memory for things. My stepmother, Sarah Bush Johnson, also encouraged me in every possible way. She urged me to read and study. She recognized that I was slow to learn, but that once I learned something, I never forgot it. She told me once that my mind is like a piece of steel. Very hard to scratch anything on it, and almost impossible after you get it there to rub it out. We couldn't afford to buy paper so I learned to write things down on a board and to keep it there until I could find some paper. I kept lots of scrapbooks as a boy and wrote words in them with definitions. I read and reread borrowed books and practiced penmanship so my words would be easily read and understood.

Author's notes:

On this date Lincoln transmitted to the Senate a report from Secretary of State Seward regarding a reciprocity treaty with the Sandwich Islands. He also sent a note to Secretary of War Stanton stating, "On principle I dislike an oath which requires a man to swear he has not done wrong. It rejects the Christian principle of forgiveness on terms of repentance. I think it is enough if the man does no wrong hereafter."

The White House – Saturday, February 6, 1864

I made a sick call upon Congressman Owen Lovejoy, who has been very ill and is not expected to recover. Owen was instrumental in the founding of the Republican Party in Illinois. I told Owen that this war is eating my life out and that I have a strong impression that I may not live to see to the end of it. He is very pale and weak. I fear he is not long for this world.

After lunch I met with the artist Francis B. Carpenter, with whom I discussed his planned painting of the Emancipation Proclamation's first reading. He is a very impressive man and I trust him to execute his assignment with great skill and perception.

Mother's reception today exceeded all that have preceded it. She is a marvelous hostess and quite the diplomat. Always the right word for the right person.

Author's notes:

On this date Lincoln wrote to General Nathaniel Banks, "The bearer, General Gustavus A. Scroggs of Buffalo, has been appointed colonel of a colored regiment, and is to report with it to you at New Orleans for assignment to Texas to collect and organize colored men of that state."

General Scroggs arrived in New Orleans on May 5, 1864, but upon withdrawal of Union troops from Texas, resigned on July 6, 1864.

The White House – Monday, February 8, 1864

I sent telegraph wires to various generals suspending the death sentences of seven soldiers for desertion and myriad other serious offenses. Today, Halleck and Stanton presented to the Cabinet a short report on the recent battle fought at Morton's Ford, Virginia, last week at and around the Rapidan River. It turned out to be a relatively inconclusive affair with casualties numbering about 300 or so. Most of our losses were from the 14th Connecticut troops. We captured 30 members of the Stonewall Brigade. After a hard day of fighting our forces withdrew during the night of the 7th.

This evening Mother and I attended "Sea of Ice" starring Laura Keane, who provided a moving performance. Mother raved about her acting. I must confess that I was tired and slept through part of the final act.

Author's notes:

Laura Keane was a famous British stage actress and theater manager. She was the lead actress in the play "Our American Cousin," which was attended by President Lincoln at Ford's Theater in Washington, D.C. on the evening of his assassination. She had a successful 20-year career as a leading actress and became known as the first powerful female theater manager in New York City.

The White House – Tuesday, February 9, 1864

This morning I reviewed 63 more court-martial cases with the judge advocate general. Sentences were reviewed, approved, remitted, commuted or pardoned. It is a slow and tedious process but a very important and necessary one. Men's lives hang in the balance. This evening Robert joined Mother and me at the largest levee of the season. He will be commissioned as a captain on General Grant's staff on Thursday of this week. I am very proud of him and know he will do an excellent job as an Army officer and prove to be a great help to Grant. In the morning I visited the studio gallery of Mathew B. Brady, who took my photograph several times. The gifted painter Francis B. Carpenter accompanied me to the studio. We must have spent two hours there.

Author's notes:

One of the photographs taken of President Lincoln was later used on the five-dollar bill.

The White House – Wednesday, February 10, 1864

Tad and I spent time at breakfast this morning talking about my father, Thomas Lincoln. Tad was curious about my father's inability to read or write. It was a common frontier failing in those days when book learning was not available to all who would have benefited greatly from it. Although my father was seriously handicapped by his illiteracy, he was strangely gifted as a storyteller. He could retell tales he had heard as a boy and young man from travelers who passed his way along the ancient Cumberland Trail. His ability to mimic voices was extraordinary. When I was nine or ten, I was able to mimic the voices of traveling Baptist preachers who came by our way from time to time. I could imitate their fire and brimstone sermons much to the pleasure of my schoolmates. Later in life I found that I, like my father, had a talent for storytelling and mimicry, which allowed me to make many friends laugh while traveling the legal circuit. I sometimes tell those same stories to members of my Cabinet, sometimes much to their chagrin. They don't always share my sense of humor. But it is my belief that a good belly laugh is worth more than riches, particularly when times are dark. And in war, times are often black as coal.

Beginning at 1 P.M. today I received the public for two hours. A few old friends came by, but mostly they were job seekers. Then 18 gentlemen from Pennsylvania, called upon me to discuss amending the Constitution in favor of freedom for all including slaves.

Author's notes:

Lincoln also explained to his son his strong aversion to killing animals. He told Tad that after shooting a wild turkey with his father's rifle when he was eight years of age, he "never again pulled the trigger on any larger game."

The White House – Friday, February 12, 1864

Mother and Tad surprised me with a birthday cake at dinner tonight. Fifty-five years of age and I am beginning to feel more like 65. For a rebellion to be defeated it takes years off one's life, I think. The touch of smallpox that I caught at Gettysburg slowed me down considerably this year. But on my day, I feel as fit as a fiddle.

Wednesday at 8:30 P.M. a fire broke out in the brick stables located between the White House and the Treasury Department where Tad's two ponies, my two horses and those of Nicolay have been kept. They all perished. When I smelled smoke I ran out, jumped over a boxwood hedge and was able to throw open the stable doors, but the flames were too far advanced to save the animals. It was a tragic fire. Tad is beside himself. He believes that the fire took place because Willie's pony was in the building. This weekend I hope to find time to look for animals to replace some of those lost. The sooner I can find one or two ponies for Tad the better he will feel. Mother has suggested we look at Shetland ponies and consider getting a cart for them to pull. Nicolay told Tad that when he was a boy his father had bought him a Shetland and that it lived to be 30 years old. He says they are generally gentle, good-tempered, and very intelligent by nature. He claims that for their size they are the strongest of all horse and pony breeds and can pull twice their weight, where a draft horse can only pull about half its own weight. In England in the mines they are used to pull carts loaded with coal. That is a terribly cruel way to treat an animal.

Author's notes:

The next day Lincoln was so busy with war matters that he was not able to examine potential horses and ponies to replace those lost in the fire. He assigned the task to Nicolay. The Washington Chronicle of February 12th reported that Patterson McGee, who had been dismissed as Lincoln's coachman on the day of the fire, was arrested on charges of having started the fire. Congress appropriated $12,00 on February 14th to replace the burned stables.

The White House – Saturday, February 13, 1864

I interviewed General Hugh Judson Kilpatrick of the Army of the Potomac. He has seen quite a bit of action in the war to date, including several wounds received as an aggressive cavalry leader. He is quite controversial but undoubtedly brave. He is called "Kill Cavalry" by his detractors, I am told. Stanton dislikes him but admits he gets results. He expects that Kilpatrick may soon be assigned by General Grant to serve under General Sherman in the west. I attended the afternoon reception but left early as I was not feeling well. One day I'm up and the next day I'm down. Before I left the reception, which was very well-attended, I had a chance to chat with General Daniel Sickes, who introduced me to three members of his staff. We spent a little time talking about my need to find horses and ponies to replace those killed in the stable fire this week.

Author's notes:

General Kilpatrick was a graduate of West Point, class of 1861, and was the first Union officer to be wounded in the Civil War. He attained the rank of brevet major general. In November of 1865 he was appointed Minister to Chile by President Andrew Johnson. He continued as minister under President Ulysses S. Grant. In Chile he married Luisa Fernandez de Valdivieso, a member of a wealthy family of Spanish origin that had emigrated to Chile in the 17th century. Kilpatrick died December 4, 1881, in Santiago, Chile. His great-granddaughter is artist and socialite Gloria Vanderbilt. His great-great-grandson is TV personality Anderson Cooper.

The White House – Monday, February 15, 1864

Yesterday, Tad and I met with Ezra Smith, a raiser of Shetland and other pony breeds who promised to bring several of his herd to the White House next week for our examination. Nicolay told us that Smith was recommended highly by several procurement officers who buy horses for our military. Tad is very excited. I hope we can find one or two good ones for him so we can replace our recent losses due to the fire. The fact that it was apparently set on purpose for reasons of revenge by a fired employee is particularly sad.

At dinner tonight Tad asked me a great many questions about my place of birth and about other early homes. I admitted to him that I do not remember my first home. I do know that it was in Hodgenville on the Nolin River. My father at that time owned 348 acres of farm land in what was then named Hardin County, Kentucky. That area is now called Larue County, I believe. In 1811, my father moved our family from Nolin River to better farm land of 230 acres on Knob Creek, 10 miles north and six miles east of Hodgenville. That place was on the Old Cumberland Road, which connected Louisville to Nashville. My earliest recollection is of the farmhouse at that location. The next year my brother, Thomas Lincoln Jr., was born. He died in infancy. In the autumn of 1815, my sister Sarah and I attended A-B-C schools. The first was taught by Zachariah Riney and the second by Caleb Hazel. Caleb lived across the road from our house. In December of 1816 we moved to Perry County in Indiana, about 91 miles. It took us five days to get there.

I ordered General Sickles to make a tour for observation and information from Cairo, Illinois to New Orleans and return by sea.

Author's notes:

On this date, Mrs. Lincoln, accompanied by her husband, son Robert and three Harvard friends attended an evening tableau at Willard's for the benefit of the Sanitary Commission. The president requested that James E. Murdoch read the poem "Am I for Peace? Yes!" at the benefit. Murdoch was a noted Shakespearean actor and considered the finest American performer of "Hamlet." When his son served in the Union Army he gave public poetry readings to aid the Sanitary Commission. Proceeds helped aid wounded soldiers. His many readings of Joseph Drake's "American Flag" were designed to invoke a sense of patriotism. Lincoln greatly admired his poetry readings.

The White House – Tuesday, February 16, 1864

I am beginning to think that sometime this month I shall ask General Grant to come to Washington to meet with me. His record of achievement has been splendid. He never complains or brags, but just pushes on against the Rebels wherever he finds them. We do not have a lieutenant general serving in our Army. The first one named was George Washington, who was recommended for that rank by President John Adams on July 3, 1798, during troubles with France. I think Grant should be raised to that rank and that Halleck should become his chief of staff to oversee all operations. I believe they would make a compatible team. Halleck and Grant have worked well together, and Halleck knows all the key players. He knows their strengths and weaknesses. I must discuss this with the Cabinet.

Author's notes:

On March 1, 1864, President Lincoln sent to the Senate the nomination of General Grant to be lieutenant general. On March 8, Lincoln met General Grant face to face for the first time at the White House. Grant was commissioned Lieutenant General on March 9, 1864. Lincoln said to Grant on the occasion, "The nation's appreciation for what you have done, and its reliance upon you for what remains to do, in the existing great struggle, are now presented with this commission, constituting you lieutenant general in the Army of the United States." Grant replied, "I feel the full weight of the responsibilities now devolving upon me and know that if they are met it will be due to those armies, and above all to the favor of that providence which leads both nations and men." Following the ceremony, the president heard a half-hour discussion of military affairs and the operations of General Sherman. On March 9, Lincoln assigned Lieutenant General Grant to command the Armies of the United States.

The White House – Wednesday, February 17, 1864

Mother reminded Tad and me at breakfast this morning that the calendar tells us that this is a Leap Year, so we will have 29 days this February rather than 28. Mother read us a report from a science book that explains why leap year occurs almost every four years. Julius Caesar figured this all out over 2,000 years ago. The Julian calendar had only one rule: Any year evenly divisible by four would be a leap year. The modern Gregorian Calendar has only 365 days in a year so if we didn't add a leap day on February 29 nearly every four years, we would lose almost six hours off our calendar every year. Leap years are therefore necessary to keep our modern calendar in alignment with the Earth's revolutions around the sun. After 100 years our calendar would be off by around 24 days. To be a leap year the year can be evenly divided by four. If the year can be evenly divided by 100 it is not a leap year unless the year is also evenly divisible by 400. Then it is a leap year. Thus 1800, 1900, 2100, 2200, 2300 and 2500 are not leap years. When I attended school, my teacher did not teach me this.

Author's notes:

It takes the Earth 365.242189 days, or 365 days, 5 hours, 48 minutes and 45 seconds to circle once around the sun. This is called a tropical year and is measured from the March equinox.

The White House – Thursday, February 18, 1864

Yesterday, I was invited to attend a lecture tomorrow evening on "The nation after the ordeal of battle," given by the Washington Lecture Association. I have invited John Hay, John Nicolay and William Stoddard to join me.

Today I officially lifted the blockade on the port of Brownsville, Texas. This is a further sign that our policy of blockade of Southern ports has worked very well. Brownsville may hereafter enjoy the benefits of uninhibited commerce. To vessels clearing from foreign ports, and destined to the port of Brownsville, opened by this proclamation, licenses will again be granted by consuls of the United States upon evidence that the vessels will convey no persons, property or information exempted or prohibited. On leaving the port every vessel will be required to have a clearance from the collector of customs showing no violation of the license.

I met with Secretary Seward and we discussed the final settlement of the owners of the "La Manche's" claims against the United States. Seward will now inform the French ambassador that this has been done in accordance with the wishes of the French government and to the satisfaction of our government.

Author's notes:

Lincoln transmitted to Congress a report from the Secretary of State, with accompanying papers, relative to the claim of this government of the owners of the French ship "La Manche" and recommended an appropriation for the satisfaction of the claim, pursuant to the award of the arbitrators. An Act approved March 22, 1864, appropriated a sufficient amount to purchase a bill of exchange for the sum of one hundred and thirty-five and fifteen one-hundredths francs, with interest as indemnity to the owners of the "La Manche," seized on August 23, 1862, and released by the Prize Court.

The White House – Friday, February 19, 1864

The Cabinet learned details of a small but lively engagement that took place on February 13 in Indian Territory near the Middle Boggy River. Union cavalry under Colonel William Phillips, made up of the 14th Kansas led by Major Charles Willets and a howitzer company commanded by Captain Solomon Kaufman, encountered a smaller and poorly armed Confederate force composed of Choctaw and Chickasaw cavalry and mounted rifles. Reports say that half the Rebel force was killed after a fight lasting less than an hour. No prisoners were taken. Two days later Phillips', troops burned the Pontotoc Court House and all the Confederate and Chickasaw buildings in the nearby town of Cochran. They also destroyed the Colbert Institute, a pre-war Chickasaw school that had been used to house Confederate troops. I am disappointed to learn that our men destroyed an Indian school. I do not believe that was necessary and so informed Halleck that in the future schools are to be spared whenever possible.

In the middle of our Cabinet meeting a fair plump woman walked into our meeting unannounced. She said she had come all the way from Dubuque, Iowa, to "see the president of the United States." I thanked her for her visit as I walked her to the door. She said two of her cousins and her son were in the Army.

Author's notes:

The Battle of Middle Boggy Depot, as it is usually called today, took place in what is now the state of Oklahoma. The battle was a defeat for the Confederates. However, the mistreatment of civilians and killing of wounded soldiers by Union troops strengthened the resolve of Confederates and their sympathizers to continue the fight. The Battle of Middle Boggy River or Middle Boggy Depot is celebrated every third year with a re-enactment. The Oklahoma Historical Society erected a marker at a small cemetery about one mile north of Atoka, Oklahoma. It honors Confederate soldiers who died in battle February 13, 1864.

The White House – Saturday, February 20, 1864

Yesterday afternoon Mother and I held a small private reception for Commodore Foote (Charles Nestel) and his sister, Eliza Nestel, world-famous midgets who are in town performing at the Odd Fellows Hall on 7th Street, North West. Tad enjoyed meeting our guests. She is billed as the Fairy Queen. Both were born in Indiana. They are both under 3-foot tall. He is 15 and she is 7. Their show is appropriately called "The Little People."

This evening we attended a performance of "King Richard the Third" at Grover's Theatre. It is one of my favorites by Shakespeare. "My horse! A horse! My kingdom for a horse!" The man knew how to bring history to life. Wit and wisdom are all there for the audience to absorb. I particularly like the lines, "Conscience is but a word that cowards use, devised at first to keep the strong in awe." And earlier, the line, "O coward conscience, how dost thou afflict me." Followed by "My conscience hath a thousand several tongues, and every tongue brings in a several tale, and every tale condemns me for a villain." What a genius of words.

Author's notes:

Charles Commodore Foote died in 1937. Eliza was so despondent she only outlived him by 10 days.

The White House – Monday, February 22, 1864

Today I read a telegram confirming that I received the endorsement of the Republican National Committee by a majority vote of four to one. This was good news. In wartime campaigning for president is not a simple matter. I have been warned that public appearances offer opportunities for assassination and are to be avoided as often as possible. I desire to be re-elected but realize that voters may reject any man they feel is a failure. The large numbers of men killed, wounded and missing in action since Fort Sumter for both North and South Halleck estimates now exceeds a million. We can now expect "peace candidates" to appear on the scene. Some citizens will gladly vote for peace at any cost. National Committee Chairman Henry Raymond has warned me that unanticipated large military defeats near election day could cost us the presidency. I do not wish to lose my bid for a second term but know that military decisions cannot be made based upon political calculations. Raymond would like me to send a commissioner to Richmond to confer with Jefferson Davis to sound him out for a negotiated way to peace. I've told Raymond that Davis will surely be unwilling to surrender but will stubbornly persist in what can only be a failed effort to sustain the Confederacy. Time is not on his side. The soldier vote will be key to victory in November. I cannot imagine how they will vote. I hope I have earned their trust.

Author's notes:

When the election was held Lincoln received 212 to 21 in electoral votes. He also received seven out of 10 soldiers' votes. After re-election, Lincoln resolved to abolish slavery throughout the United States via the Thirteenth Amendment, which was introduced on January 6, 1865. The amendment was ratified by three-quarters of the states in December 1865.

The White House – Tuesday, February 23, 1864

Secretary Welles and several high-ranking officers reviewed Navy matters with me and the Cabinet. They reported that the U.S.S. Housatonic was blown up by a mine while on blockade patrol off Charleston Harbor on the 17th at 9 P.M. Two officers and three enlisted men died. The crew managed to get off two boats and rescued most of the ship's company. A few seamen were removed from the rigging where they had remained after the ship sank and settled on the bottom in shallow water.

Author's notes:

The Housatonic was the first ship to be sunk by a submarine. The C.S.S. Huntley rammed her spar torpedo into the starboard side of the hull of the U.S.S. Housatonic, forward of her mizzen mast, and blew her up. The Confederate submarine, The Huntley, named after her inventor, sank in the explosion and all hands were lost. In 2017, researchers from Duke University estimated that the Huntley crew were most likely killed immediately at their posts by the blast's pressure wave damaging their lungs and brains. The anchor of the Housatonic can be found at the office of Wild Dunes on the Isle of Palms, South Carolina.

The White House – Wednesday, February 24, 1864

The White House reception last evening was undoubtedly the largest that has taken place this winter. Mrs. Keckley created a pale green gown for Mother that drew oohs and aahs from the onlookers. She is a wonderful dressmaker and devoted companion for Mother.

I wrote a note to Master Willie Smith, a 12-year-old friend of Leroy C. Driggs. Driggs tells me the lad has taken a lively interest in political affairs. I told young Willie that he and those of his age are to take care of this country when we older ones are gone; and I am glad to learn that he already has taken an interest in what just now so deeply concerns us.

Tonight, we attended Grover's Theatre for a performance by Edwin Booth in the role of Brutus in "Julius Caesar." A powerful display of acting. Every seat was taken because Booth is without peer when it comes to Shakespeare. I love to hear the lines, "Yond Cassius has a lean and hungry look; He thinks too much; such men are dangerous." I also enjoyed hearing the lines, "There is a tide in the affairs of men, Which, taken at the flood leads to fortune; Omitted, all the voyage of their life is bound in shallows and in miseries." How very true that is. Life is one surprise after another. One cannot take anything for granted, particularly in times of war.

Author's notes:

Often President Lincoln would deliver from memory Shakespearean verses for his associates. At home he frequently read or recited them for Tad, Mary and for Robert, when he was home from college.

The White House – Thursday, February 25, 1864

I telegraphed General Frederick Steele informing him that General Sickles is not going to Arkansas but instead will probably make a tour down the Mississippi to include Vicksburg on his way to New Orleans. I expect he will make his way back to Washington by way of the ocean. I advised Steele that Sickles will not meddle in his affairs.

Tad and I got to discussing grammar today. He is good at his lessons but weak in grammar. I told him that when I was his age, I lacked formal training in grammar. The proper use of commas and semicolons confused me. The schoolmaster in New Salem recommended that I read "Kirkham's English Grammar," which I borrowed from a kind gentleman who lived 5 or 6 miles away. I now have my own copy of it in the library and when in doubt I will pick it up and read it again. I am always willing to refer to it, particularly when it comes to adverbs and adjectives. I suggested to Tad that he read my old book, which he promises to do.

My loyal friend Simon Cameron stopped by to say hello and ask for a pass to visit Fortress Monroe in Virginia. Cameron has kept up correspondence with friends in our offices in St. Petersburg, where he served for a short time as minister to the Russian court. He believes Tsar Alexander II of Russia to be a true friend of America and a staunch supporter of our side in the Civil War. I trust Alexander will continue his friendly attitude. I admire him greatly for freeing the serfs.

Author's notes:

On this date President Lincoln issued a pass authorizing former Secretary of War Simon Cameron and friends to visit Fortress Monroe in Virginia and return to Washington. Cameron was still a powerful political figure in Pennsylvania. Like Lincoln, Tsar Alexander would also be assassinated. He was blown up on March 13, 1881, in St. Petersburg.

The White House – Friday, February 26, 1864

I signed General Order Number 76 today. It specifies sentences for deserters. Those sentenced to death are instead to be sent to Fort Jefferson Prison in the Dry Tortugas, which is in the Gulf of Mexico off Florida. Some may be restored to duty if in the opinion of the commanding generals the military service will benefit.

Author's notes:

Dr. Samuel Mudd, who treated John Wilkes Booth for injuries after the assassination of Abraham Lincoln, was sentenced to life imprisonment at Fort Jefferson in the Dry Tortugas. For his bravery in treating yellow fever patients there, Dr. Mudd was pardoned in 1869 by President Andrew Johnson.

The White House – Saturday, February 27, 1864

On February 22, I received a hand-delivered letter from Secretary Chase in which he offered to resign as secretary of the treasury. Chase is an exceedingly ambitious man, but a bright individual as well. His letter was prompted by the mailings by Kansas Senator Samuel Pomeroy of circulars recommending to prominent Republicans that Chase be the party's candidate for president this year and not Abe Lincoln. The gist of the Pomeroy messages: I am intellectually wanting, that I vacillate and am a man of indecision whose re-election is "practically impossible." Chase was obviously embarrassed by Pomeroy's messages and ashamed to be seen as disloyal, and thus offered to resign. If I were to accept his resignation, he would be free to run for the Republican nomination. I do not plan to accept his resignation. It is the third he has submitted to me since joining the Cabinet. Chase has wanted the nomination since 1859. Today, Congressman Francis Blair spoke against Chase from the floor of the House of Representatives.

This afternoon Tad, Mother and I visited an exhibit in the Capitol to see an oil painting of General Grant made by John Antrobus. In it he is shown holding field glasses in his left hand. We were met at the exhibit by J. Russell Jones, a friend from Galena who commissioned the portrait. I have not met the general, so I will soon be able to judge if the picture is a good likeness of him.

Author's notes:

On February 25th, at Lincoln's urging, the Republican Convention, held in Ohio, Chase's own state, endorsed the president's nomination. On February 29th Lincoln wrote to Chase that he wished him to remain as secretary of the treasury.

The Grant portrait was a three-quarter view of the general. Grant's posture reflects the same stance held by George Washington in an earlier painting. The artist traveled to Chattanooga, Tennessee, where Grant was headquartered and made sketches of the general. The painting measures 50 by 40.5 inches and is in the possession of the Chicago Public Library, Grand Army of the Republic Collection, gift of J. Russell Jones. Chicago artist John Antrobus (1837 to 1907) also painted a second full-length portrait of Grant.

The White House – Monday, February 29, 1864

Tad reminded me this morning that this is "leap day." On this "extra" day of the year I will be sending a copy of my Gettysburg Address to George Bancroft in New York City. This is the fourth copy I have made of my remarks. It will be sold at a Soldiers' and Sailors' Sanitary Fair in Baltimore to raise money for the care of the wounded men of the Union Army.

I wrote to Secretary Chase that neither of us can be justly held responsible for what our respective friends may do without our instigation or countenance. I advised him that I do not accept his resignation. I informed him that whether he stays at treasury or not is a question which I will not allow myself to consider from any standpoint other than my judgment of the public service; and in that view, I do not perceive occasion for a change.

Author's notes:

After Lincoln's assassination, Bancroft was chosen by Congress to deliver a special eulogy on Lincoln. Bancroft, as secretary of the Navy, established the U.S. Naval Academy at Annapolis in 1845. He served as U.S. minister to the United Kingdom, Prussia and the German Empire. The United State Navy has several ships, U.S.S. Bancroft and the nuclear submarine George Bancroft SBN-643, named after him. The United States Coast Survey Schooner Bancroft was also named after him in the mid-19th century. Bancroft Hall at the Naval Academy is named in his honor.

The White House – Tuesday, March 1, 1864

Southern newspapers report that the recent sinking on February 17th of the U.S.S. Housatonic in Charleston Harbor was not by a Confederate mine, as originally thought by our naval people, but by an ill-fated eight-man submergible craft. The Hunley was a revolutionary underwater ship that was invented by Horace Lawson Hunley. He went down with the ship following its attack on the Housatonic.

Hay hand-delivered to the Senate my nomination of General Grant to the rank of lieutenant general. This is the first such appointment at that grade since George Washington was awarded the rank by President John Adams. I pray that he will provide to our cause the victories we hope will flow from his sword. I have full confidence in the man.

Tomorrow we plan to attend a performance of "Hamlet." I recited my favorite lines in that play to Tad this morning. They are from Act III, scene iii, line 36: "O! My offense is rank, it smells to heaven; It hath the primal curse upon 't, A brother's murder!" Tad's favorite line from the play is, "A man may fish with the worm that hath eat of a King and eat of the fish that hath fed on that worm" (Act IV, scene iii, line 29). Mother prefers the line from Act II, scene ii, line 211, "Though, this be madness, yet there is method in 't."

Author's notes:

On this date the president and Mrs. Lincoln entertained at the Executive Mansion members of Congress and their families. No cards of invitation were issued to any other persons.

The White House – Wednesday, March 2, 1864

A Cincinnati newspaper editor commented this week that he believed that I was the "poorest dressed president in history." I am afraid that a man of my long length often looks ill-dressed. I remember vividly that when I won my first election back in 1834 to the Illinois state legislature that I possessed no clothes worthy of the position I was about to fill. I was only able to go and take my seat in the capital without embarrassment because my friends and neighbors in New Salem were generous enough to chip in and purchase suitable clothing for the occasion. In that way I was able to maintain my dignity and represent them in an acceptable fashion. It was at that time in my life that I began to seriously read the law at night while working days as a surveyor and postal clerk. John Stuart generously allowed me to read law books from his library. John was a very impressive man, a good legislator, a smart attorney and a lifelong friend. We became law partners in time. Later William Herndon became my partner. My hope is that when my term in office ends that I shall be again working from an office in Springfield with his name and mine on the shingle again. This diary I am keeping was given to me by William Herndon.

Author's notes:

William H. Herndon, Lincoln's law partner after Stuart claimed that Stuart said Lincoln always "denied that Jesus was the son of God as understood and maintained by the Christian Church." Judge David Davis disagreed, stating that "The idea that Lincoln talked to a stranger about his religion or religious views, or made speeches and remarks about it as are published, is to me absurd. I knew the man so well; he was the most reticent, secretive man I ever saw or expect to see. He had no faith, in the Christian sense of the term – He had faith in laws, principles, causes and effects."

The White House – Thursday, March 3, 1864

General Halleck and staff members from the War Department reviewed recent events in Meridian, Mississippi, and Olustee, Florida, with the Cabinet this morning. The Meridian Expedition from Vicksburg to Meridian, Mississippi, captured Meridian and destroyed much of the enemy's infrastructure. General Sherman reports that Meridian was an important railroad center, an arsenal, military hospital and prisoner-of-war stockade. No longer. All has been eliminated. Our troops eliminated 115 miles of railroad, 61 bridges, over a mile of trestle work, 20 locomotives, 28 railroad cars and three steam sawmills. Sherman reports that "Meridian no longer exists." He is now heading toward Canton, Mississippi. His Army now numbers over 25,000 men.

The Battle of Olustee, fought in Baker County, Florida was a strong defeat for our forces. The battle was fiercely fought in a pine forest with heavy losses on both sides. General Truman Seymour reports casualties of 1,861 out of 5,500 troops engaged. He estimates Rebel losses were about half of ours. Our forces retreated back to Jacksonville, Florida. They included Negro soldiers of the 54th Massachusetts Volunteer Infantry Regiment and the 35th U.S. Colored Troops.

Author's notes:

The Battle of Olustee was the only major battle fought in the state of Florida during the Civil War. The repulsed Union forces stayed in Jacksonville for the remainder of the war.

The White House – Friday, March 4, 1864

Henry Villard of the New York Herald came by and we discussed the Pomeroy circulars for an hour or more. Villard is one of the best journalists in that city. I told him that I had no wish for the letters between Secretary Chase and me to be published, but that I had no problem if Chase wished to have such publicationmade. I wrote to Chase today confirming my position but advising him that if he wished his correspondence to be made public, he was free to do so.

I issued a memorandum about churches. It informs our officers that the U.S. government must not undertake to run the churches for any reason. We cannot appoint trustees, supervisors, or agents for the churches. If the military have need for a church building let them keep it and use it, otherwise leave it alone except for causes that justify the arrest of any one. Freedom of religion is just that – freedom.

Admiral Dahlgren visited with me today seeking news of his son, Colonel Ulric Dahlgren, who was involved in the fighting at the James River outside Richmond. I hope we will soon get good news about his fate.

Author's notes:

On March 4, 1864, General Benjamin Butler wired Lincoln that "Col. Dahlgren was directed to make a diversion with 500 men on the James River. He attacked at 4 p.m. Tuesday evening; drove the enemy in on Richmond. The main attack failed, Col. Dahlgren attempted to rejoin me...He and Major Edwin F. Cooke were with the advance guard...became separated from his main force. Since, nothing has been heard." On March 7, Lincoln advised General Butler that "Gen. Meade has Richmond Sentinel, saying that Col. Dahlgren was killed and ninety of his men captured."

The White House – Saturday, March 5, 1864

My law partnership with Stephen T. Logan lasted about three years. When we broke up in 1844, he reminded me that it had always been his intention to take his son David into the firm. Stephen was a very good teacher of the law. He was excellent in writing documents that would satisfy the courts. He was meticulous in his court briefs. Our breakup was amiable and in friendship. Stephen was at the time the leading attorney in the county. While I was with him, I gained greater confidence in myself as a lawyer and felt that I could ultimately run as a Whig for the House of Representatives and win the seat for the 7th Congressional District of Illinois. My single term in Congress was generally regarded by my constituents as a failure. I didn't set the world on fire. I had hoped when I returned to Springfield the Taylor administration might offer me a federal position. I had sought the post of commissioner of the Land Office. When I didn't get the job, my new law partner, Bill Herndon, tried to cheer me up, but he didn't succeed. For many months I was down in the mouth about my political prospects. But once I got back on the traveling circuit, again meeting the public for eight weeks each spring and fall, I soon cheered up and put a federal appointment out of my mind.

Author's notes:

From 1834 to 1840 Lincoln served in the Illinois Legislature. He began to practice law in 1837. In 1840, he declined re-election and for the next five years focused on his law practice and the beginning of his family. In 1846 he was elected and served one term from December 1847 to March 1849 in the United States Congress. While in Congress he unsuccessfully introduced a bill to abolish slavery in the District of Columbia.

The White House – Monday, March 7, 1864

Secretary Seward amazed Mother and me with a gift copy of Niccolo Machiavelli's book, "The Prince." It is in a light brown leather-bound edition with the title in gold lettering. We were both surprised and very pleased to add it to our library. Mary told him that she considered it to be especially timely, inasmuch as we are now in that political season when a president must be picked. Seward suggested that we both read it carefully, for there may be some valuable lessons found within its pages. Machiavelli is considered by most historians to have been unscrupulously cunning, deceptive and expedient in seeking to achieve some end. But he was also the secretary of the Florentine Republic, and in time his sponsor, Lorenzo de Medici, the Duke of Urbino disregarded his opinions and writings. I plan to read some of the book next weekend. I am always in awe of a richly printed edition. I remember my humble roots when any book I read had to be borrowed and often came from some trusting soul who may have lived many miles from me. Machiavelli taught how to be a powerful autocrat. He believed that it is difficult to be feared and loved at the same time, but it is safer to be feared than loved if one had to lack one of the two. My sense is that few in my administration fear Abraham Lincoln. But then, I'm not a "Prince" but merely a man who only serves at the wishes of the electorate. And in times of war an electorate can be mighty fickle!

Author's notes:

Last evening Secretary Stanton and the president called upon Rear Admiral Dahlgren's residence with a telegram from General Butler announcing that Dahlgren's son on a raid against Richmond was alive. Later they would learn that the report was in error and that his son, Ulric, had been killed in battle.

The White House – Tuesday, March 8, 1864

This was a red-letter day for me and Mother, for today we finally met soon-to-be-Lieutenant General Ulysses S. Grant face-to-face. We had a large reception in the White House, which began at 8 P.M. The general arrived an hour and a half later. We briefly discussed arrangements for the ceremony on Wednesday when he will be presented with his commission of lieutenant general. Mother, Mrs. Seward and I promenaded around the room with the general. I feel a large load has been removed from my shoulders and that many of my cares and fears may now be abated by Grant's presence in command of our forces. Mother is very impressed by the general's looks and demeanor.

Yesterday morning, Mother and I discussed our sympathies for Queen Victoria, who has been in mourning ever since the sudden and unexpected death of Prince Albert in December of 1861. He was a true friend of the United States and we owe him our sincere gratitude for helping defuse tempers during the Trent Affair. We drafted a letter to her, to be mailed tomorrow, congratulating her upon the birth of a grandchild who is the daughter of the Prince of Wales, Edward Albert.

Author's notes:

Today, the president mailed a letter to Queen Victoria, which he addressed to his "Great and Good Friend," in which he congratulated the queen upon news that the Princess of Wales delivered of a prince on January 8, 1864. On December 14, 1861, her husband, Prince Albert died. It was believed at the time that he died of typhoid fever. There was no autopsy performed. Recently, medical experts have concluded that Prince Albert may have died of Crohn's Disease.

The White House – Wednesday, March 9, 1864

The presentation of his new commission to General Grant took place as scheduled at 1 P.M. In attendance were the full Cabinet; General Halleck, who will be Grant's chief of staff; John Rawlings, his good friend; Congressman Lovejoy, of Illinois; and John Nicolay. Later we had a full discussion of the role to be played in the West by General William Sherman. His new assignment will be commander of the Military District of Mississippi, composed of the Ohio, the Cumberland, the Tennessee, and the Arkansas. It was decided that Grant will now be headquartered in the East and serve as commander of the Armies of the United States.

I sent a telegram to General Meade notifying him that New York City voted 9,500 majority for allowing soldiers to vote in the presidential election, and that the rest of the state voted nearly all on the same side. I instructed Meade to notify the troops of their right to vote. I consider this good news as I trust that the men in uniform may support Old Abe in November. However, if the Democrats nominate General George McClellan, the soldier vote might very well be divided.

Author's notes:

In the late afternoon Lincoln received a letter from Salmon Chase notifying him that he was withdrawing from the 1864 presidential race. Chase was an ambitious man, but also a man whom Lincoln considered to be of great talent and devotion to the ultimate effort of achieving victory.

The White House – Thursday, March 10, 1864

At the theater tonight I again relished hearing lines from "King Richard III," particularly these words, "An honest tale speeds best when plainly told." And, "Thus far into the bowels of the land we have marched without impediment." I have often recited the lines, "conscience is but a word that cowards use, devised at first to keep the strong in awe." Shakespeare gives me great comfort in the reading and in the reciting. I keep his book near my bed table so that I may read from it whenever I feel the need. Tonight, was the last in a series of Shakespearean dramas in which the celebrated actor Edwin Booth graced the stage. He has no peer.

Today the president and vice president are provided free postage courtesy of a bill passed by the Senate.

Mother and I invited General Grant and his son to join us at the theater, but he did not attend. I believe he is incredibly busy at his time here in Washington, what with all the new duties we have heaped upon him.

Author's notes:

The president and Mrs. Lincoln sent a note to General Grant inviting him and General Meade to join them for dinner on Saturday, March 12, 1864.

The White House – Friday, March 11, 1864

At an early morning Cabinet meeting yesterday, General Grant notified me that he was returning at once to Nashville to coordinate important arrangements with General Sherman and regrets that he will not be able to join Mrs. Lincoln and me for dinner with General Meade. He is rightly concerned that matters in the West deserve his immediate attention. He will soon be back in Washington in command of all our forces. Before he left, we discussed the appointment of General James B. McPherson to command the Department of Tennessee.

After lunch I met with General Lewis Wallace, who will be joining other officers at the White House for dinner this evening at 6:45 P.M. I expect about 15 officers will be with Mother and me. Generals Meade, Wool, Sickles, Doubleday and McCook are joining us.

Author's notes:

James Birdseye McPherson (November 14, 1828 – July 22, 1864) was a career Army officer who graduated from the United States Military Academy in 1853, first in his class. His classmates included Philip H. Sheridan, John M. Schofield and John Bell Hood. For a year after graduation he was assistant instructor of practical engineering at the Military Academy, a position never before given to so young an officer. In September of 1862 he assumed a position on General Grant's staff. For bravery at Corinth he was promoted to brigadier general. On October 8 he was promoted major general and given command of the XVII Corps of Grant's Army of the Tennessee. In the Atlanta campaign his Army was the Right Wing of Sherman's Army. He was killed during the first day of the Battle of Atlanta by enemy skirmishers. Confederate General John Hood wrote, "Since we graduated it has not been our fortune to meet. Neither the years nor the difference of sentiment that had led us to range ourselves on opposite sides in the war had lessened my friendship; indeed, the attachment formed in early youth was strengthened by my admiration and gratitude for his conduct toward our people in the vicinity of Vicksburg."

The White House – Monday, March 14, 1864

General Halleck and his staff presented to the Cabinet a comprehensive review of recent military actions in Okolona, Mississippi, Dalton, Georgia, and Walkerton, Virginia. All were Confederate victories. In the battle at Okolona, according to Sherman, General William Sooy Smith failed to set off on his march when ordered and became engaged in a running battle with Nathan Bedford Forest's cavalry for three days. Forest routed Smith's larger-sized force but ran out of ammunition and abandoned the field.

The fighting in Dalton took place on February 22 through February 27 in Whitfield County, Georgia. It is estimated that as many as 65,000 men may have been involved on both sides. General George H. Thomas attempted to probe General Joseph Johnston's strength to see if the loss of two divisions to reinforce Confederate forces elsewhere had made the Southerners vulnerable to attack. After several days of intense skirmishing, Thomas withdrew upon realizing Johnston was situated in way that he could repel any assault we launched against him.

The Battle at Walkerton, in King and Queen County, Virginia, occurred on March 2nd. In it forces of Brigadier General Hugh Judson Kilpatrick rode along the track of the Virginia Central Railroad tearing up track and equipment, while an advance force was sent south along the James River under Colonel Ulric Dahlgren. Kilpatrick found he could not penetrate Richmond's defenses and withdrew when challenged by Rebel cavalry under Wade Hampton. Dahlgren was killed and most of his men captured.

Author's notes:

Papers found on Dahlgren's body allegedly contained an official Union order to burn Richmond and assassinate Jefferson Davis and his Cabinet. Meade, Kilpatrick and Lincoln disavowed any knowledge of the Dahlgren papers and their authenticity was disputed.

The White House – Tuesday, March 15, 1864

Tad, who has been reading Caesar's history, called to my attention that today is the Ides of March. Tad said I should be forewarned. I will heed his warning and see if I can speed up my Cabinet meeting today. Lately they seem to go on and on without end.

At the Cabinet meeting, we reviewed at length the need for a draft call to total 200,000 men. I instructed Hay and Nicolay to prepare it for signature tomorrow. In the final analysis our ability to enroll large numbers when needed and the Confederate's inability to do the same means in time that this war of attrition will prove unsustainable for the South. The steady drain from its manpower source of thousands of liberated slaves means that its Army and agricultural society must be weakened every day.

Later Seward came by and we discussed the treaty now being prepared for transmission to the Senate as relates to claims of Hudson's Bay and Puget's Sound Agricultural Companies. Our papers include the appropriations required to carry into effect the first, second and third articles thereof. At the same time Seward and I discussed the convention with Ecuador, which requires the appointment of a commission to adjust claims.

Author's notes:

On March 15th Lincoln directed land and naval forces to assist General Sickles on his official tour from Washington by way of Cairo, Illinois.

The White House – Wednesday, March 16, 1864

Today I had reason to remember Jack Kelso, a proud Scottish American who introduced me to his favorite poet, Robert Burns, back in 1831, when I reached my 21st year in New Salem, Illinois. Jack possessed books by Shakespeare and Burns and gladly lent copies to me. Jack was a teacher in his homeland and owned the largest library in our poor little town. Now and for many years I have kept a copy of his poetry in my bedroom. When I need a lift, I often recite this verse:

> The year's at spring
>
> And days at the morn;
>
> Morning's at seven;
>
> The hillside's dew-pearled;
>
> The larks on the wing;
>
> The snails on the thorn;
>
> God's in His heaven –
>
> All's right with the world!

Thanks to Jack Kelso I can still recite Burns by the hour. He was a man who never touched sentiment without carrying it to its ultimate expression and leaving nothing to be said. I knew Burns by heart and his words have given me much joy throughout my life. When I was practicing law before my election to Congress, a copy of Burns was my inseparable companion on the circuit. I knew by heart every line of his. In 1859, I attended the Springfield Centenary celebration of Burns' birthday and gave a formal toast to his memory.

Author's notes:

Scotland erected the first heroic statue to Lincoln in the Old Carlton Hill Burial Ground in Edinburgh in 1893. Twelve American cities including New York, Denver and Cheyenne house heroic statues to Robert Burns. When the National Park Service refurbished the Lincoln family home in Springfield in 1988, it picked busts of Shakespeare, Dickens and Burns, his favorite writers, to display in the Lincoln parlor.

The White House – Thursday, March 17, 1864

Today is St. Patrick's Day. The Patron Saint of Ireland is well-honored by the Irish American soldiers and sailors who celebrate his anniversary on this date. Some Irishmen, who are recent immigrants to our shores, and who are now serving in New York regiments came by the White House this morning and sang several Irish tunes to the enjoyment of Mother and Tad. They had two bagpipers playing, which I found very uplifting. Sadly, I have received no word as to the status of our getting the body of Colonel Dahlgren returned from the war zone where he was killed. General Butler expects that the body may be in Union hands as of this Sunday. I hope so for the family's sake. Tomorrow, General Halleck will be acquainting the Cabinet with our current military plans and activities in the Red River area of Louisiana.

Author's notes:

The Battle of Fort DeRussy was the first engagement in the Red River Campaign. The operation was led by General A.J. Smith's Trans-Mississippi Department, headquartered in Shreveport, Louisiana, in early 1864. Major General Nathaniel Banks and Rear Admiral David D. Porter jointly commanded the combined federal force. The Army set out on March 12, 1864, up the Red River, the most direct route to Shreveport. After removing obstruction, the Rebels had placed in the river, the major impediment to the Union expedition was the formidable Fort DeRussy, an earthen fortification with a partly iron-plated battery designed to resist the fire of Union iron-clads that might come up the river. On March 14, upon arriving at the fort the enemy garrison of 350 men opened fire. Smith's XVI Division at around 6:30 P.M. charged the fort and about 20 minutes later his men scaled the parapet, causing the enemy to surrender. The Red River was now open to Alexandria.

The Civil War Trust and its partners have acquired and preserved 73 acres of the Fort DeRussy Battlefield.

The White House – Friday, March 18, 1864

Tad and Mother were curious about my parents' backgrounds and appearances. I discussed them this morning. My father, Thomas Lincoln, was born in Virginia and moved to Hardin County, Kentucky, when 3 years old. When he was 6 years old, his father, Mordecai, was killed by hostile Indians. Thomas married Nancy Sparrow in Mercer County, Kentucky. She was born of Lucy Hanks in Hampshire County, Virginia, on February 5, 1784, and died October 5, 1818. Thomas was black-haired, heavyset, fleshy and weighed about 180 pounds. He was a quiet man, a good citizen, with good moral habits and sound judgment. He was a kind husband to my mother. His disposition was even and good, lively and cheerful. My mother had dark hair, hazel eyes, and was 5 foot 7 inches tall. She had a spare, delicate frame and weighed about 120 pounds. She had a clear intellectual mind, was amiable, kind, charitable and affectionate. She was dearly loved and revered by all who knew her. My sister, Sarah was born on February 10, 1807, and died January 20, 1828. My brother, Thomas, died in infancy in 1812.

The Cabinet met at 4 P.M. and Seward proposed a bill on emigration, consideration of which we shelved for further discussion. Later Mother and I went to the closing night of the Christian Commission and District Fair volunteers held in the Patent Office. I was asked to say a few words. My closing comments emphasized the extraordinary developments for the relief of suffering soldiers and their families. The chief agents in these fairs have been the women of America. I closed by saying "God bless the women of America." That last line was received with loud applause.

Author's notes:

On this date Lincoln wrote to Secretary Stanton regarding prisoners of war then in Union custody whose homes were within Union lines, and who wished to not be exchanged, but to take the oath and be discharged. Lincoln suggested to Stanton that these men be not be exchanged but be freed by discharge. He thought they would not be in large enough numbers to do considerable mischief in any event.

The White House – Saturday, March 19, 1864

William O. Stoddard returned to the White House early in the day. He has been seriously ill with suspected typhoid. I am glad to have him back. He is weak and will be encouraged to work fewer hours until he feels his normal self. I attended a reception given by Mother, which was very well-attended. I also sent to our Indian Affairs people authorization to discharge 16 named Indians who are not considered a threat to the peace.

Author's notes:

Typhoid fever was a major killer during the Civil War. It was the result of contaminated water and food. It is estimated to have killed 30,000 Confederate and 27,000 Union troops. One out of every three soldiers or sailors who contracted the disease died of it. During the first year of the war 2 percent of the entire Union Army died from it. During the second year of the war 4.9 percent of the Union Army had the disease and 1.7 percent died of it. Confederate forces suffered at about the same rates throughout the war. There were no effective treatments for the disease. Some physicians prescribed calomel for the disease, causing mercury poisoning in many patients. Lincoln's son, Willie Lincoln, died of the disease at age 11.

Pneumonia is estimated to have killed 17,000 Confederates and 20,000 Union troops. Measles killed about 11,000 soldiers in total or about one in 20 who got the disease. Tuberculosis killed about 14,000 soldiers. Malaria killed approximately 30,000 soldiers.

The White House – Monday, March 21, 1864

I approved an Act to enable the people of Nevada to form a constitution and state government, and for the admission of that state into the Union on an equal footing with the original states. At noon I was called upon by the committee from the New York Workingmen's Democratic Republican Associations. I was given an honorary membership for which I expressed my appreciation. I told them that I appreciate that they realize that the current rebellion is a war upon all working people. I pointed out that the hanging of some working people in their city by other working people was a great tragedy not to be repeated. I wrote to Clara and Julia Brown from Buffalo, thanking them for the afghan they thoughtfully made and sent to me. It will be provided to a soldier in a military hospital. They wrote that they are "little friends who pray for me, that I may be cheerful, strong and wise."

Author's notes:

On this date, Lincoln made a note which read, "I never knew a man who wished to be himself a slave. Consider if you know any good thing, that no man desires for himself. A. Lincoln." The item was identified in an autograph for a Sanitary Fair. He was often requested to send notes to the fairs. They were typically auctioned off and the proceeds used to aid wounded soldiers.

The White House – Tuesday, March 22, 1864

Today was spent with Navy Secretary Gideon Welles, or as I call him, Father Neptune. With his long white beard, he surely looks the part. Although he initially opposed the Anaconda Plan, which was devised by General Winfield Scott, he has carried it out with great success and efficiency. He gave the Cabinet his best estimates as to the number of vessels intercepted or destroyed (1,500) with our boycott of Southern ports, and how many bales of cotton we have denied to foreign markets. My view from the start is that the Anaconda Plan has been one of the major causes of our success in the war. The South cannot long exist without foreign income to pay for weapons and other materials of war from cotton sales, which are now negligible as we seal more tightly their seaports and coastal rivers.

Author's notes:

By war's end Welles had overseen the construction and launching of enough ships to increase the size of the pre-war Navy by 10-fold. He was instrumental in the Navy's creation of the Medal of Honor. After Lincoln's death, President Andrew Johnson kept him on as Secretary of the Navy. Welles remained loyal to Johnson and supported him through his impeachment ordeal. In 1874 he edited a biography, "Lincoln and Seward." He was the seventh generation of a family that arrived in America in 1635. His original immigrant ancestor was Thomas Welles, who was the only man in Connecticut's history to hold all top offices: governor, deputy governor, treasurer and secretary. (Born July 1, 1802 – died February 11, 1878)

The total war expenditures of the U.S. government in the Civil War were $6.8 billion – of that amount the cost of the Navy was $587 million or one-twelfth of the total. The Union Navy operated 671 warships mounting 4,610 guns. All but 112 of these were steamers. 71 were ironclad. The Navy Department purchased 418 ships and contracted for the construction of 208 more. The Confederate Navy consisted of 121 warships carrying about 400 guns, including 20 ironclads, eight torpedo boats, and two submarines. Confederate raiders destroyed or captured 252 merchant ships and whalers.

The White House – Wednesday, March 23, 1864

Senators Wade of Ohio and Chandler of Michigan called upon me yesterday demanding the removal of General George Meade. I listened to their views and told them that any decisions on the matter would only be made after consultation with Generals Grant and Halleck. Both of those officers are not displeased with the performance of General Meade, whose victory at Gettysburg still rings true to my mind and deserves the gratitude of the nation.

General Carl Schurz would like to get involved in the upcoming political campaign. I advised him that as a serving officer to act in any partisan manner is inappropriate and would require his resignation from the Army first.

I spent a profitable evening meeting with Generals Grant and Halleck. I am finding Grant to be very precise in his thinking on military matters. He quickly gets to the nub of any problem and acts to solve any problems he encounters. He has the unique ability to keep focused on the overall target, the armies of the enemy and on the myriad steps we can take to destroy them and their resources. He relies heavily on General Sherman and I rely heavily upon them both. Later John Hay joined us and filled us in on political matters in the state of Florida.

Author's notes:

On this date, Lincoln advised Major General George C. Meade, "Do not change your purpose to send Private Orton, of Twelfth U.S. Infantry, to the Dry Tortugas."

The White House – Friday, March 25, 1864

Late this evening at the telegraph office we learned that our forces fared badly in Paducah, Kentucky, earlier this week when a Confederate cavalry force led by General Nathan Bedford Forrest, which had moved into Kentucky to capture Union supplies, launched a raid at Paducah on the Ohio River. It is estimated that our forces, which were occupying Fort Anderson, were greatly outnumbered. Fortunately, the fort was supported by two Union gunboats, which were able to effectively shell the Rebel attackers. Colonel Stephen Hicks in command of the fort reports 90 casualties. The ships engaged were the U.S.S. Peosta and the U.S.S. Paw. Earlier in the war we lacked such cooperation between our land and river forces. Where it can be organized the enemy will typically lack the ability to succeed against us.

I issued a Proclamation About Amnesty today. It carefully defines those cases in which insurgent enemies are entitled to benefits and the way they shall proceed to avail themselves of those benefits. It will hopefully end confusion on the matter.

Author's notes:

On this date Lincoln met with Secretary of the Navy Welles relative to the transfer to the Navy of 12,000 men currently serving in the Army.

The White House – Saturday, March 26, 1864

I discussed at length Negro enlistments in Kentucky with Governor Thomas Bramlette, Attorney General Edward Bates, former Senator Archibald Dixon of Kentucky and Albert G. Hodges, editor of the Frankfort, Kentucky, "Commonwealth." The consensus is that colored enlistments are growing in a healthy manner and that the quality of the troops raised has been significantly improving each enrollment period. Who could have imagined that our Army would be so positively enhanced by the enlistments of colored men of limited education? They are proving to be very accepting of strict training and quickly become well-disciplined and often eager to experience action under fire.

I requested Navy Secretary Welles and Assistant Navy Secretary Gustavus Fox to proceed with the orders to transfer 12,000 soldiers into the Navy.

Author's notes:

On March 26, 1864, Presidential Secretary John Nicolay arrived in New York to represent the president at a conference with Thurlow Reed concerning political conditions in New York and patronage appointments.

The White House – Monday, March 28, 1864

Lack of strict tight security at the White House can often result in odd occurrences. Today a mild-mannered but confused gentleman by the name of Francis Xavier arrived at our offices in a disturbed estate. He insisted that he had won the presidential election in 1856. He was harmless, but his presence demonstrated just how very weak our security arrangements are. Had he been carrying a gun he could have easily killed someone. Marshall Ward Lamon has been asked to study the matter and get back to the Cabinet and me about steps we can take to avoid occurrences like the Xavier affair.

I received a letter from Peter McConnell of Kansas – he wishes to give a Rocky Mountain pony to Tad. Since the recent deadly barn fire, we have been anxious to have another pony in the stable. We will watch Tad ride the animal and determine if he is safe enough for Tad to ride.

Author's notes:

As plans were firming up for spring campaigning, Lincoln approved Grant's plan to move in three directions at once; the Army of the Potomac would strike Lee head on, forcing him to retreat south toward Richmond; Sherman would move through Georgia from west to east, with the initial goal of capturing Atlanta; meanwhile, General Butler would move northeast against Richmond from the James River. Lincoln believed Grant's plan would assure accomplishments from the great advantages in numbers. With seven weeks of the commencing of combat 86,000 Union and Confederate casualties would take place. Grant's famous dispatch of May 1, "I propose to fight it out on this line if it takes all summer," convinced Lincoln that he had the right general in command.

The White House – Tuesday, March 29, 1864

At our Cabinet meeting Secretary Welles brought these guests: Hiram Paulding, retired commander N.Y. Navy Yard; C.H. Davis, Chief Bureau of Navigation; S.H. Stringham, retired, Francis Gregory, retired and superintending construction of gunboats. We had a good talk about various naval matters. We've never had so many admirals in our offices before. I sent to Congress a report of Charles B. Stuart, consulting engineer of New York City, regarding improvements to pass gunboats from tidewater to northern and northwestern lakes. General Meade asked that a Court of Inquiry be established to deal with charges that he did not act properly at Gettysburg. I advised him that I am satisfied he performed admirably and that an inquiry would be a waste of his time. He believes General Sickles is the troublemaker. I fail to see the need for Meade's time to be diverted by such distractions. I trust Meade.

The Rev. M.R. Watkinson of Ridleyville, Pennsylvania, has recommended that the American flag be imprinted on U.S. coins with the words "God, Liberty, Law" within the flag's bars. He writes this would "place us openly under the Divine protection we have personally claimed." Chase has asked James Pollock, the director of the Philadelphia Mint, to write a suitable motto. I like the idea.

Author's notes:

On April 22, 1864, Lincoln signed the Mint Act, which authorized the U.S. Mint to imprint the word, "In God We Trust" on American coins. The first coin selected was the two-cent piece. The penny with Lincoln's image on it began carrying the motto in 1909. It began to appear on paper money in 1956.

Wednesday, March 30, 1864

Today's weather was superb and motivated me to take Mother and Tad out riding in our carriage. I did so and it was very pleasant. There were no visitors at my office this morning because on Tuesday, my doorkeepers had asked many who were then standing in a long line to return not today, but Thursday. They also put up a sign this morning which read in bold type, "No Visitors Today." We must have ridden a good six or seven miles. Many who saw us waved or shouted greetings. Tad was most enthusiastic in his acknowledgments and waves. I can always count upon Cornelius O'Leary, the doorkeeper and Thomas Burns, the second-floor guardian of my privacy to deal with visitors diplomatically. O'Leary's predecessor, Edward McManus had served presidents going as far back as Jackson or Polk. McManus had a remarkable sense of humor and a wonderful Irish accent to go with it.

Author's notes:

Lincoln had many Irish Americans on his White House staff. When he lived in Illinois, he had hired many Irish maids to assist Mary Lincoln. In 1855 he had written to his good friend Joshua Speed, who had questioned Lincoln about the Know-Nothings, whose anti-immigrant rhetoric was anti-Negro, anti-foreigner and anti-Catholic. Lincoln wrote Speed that "As a nation, we began by declaring that 'all men are created equal.' We now practically read it, 'all men are created equal, except negroes.' He added, "When the No-Nothings get control, it will soon read, 'All men are created equal except negroes, and foreigners and Catholics.' He said he'd rather move to Russia where they make no pretense of loving liberty – where despotism can be taken pure, and without the base alloy of hypocrisy.

The White House – Thursday, March 31, 1864

I received from Reverend Frederick A. Farley, D.D., a handsome bedspread or quilt made by his fellow citizens. They are members of the Brooklyn and Long Island Sanitary Fair. It is a silk masterpiece formed in the national colors and emblemed with the stars and stripes and the national eagle. It is a work of art. Mother suggests that we donate it to the Smithsonian Institution for permanent display there. She intends to show it to our guests at her Saturday reception. I agree it deserves to be seen by as many people as possible and the Smithsonian would seem to be such a setting. Stanton suggested that perhaps it should first be sent around the nation to be shown at various Sanitary Fairs as a symbol of patriotism and sacrifice by our brave servicemen.

Author's notes:

On this date Lincoln granted a pardon to Franklin B. Furlong, imprisoned for bank robbery. He also accepted the recommendation of Captain Ezekiel R. Mayo, Third Maine Battery, for the pardon of Private Edward Avery, sentenced for desertion on October 29, 1863.

The White House – Friday, April 1, 1864

Tad reminded me that today is April Fool's Day by handing me a sealed letter I was supposed to give to his teacher. When I opened it, the message read: April Fool! No School Today! Tad and his mother had a good laugh about it. He has a keen sense of humor. Perhaps he takes after his father in that regard. I firmly believe that each day should have its fair share of laughter, particularly on those grim days when there is little reason to smile.

I met with Senator James Harlan of Iowa, who asks that I nominate Colonel Edward Hatch brigadier general. I told him that I would gladly do so. Hatch has a good record as an officer with the 2nd Iowa Cavalry. Grant tells me he likes Hatch very much. Before joining the Senate, Harlan was president of Iowa Wesleyan Collegein Mount Pleasant, Iowa. He is a fine man who tried his best to arrange a compromise to prevent the Civil War.

Author's notes:

In 1865 Harlan resigned from the Senate when he was appointed secretary of the interior under President Andrew Johnson. He fired Walt Whitman, who was working as a clerk in the department. Twenty-nine years later he defended the firing by saying that Whitman was fired solely "on the grounds that his services were not needed." He resigned from the Interior Department when he no longer supported the policies of President Johnson. In 1868 his daughter, Mary Eunice Harlan, married Lincoln's son, Robert Todd Lincoln.

After the war, Edward Hatch became the first commander of the 9th U.S. Cavalry Regiment, a Buffalo soldier regiment with African American troops commanded by white officers. He became known as an Indian fighter. He negotiated treaties with the Ute Indians in 1880. He achieved the rank of major general.

The White House – Saturday, April 2, 1864

This morning I discussed future judicial appointments with Treasury Secretary Salmon Chase and Attorney General Edward Bates. To the United States Supreme Court, I have already appointed Noah Haynes Swayne, Samuel Freedman Miller, David Davis and Stephen Johnson Field. If nature takes its course, we expect one of these days that the seat now held by Chief Justice Roger B. Taney will have to be filled. So far this year I have nominated these Federal District judges: Andrew Wylie, John Curtiss Underwood, Edward Henry Durell, Mark W. Delahay, Thomas Jefferson Boynton, Richard Busteed and Albert Smith White. I was surprised to learn that I had appointed so many judges. Had the rebellion not occurred the number would be significantly higher.

This evening Mother and I escorted Mrs. Ulysses Grant (Julia) to join us at Grover's Theatre for a performance of the tragic play "Faust." Mother and I were very familiar with Johan Wolfgang von Goethe's tragic play. For the general's wife, it was the first time she had seen it. I believe she enjoyed herself. Her husband had to return to the West to discuss with General Sherman his next movements. One thing I admire about Grant; he lets nothing interfere with his duties. He is where he needs to be – with his armies urging them ever forward against a determined foe.

Author's notes:

During his presidency, Lincoln appointed 32 Article III federal judges, including four Associate Justices and one Supreme Court Justice (Salmon Chase) to the Supreme Court, and 27 judges to the United States district courts. He appointed no judges to the United States circuit courts during his time in office. In 1863 the U.S. Circuit Court for the District of Columbia, which had existed since 1801, was abolished. The United States Direct Court for the District of Columbia was established in its place with one Chief Justice and three Associate Justices, all four positions being filled by Lincoln. These four positions are included in the 27 District Judges appointed by Lincoln. He appointed 4=four judges to the U.S. Court of Claims, an Article I tribunal. He later laterally reappointed one of those judges as Chief Justice of the same court. They were Joseph Casey, Ebenezer Peck, David Wilmot and Charles C. Nott.

The White House – Monday, April 4, 1864

Secretary Seward and I discussed America's increasingly positive relationship with Spain. I also signed a letter he had brought with him addressed to Isabel II, Queen of Spain, expressing our congratulations upon the birth of a daughter who received in baptism this name: Maria, Eulalia, Francisco de Asis, Margarite, Roberta, Isabel, Francisca de Paula, Cristrina Maria de la Piedad. What ever happened to just plain old Mary!

Earlier this evening, Senator Orville Browning of Illinois came by and we had a pleasant and relaxed chat. I confide in Orville more than any other member of the Senate. I trust him implicitly. The saying in this town is, "If you want a trusted friend, get a dog!" There is much truth to that advice. Orville came by to see if I could do something to help Ludwell Y. Browning, who is a prisoner at Camp Douglas in Illinois. This camp has had nothing but problems since it was established. There have been too many deaths of prisoners. The camp was built on bad ground and the buildings set up have been inadequate to the needs of the men confined there.

I was introduced to General Philip Sheridan today by General Halleck. He is an impressive officer for whom Grant has expressed high hopes. When he appeared in my office, I said to Halleck that the man may be very short of stature, but I have high hopes for him.

Author's notes:

On this date the president laid before Congress for its approval, a treaty concluded June 9, 1863, between C.H. Hale, superintendent of Indian Affairs, Charles Hutchins and S.D. Howe, Indian agents on the part of the United States, and the chiefs, headmen and delegates of the Nez Perce tribe of Indians in the Washington Territory. The treaty was ratified on June 26, 1866.

The White House – Wednesday, April 6, 1864

Yesterday we received by telegraph confirmation of a victory for our forces at Elkin's Ferry in Clark and Nevada counties in Arkansas. Major General Frederick Steele led the 3rd Division of the Seventh Army Corps and two cavalry brigades against the forces of three cavalry brigades under Confederate General, John S. Marmaduke. The number of men on both sides is estimated to have totaled over 16,000. Fighting took place on the 3rd and 4th of April. The events showed the superiority of our artillery in the battles here. Losses on both sides were light. The enemy withdrew 16 miles to Prairie D'Ane the following morning.

I mailed a long letter today to A.G. Hodges, Esq., editor of the Frankfort, Kentucky, "Commonwealth," outlining my comments made earlier in the week to him and to Kentucky Governor Bramlette and former Kentucky Senator Archibald Dixon. I reiterated my long-held belief that if slavery is not wrong, then nothing is wrong. I confessed that I have always been naturally anti-slavery. I explained that now, a year after the Emancipation was issued, there has been no loss in our foreign relations, none in our home sentiment, none in our white military force and a gain of 130,000 soldiers, sailors and laborers. We have the men, and without the measure we would not.

Author's notes:

The Civil War Trust, a division of the American Battlefield Trust, and its partners have acquired and preserved 442 acres at the Elkin's Ferry Battlefield.

The White House – Thursday, April 7, 1864

I received a thoughtful letter from my first cousin Dennis Hanks, one of my truest lifelong friends. In it he thanked me for sending him a check for $50. Dennis is a Rara Avis…the kind of special person who never disappoints. I miss his company and good humor. The last time he was in Washington, which was last year, I gave him a silver pocket watch because I learned that he did not own a timepiece. The watch had been given to me several years ago by a law client and a jeweler, who was short on cash but long on watches. Dennis was thrilled to get it. He has simple tastes and a marvelous country wit. He helps take care of my dear mother and for that I am eternally grateful. I showed him a petition that I had received. It was signed by 195 young children from Massachusetts, asking that I free all slave children. It had been sent to me by Mrs. Horace Mann.

I read a statement by Horace Mann that I think should be widely distributed. He said at the commencement in 1859 to the graduates at Antioch College, "Be ashamed to die until you have won some victory for humanity." When Mann served in Congress as a Whig in 1848, he was relentless in his opposition to slavery. He had said, "I consider no evil as great as slavery." As an attorney he had volunteered as counsel for Drayton and Sayres, who were indicted for stealing 76 slaves in the District of Columbia in a trial that lasted 21 successive days in their defense.

Author's notes:

In 1843 Mann traveled to Germany to investigate how the educational process worked. Upon his return to the United States, Mann promoted the creation of Normal Schools and well-appointed, safe and well-resourced schoolhouses. Unlike German schools, Mann favored a female-only teaching force. In 1852 he was chosen president of Antioch College at Yellow Springs, Ohio. He continued here until his death in 1859. Most historians treat Mann as one of the most important leaders of education reform in the antebellum period. His statue stands in front of the Massachusetts State House.

The White House – Saturday, April 9, 1864

Last evening at Ford's Theatre, Mother and I, with Secretary Seward and his wife, attended a performance of "King Lear." Edwin Booth's performance as Lear was superb. This morning George Thompson stopped by for a brief visit. Seward and Stanton joined us. This Englishman and former member of Parliament has been on a successful lecture tour of the United States. This week he spoke to audiences in Philadelphia and Washington. For decades his subject has been the evil of slavery and the justness of the abolition movement. He has been a powerful voice for the liberation of slaves. Before the Civil War he was often threatened for expressing his views by advocates of slavery. We discussed the Emancipation document and I autographed a printed copy for him. He will soon be back in Great Britain, where his voice in support of the Northern cause will be greatly appreciated by me and Seward.

After lunch, Massachusetts Senator Sumner came by to discuss military matters related to soldiers from his state and the use of Negro troops in some of their regiments, who are doing a fine job when in action. We also discussed a letter sent by Mrs. Horace Mann to me which included a petition from almost 200 youngsters urging the freeing of all slave children.

Author's notes:

On this date the president spent more time than usual with guests at the last afternoon reception of the season. He signed a letter to Mrs. Horace Mann thanking her for sending a petition signed by 195 children, asking that he free all slave children. Lincoln wrote, "While I have not the power to grant all they ask, I trust they will remember that God has, and that, as it seems, He wills to do it."

The White House – Monday, April 11, 1864

Mother is feeling ill today, so I canceled a trip that I had planned to take to Fortress Monroe, Virginia. She does not have a fever but has a bad cough. I had wanted to see General Butler but that can now wait for a more convenient time. Simon Cameron wrote to me warning that some in the Republican Party of New York are urging that the nominating convention be postponed until September. Cameron opposes any delays in the nominating process, and I agree with his thinking on the matter. He has just been to Fortress Monroe, where he met with Butler. They are both loyal men whose help and concerns for my presidential bid in November I greatly appreciate. Waging war and politicking at the same time is a difficult trick to pull off.

Author's notes:

Former Secretary of War and Minister to Russia Simon Cameron wrote Lincoln, "It is well known that Mr. Seward has never ceased to think he will succeed you, and that his faithful management hopes to carry him into the presidency next March, by his skill, aided perhaps by the millions made in New York by Army and Navy contracts. I am against any postponements & presume you are, but I look upon this movement as being so formidable that I should like to have a full and free conversation with you concerning it and the campaign. There are many points which would enable me to do more service - & as I am in the contest, with no wish saving your success – and with little business to interfere, I desire to guard against all surprises."

The White House – Tuesday, April 12, 1864

Mother and Tad are feeling much better. Mother had a nasty cold and sore throat; Tad had the sniffles. Mother believes that beef tea will cure just about anything and all of us have been treated to ample quantities of it this week.

I mailed a letter today to Tsar Alexander II, congratulating him upon the birth of a son to Madame the Grand Duchess Alexandra Petrovna, Spouse of his Imperial Majesty's well-beloved brother, the Grand Duke Nicholas Nicolaewitch. Alexander II is the most supportive of all the major rulers in Europe to our cause. His friendship is extraordinary. His sending vessels of the Russian Navy to visit the United States was a noble act and of great importance to our nation. He has liberated the serfs and done much to improve the judicial system; an inspired and enlightened leader.

Author's notes:

Secretary of State William Seward remained in office after the assassination of President Abraham Lincoln. Under President Andrew Johnson, Seward negotiated the acquisition of Alaska from Russia. It was purchased under a treaty signed on March 30, 186,7 in which the United States paid Russia $7.2 million dollars for 586,412 square miles of new territory of the United States of America. It became the modern State of Alaska upon being admitted to the Union in 1959. A majority of American newspapers supported the acquisition.

The White House – Wednesday, April 13, 1864

I have been giving more than the usual amount of thought to the upcoming nominating convention to be held in Baltimore on the 7th of June. The Democrats will be holding their event at the end of August. Our event will be called the National Union Convention rather than the Republican Convention. Instead of Judge Davis, my personal emissary will be John Nicolay. My contacts in all of the 25 states that will be sending representatives advise me that there may be no opposition candidate. That is reassuring because there have been signs that some ambitious parties were eager to be nominated. Apparently, they have had a change of mind. The party will, among other matters, be asked to formally resolve that slavery will be forever prohibited in the United States.

From 1 o'clock on today I reviewed 67 court-martial cases. Most resulted in pardons, commutations, remissions or approvals of sentence with two exceptions.

I spent time in preparation of comments to be made in Baltimore on the 18th at a celebration of the Sanitary Fair opening there. I will be reminding my audience that three years ago our soldiers and I could not pass safely through their city. At the time slavery was still in existence in the states. I plan to also speak of liberty as understood by me and as understood by those who have owned slaves. With some the word liberty may mean for each man to do as he pleases with himself, and the product of his labor; while with others the same word may mean for some men to do as they please with other men, and the product of other men's labor. Here are two, not only different but incompatible things called by the same name – liberty. And it follows that each of the things is, by the respective parties, called by two different and incompatible names – liberty and tyranny.

Author's notes:

Governor Bradford of Maryland delivered an eloquent speech before a crowd of 6,000 to 8,000, followed by a 15-minute speech by Lincoln at the opening of the Sanitary Fair in Baltimore. Lincoln noted that when the war began no one expected it would last until now…he said," So true is it that man proposes, and God disposes." Mrs. Lincoln did not attend the fair opening.

The White House – Thursday, April 14, 1864

Today I met with Henry G. Lee, an officer of the recently organized the Union League of Philadelphia, a patriotic society of distinguished gentlemen of that city. Lee is, among other things, a busy pamphleteer who has done much to encourage men of his city to enlist in the Army and Navy. Each July 4th the Union League plans to hold elaborate demonstrations with parades, marching bands and evening fireworks. It is only fitting that this all take place in the city of America's independence and the Liberty Bell. When last in Philadelphia, Mary took Tad to see the bell. It is no longer rung for fear that the crack in it may crack even further. Abolitionists have long considered the Liberty Bell a symbol of freedom and point to its inscribed message, "Proclaim Liberty Throughout All the Land Unto All the Inhabitants Thereof."

Author's notes:

The Bell's inscription is from the King James version of the Bible and refers to the Jubilee, or the instructions to the Israelites to return property and free slaves every 50 years. After the American Revolution, abolitionists seeking to end slavery in America were inspired by the bell's message. Beginning in the late 1800s the Liberty Bell traveled across the country for display at expositions and fairs. For a nation recovering from wounds of the Civil War, the bell served to remind Americans of a time when they fought together for independence. Movements from women's suffrage to civil rights embraced the Liberty Bell in both protest and celebration.

The White House – Saturday, April 16, 1864

Yesterday Nicolay helped me put together the final documents concerning the supplemental treaty with the Chippewa Indians, which were then delivered to the Senate. The Cabinet met with Blair, Chase and Stanton absent. Today I authorized the transfer of Fort Smith, Arkansas, and the Indian Territory to the Department of Arkansas.

Later in the day, news of a military disaster of the Red River expedition reached the War Department. It was a complete Confederate victory on April 8th as best as I can tell. Halleck estimates that as many as 26,000 men may have been engaged on both sides. It took place in De Soto Parish, Louisiana. Confederate forces were from the West Louisiana, Trans-Mississippi Department. Union troops were with the Army of the Gulf, supported by gunboats under the command of Admiral David Porter, which had ascended the Red River. Halleck believes our casualties may top 1,500 men. We also lost 20 cannons, over 150 wagons and thousand of horses and mules killed or captured. The Confederate were under the command of General Richard Taylor. Our men were led by General Nathaniel Banks.

Author's notes:

The battle of April 8th is known as the Battle of Mansfield or the Battle of Sabine Crossroads. 421 acres of land have been acquired by the American Battlefield Trust

The White House – Monday, April 18, 1864

News over the telegraph tells of significant fighting in the area of Prairie D'Ane in an open grassland area of the state of Arkansas. When I mentioned the name of the battleground to Mother, she told me that in French it means "donkey's prairie." Here an estimated 13,000 of our men prevailed over about 7,000 Confederate soldiers. Our forces were under the command of Major General Frederick Steele. The Rebels were led by Major General Sterling Price. Both sides have suffered from a host of diseases including typhoid, yellow fever, influenza and chronic diarrhea. One factor in Steele's success was the arming of men of the 36th Iowa with the new Springfield .58 caliber rifled muskets before they left Little Rock. When employed, its heavy and accurate musketry fire demoralized the enemy. Unfortunately, our forces were poorly provisioned and this in the end may force Steele to retreat from South Arkansas. The ordering of more of the powerful Springfield muskets seems in order. I've asked Halleck and Stanton to get back to me with information on how quickly this can be achieved.

Author's notes:

Union General Frederick Steele suffered a loss of nearly 500 supply wagons and 1,200 mules in bitter and ferocious cavalry ambushes upon Union supply trains at Poison Springs on April 18, and at Marks Mills on April 25. Thus, the use of the word Ane, meaning donkey, was very prescient.

The White House – Tuesday, April 19, 1864

Yesterday I returned in the morning by train from Baltimore, where I had made brief comments at the opening of the city's Sanitary Fair event. It was well attended by enthusiastic citizens of that city who gave generously to the Fair in order to help wounded soldiers and sailors. Mother was not able to join me. Many who greeted me asked me to give their best wishes to Mrs. Lincoln. She is feeling much better today. The rest has done her good.

I also interviewed Chippewa Indian chiefs in the East Room of the White House. They were a noble-looking assembly whose leaders stand tall and command respect by their words and overall behavior. I trust that our agreements with the tribes will prove successful. In the past we have failed to honor too many of our promises. I endeavored to reassure the men that I would do all I could to ensure that our word would be honored in the future. They fear the continued loss of hunting grounds as do I. Immigrants from Europe arriving on our shores have an almost insatiable appetite for Western lands for homesteading. It is up to the federal government to see that both parties understand and respect the rights of the other.

Author's notes:

On this date a large crowd overran the last reception of the White House for the season.

The White House – Wednesday, April 20, 1864

The Cabinet met to hear more news of our Red River campaign. This time we learned of activities on the 9th and 10th of the month in Pleasant Hill, Louisiana. Our generals have described it as a Union victory, but I sense that it was probably more of a draw with heavy casualties on both sides. The battle itself lasted about two hours. Halleck reported that the 32nd Iowa Infantry sustained especially heavy losses and was cut off from the rest of the Union forces during the battle. The Southerners launched their attack at 5 p.m., charging our lines. The Union right held its ground but the left and center were overrun and forced backward. During the struggle the Confederates were initially very successful and many of our positions were overrun. However, the Union side succeeded in halting the Rebel advance, and ultimately regained the left and middle ground before finally driving the enemy from the field. General Banks and his Army began its retreat from Pleasant Hill at 1 a.m. on the morning of the 10th, just a few hours after the battle ended. Halleck advises the Cabinet that Union forces then retreated to Grand Encore and abandoned plans to capture Shreveport, the capital of Louisiana. One of the significant problems for our Army was the lack of enough water to sustain the men.

Author's notes:

The Red River Campaign would ultimately prove to be a Union failure.

The White House – Thursday, April 21, 1864

Last evening, I had a recurring dream. In it I was wrestling Lorenzo Dow Thompson from St. Clair County. He was as strong or stronger than Jack Armstrong. The first time we went at each other Lorenzo brought me to the ground with great force with me landing on my back. The force of the exchange took my breath away, and as I rose to get up, Lorenzo immediately put me down again. The crowd was cheering for him and not for me. I later learned that the "smart money" was on Thompson and not Abe Lincoln. Lorenzo was a large and powerful man, but a little on the slow side. The match had taken place in a cleared area with no grass, only hard clay soil on the ground we wrestled upon. It seemed to me that every citizen of Beardstown must have been watching the match. At the time Lorenzo and I were both awaiting orders to march against Blackhawk and his warriors. In our first match he was the clear winner, but in the next two I managed to hold my own and ultimately not only put him down but did so with enough force that he had trouble getting to his feet. Throughout the Blackhawk campaign Lorenzo and I got to know each other well and became good friends. I understand that he became a successful farmer in Southern Illinois and has a great many children. I wonder if any of them are as big as him.

Author's notes:

Lincoln enlisted in the Blackhawk war as a private and was elected captain of his company. When he returned from the war he became, in 1832, a candidate for the legislature. He was defeated in that election even though the people around New Salem's precinct voted for him 275 out of 278 voters, so popular was he. He was elected in 1834 and went to Vandalia in December of 1834. He soon became a leading member of the state legislature. In the years 1833 and 1834 he fell in love with Ann Rutledge of New Salem. She died suddenly of brain fever.

The White House – Friday, April 22, 1864

I instructed General Meade to commute death sentences by court-martial to imprisonment on Dry Tortugas, Florida, for the duration of the war under Special War Department Order. Today I was shown prints of photos taken on Wednesday in my office by the painter F.B. Carpenter. He will be using them as he prepares to do his painting of the Cabinet members at the time of the issuance of the Emancipation Proclamation. Carpenter is a very thorough man and is determined to create a painting that will be as accurate as possible. After the photos were taken, I had an opportunity to visit with General Grant, who has returned to be with the Army of the Potomac.

Among other things we discussed with Secretary Stanton and General Halleck were the battles fought at Fort Pillow and Blair's Landing earlier in the month. Blair's Landing in Louisiana was a Union victory. Events at Fort Pillow, in Lauderdale County, Tennessee remain clouded as reports slowly come to our attention. We have good reasons to now believe that the battle may have ended with the massacre of black troops under the command of Confederate Major General Bedford Forrest. The event may have been caused by the rage of Rebel soldiers seeing former slaves fighting them with guns. The question to be answered is were the officers in charge of the Confederate troops responsible for the atrocities that occurred.

Author's notes:

Following cessation of hostilities at Fort Pillow, Forrest transferred 14 most seriously wounded United States Colored Troops to the U.S. Steamer Silver Cloud. President Lincoln asked his Cabinet for opinions as to how the Union should respond to the massacre at Fort Pillow. General Sherman headed an investigation into the event and the extent of Forrest's culpability for it, in which Forrest was found blameless, as he was, "to the rear and out of sight if not of hearing at the time" and "stopped the firing as soon as he could." Additionally, Sherman was told by hundreds of Union soldiers that they were well treated, while prisoners under Forrest at various times during the war. After the war, Grant wrote in his memoirs that Forrest in his report of the battle had "left out the part which shocks humanity to read." The Fort Pillow massacre became a major political issue in the North and increased public support for the war effort.

The White House – Saturday, April 23, 1864

Partly because General Nathaniel Banks has not been successful in his Red River campaign, General Grant has decided that the spring campaign should be directed against the South's two largest Armies, those of Lee and Johnston. It is our hope that there will be no more uncoordinated battles in various places in the South. That is why on April 3rd he ordered Sherman to leave Chattanooga and head with his 98,000 troops for Atlanta, Georgia. Sherman is unlikely to get confused or sidelined. He has a reputation for always moving forward with an ability to live off the land.

Edward Lyulph Stanley, the younger son of British Postmaster General Lord Stanley, arrived in our city on the 14th and has been shown around Washington by John Hay at my request. His father is in Lord Palmerston's Cabinet. Charles Francis Adams escorted Stanley to Brandy Station in Culpepper County, Virginia, where he was introduced to Generals Meade and Grant. Grant explained to Stanley how his views on Negroes in the Army had changed since he observed them in action at Vicksburg. He is now assured that they can perform front line duty with bravery and skill. This fact alone means that the freeing of slaves of military age will allow the Union to add to its forces at a time that the South will lose the labor of the slaves who come into our lines and join our Army.

Author's notes

Grant directed that Sherman "move against Johnston's Army to break it up and get into the interior of the enemy's country as far as you can, inflicting all the damage you can against their war resources." Ultimately Sherman was to march to Savannah and the up the coastline through South and North Carolina, where in time he was to unite with Grant at Richmond.

The White House – Monday, April 25, 1864

From the Eastern Portico of Willard's Hotel, Mother, Tad and I reviewed 30,000 of General Burnside's troops as they passed through Washington from Annapolis on their way to join the Army of the Potomac. I ordered Dr. John Gray to go to Elmira, New York to examine and decide upon the sanity of Private Lorenzo C. Stewart, who is under the sentence of death. He is to determine his current sanity and to advise if he believes Stewart may have been insane at the time the crime was committed.

Since General Burnside once outranked General Meade and will now be inferior to him in grade, this situation requires Burnside's agreement to this change in status. Burnside has advised Stanton that he is willing to be subordinate to Meade and therefore we can expect complete cooperation between the two men.

Author's notes:

President Lincoln wrote to John R. Woods, secretary of the Illinois Sanitary Commission, expressing his regrets that he was unable to attend the inauguration of the Soldier's Home that week in Springfield, Illinois.

The White House – Wednesday, April 27, 1864

We had a good Cabinet meeting yesterday, albeit Chase, Stanton and Blair were absent. Secretary Wells described for us the battle fought 10 days ago in North Carolina at Plymouth. This was an unexpected victory for the Confederates. The Rebel ironclad Albemarle drove off the Union naval squadron on the Roanoke River that was supporting the Union defenders of Plymouth. That in turn ensured the success of an enemy infantry assault. The Albemarle sank the USS Southfield and heavily damaged the USS Miami. On the 20th, General Hoke captured two of our forts, all our troops and 25 artillery pieces.

I conferred with Congressman Albert G. Riddle, who will be assuming duties as U.S. consul at Mantazas, Cuba. Reportedly Reb ships are still visiting the island of Cuba to pick up arms and munitions despite our blockading efforts along the Southern coast of the United States.

I reviewed 27 court-martial cases – never a pleasant task, but a vital one.

Author's notes:

The Confederates held the town of Plymouth until the Albemarle was sunk in late October of 1864. With the support of the ironclad ship gone, the Rebels abandoned Plymouth, which remained in federal hands for the duration of the war. The federal garrison at Plymouth under Brigadier General Henry Wessels of 2,834 men was outnumbered by the Confederate forces, which totaled three brigades of about 10,000 troops commanded by Brigadier General Robert F. Hoke. Commander James Cooke commanded the CSS Albemarle.

Albert Gallatin Riddle served only one term in the House of Representatives, from 1861 to 1863. He was succeeded by James A. Garfield. He served in Cuba until 1864 as consul. When he returned to Washington, he was retained by the State Department to aid in the prosecution of John H. Surratt as one of the accomplices in the murder of President Lincoln. He oversaw the law office at Howard University for several years after its establishment.

The White House – Thursday, April 28, 1864

Mother and Tad are visiting several good friends in New York City and are staying at the Metropolitan Hotel. She telegraphed for $50.00 and Tad inquired as to the condition of his goats. I advised him that a draft was on the way for Mother and that the goats are thriving. I congratulated Governor Isaac Murphy on the successful organization of the state government of Arkansas. The immediate relief of the citizens in the Midwest can best be managed via the construction of a railroad to service people located between Knoxville, Tennessee, and Cincinnati, Ohio, by way of central Kentucky.

Reports received by the War Department tell of another massacre of black soldiers by Rebels at the Battle of Poison Spring in Arkansas 10 days ago. We are asking for more information before considering what steps may be taken to resolve this recurring problem. The Red River campaign has been a fiasco from day one.

Author's notes:

On May 25th a resolution about a railroad being built to serve the areas from the valley of the Ohio to Eastern Tennessee passed the House of Representatives but failed to pass the Senate when voted upon there. The matter was first raised by the Congress in December of 1861.

The Metropolitan Hotel in Manhattan was located on Broadway and 200 feet on Prince Street. It was built in a grand commercialized style reminiscent of Roman palazzos, with many fine furnishings imported from Europe, including the largest plate-glass mirrors in the United States. The interior decorations were claimed to have cost $200,000. It could shelter 600 guests in steam-heated rooms. It operated on the American Plan, which included three meals a day. Mary Lincoln and her black seamstress stayed there often. After the Civil War the hotel was managed by William M. Tweed, the son of "Boss Tweed," who became the hotel's proprietor. It was closed in 1895 and destroyed that year.

The White House – Saturday, April 30, 1864

Today as I looked out of my office windows, which face south, I was able to clearly see the Washington Monument. It remains uncompleted. Construction began in 1848 and has been halted since 1854 due principally to a lack of funds. When it is finished after this awful war, I am told it will be the tallest building in the world. The cornerstone was laid on July 4, 1848. I always find it an inspiring sight.

My view of George Washington has not changed since I was a young boy and read Parson Weems' book, "The Life of Washington." Hay went to the Library of Congress and borrowed a copy for me, which I intend to read to Tad. I believe that George Washington was our greatest president.

Author's notes:

The capstone of the monument was set on December 6, 1884; the completed Washington Monument was dedicated on February 21, 1885, and officially opened to the public on October 9, 1888. Today, 50 American flags fly 24 hours a day on a large circle of flag poles centered on the monument. It is the tallest monumental column in the world. It was the tallest building in the world from 1884 until 1889, when it was overtaken by the Eiffel Tower in Paris.

The White House – Monday, May 2, 1864

Today the full Cabinet met to discuss, among other things, the status of railroads in the seceded states. We have learned a great deal from captured prisoners and spies about the weakening condition of railroads in the Confederacy. While the North has expanded its rail resources, the South has suffered significant damage to equipment and trackage due to our aggressive policy of destroying bridges, captured rolling stock and rails themselves. Because the South lacks large steel manufacturing assets, it is now faced with an inability to replace destroyed rails and engines, thus losing the use of its rail lines. When the war began, the South's railroads were inefficient compared to ours. The Rebels had insufficient mileage, had gaps between key lines, inability to repair and maintain track and rolling stock, differences in gauge, and the inability to build new lines. We believe these shortcomings will only intensify for the Confederates as forces like Sherman's emphasize track and equipment destruction as a determined war policy. The typically small repair shops of their railroads have been cut off from all sorts of supplies of railroad material but what their shops can produce. We learned from a captured Rebel officer that James Longstreet's First Corps, when traveling from Northern Virginia to reinforce Braxton Bragg's troops in northern Georgia by rail last year, traveled 852 miles in 182 hours, or just about 4 1/2 miles an hour. By contrast, our trains run on time and at peak speeds when carrying troops, horses and artillery and rations to key battle areas.

Author's notes:

On April 12, 1864 General Robert E. Lee implored Secretary of War James A. Seddon to address the management of railroads in the Confederacy. Problems of supply plagued the Army of Northern Virginia, and Lee wanted all obstacles to deliveries removed. He wrote, "I earnestly recommend that no private interests be allowed to interfere with the use of all the facilities of transportation that we possess until the wants of the Army are provided for. The railroads should be at once devoted exclusively to this purpose, even should it be found necessary to suspend all private travel for business or pleasure upon them for the present." Historians have concluded that Jefferson Davis and the Congress in Richmond were loath to enforce the kind of transportation policy the war effort demanded. The South lacked wholehearted public cooperation and government coercion needed to wage a modern war. The conclusion: Collapse of Confederate railroad service was of immense importance in hastening the breakdown of the rebellion.

The White House – Tuesday, May 3, 1864

I asked the Cabinet members to give me their written recommendations on what our policy should be concerning the killing of surrendered black Union soldiers by Confederate forces at Fort Pillow, Tennessee, and apparently at Poison Spring, Arkansas. Murder in war is never to be condoned on either side of the conflict. My sense is that we must put Jefferson Davis and his government on notice that such behavior will be met with the severest retaliation on our side. I've always viewed Davis as an honorable gentleman and cannot believe he views this behavior by his officers and men as allowable. The problem with retaliation is that if we shoot a Southerner who had nothing to do with the crime, we are executing an innocent man instead of a guilty one. Secretary Wells said that "The idea of retaliation – killing man for man – which is the popular noisy demand is barbarous. We cannot yield to any such inhuman scheme of retaliation." I believe Welles has the right attitude in this sordid matter.

Author's notes:

The Cabinet decided to have General Forrest's officers and men tried for murder if caught and agreed to formally notify the Confederate government that the U.S. would set aside Southern officers being held in Northern prisoner camps as hostages against such occurrences in the future.

The White House – Wednesday, May 4, 1864

Richard H. Dana Jr., the U.S. district attorney for Massachusetts, visited me today. I hadn't seen him for a year. He is a very engaging man. His writings have made him famous. Mary and I have both read "Two Years Before the Mast." All his adult life he has been a champion of the downtrodden, from seamen to fugitive slaves and freedmen. His book "The Seaman's Friend" is considered the standard reference for lawyers on the legal rights and responsibilities of sailors. We discussed some of his court cases in which he defended wronged seamen. He defended the United States in the Supreme Court in the matter of the legality of rightfully blockading Southern ports.

I wrote to General Sherman at Chattanooga to do whatever he can for the suffering people in the Nashville area.

Lucius Chittenden, registrar of the Treasury, came by my office at 4 P.M. We discussed the terrible condition of exchanged prisoners. Too few are being exchanged and many of those exchanged are desperately ill from lack of food, awful sanitary conditions and poor medical attention. I asked that he leave at once and visit Annapolis, Maryland. He is to report back conditions he finds there among Rebel prisoners being held.

Author's notes:

After the close of the Civil War Dana resigned his office because he did not approve of President Andrew Johnson's regressive reconstruction policies. From 1867 to 1868 he was a member of the Massachusetts legislature and served as a U.S.counsel in the trial of Confederate President Jefferson Davis. In 1876, his nomination as ambassador to Great Britain was defeated in the Senate by political enemies.

The White House – Friday, May 6, 1864

Yesterday I authorized Secretaries Chase and Stanton to allow the export of fine horses bought for the personal use of the emperor of France and the captain general of Cuba. It reminded me of the terrible fate of so many fine horses that are forced to pull cannon or supplies often under difficult combat conditions. I believe that Confederate officers own their own horses, whereas Union cavalry officers utilize horses provided to them by the quartermasters. I would think that the fact that a horse is owned by its rider would mean it will probably get better food and care than one provided by the government at no expense to the cavalryman. I must remember to ask General Sheridan about this when I next see him.

Last evening, I interviewed Congressmen Green Clay Smith of Kentucky and James Ashley of Ohio. Both men are strong supporters of my candidacy for president.

Author's notes:

On this date, Lincoln wrote a letter to Mrs. Abner Bartlett of Medford, Massachusetts, an elderly woman who had knitted the president a pair of socks. They were too small for him, so he gave them to Hay to wear.

The White House – Saturday, May 7, 1864

Stanton and Halleck presented a detailed report describing four recent battles fought in Arkansas and Louisiana, including Poison Springs, Monett's Ferry, Marks' Mills and Jenkins' Ferry. Two were wins and two were losses. Later, I received a first-hand account of fighting during the Wilderness campaign from Henry E. Wing, the correspondent of the New York Tribune who had traveled directly from the fighting by special locomotive. He arrived at 2 A.M. and came directly here. There have been heavy losses on both sides of this difficult struggle. Grant is determined to stick to his plan of aggressive warfare against Lee despite the costs.

Mother and Tad joined me for a performance by the Marine Band on the lawn of the White House with several hundred in attendance. I had them play "Dixie," one of my favorite tunes. They hadn't performed in quite a long while, so it was a special treat for the public and for Tad in particular. He can carry a tune very nicely, unlike his father, who I think is tone deaf!

The crowd repeatedly called for me to speak and I accommodated them as best I could. I specifically proposed that they give three cheers for General Grant and all the armies under his command. The crowd did so noisily and with great enthusiasm for our new military commander.

Author's notes:

The Battle of the Wilderness was fought over the same ground where General Joseph Hooker had been defeated by Robert E. Lee the year before. The struggle lasted two days, May 5 and May 6. Grant assured Lincoln that there would be no turning back. Instead he would continue to pressure Lee and engage him two weeks later at Spotsylvania, where almost two weeks of heavy fighting would exact another 20,000 casualties by both armies combined. Grant's message to Lincoln read, in part, "I propose to fight it out on this line if it takes all summer. Lincoln told Hay and Francis Carpenter that, "The great thing about Grant is his perfect coolness and persistency of purpose...he has the grit of a bulldog! It is the dogged pertinacity of Grant that wins."

The White House – Monday, May 9, 1864

Speaker of the House Colfax of Indiana came by the White House yesterday to discuss recent events and the heavy casualties experienced by our forces and the enemy. He strongly supports our more concerted and better-coordinated war efforts. He spent just little over an hour with me. He tried to cheer me up, but the number of dead and wounded is just too oppressive to contemplate. I attempted a bit of country humor as an anecdote, but it did not work. The number of casualties flowing into Washington seems to be beyond count.

Gwinn Heap, clerk to Rear Admiral David Porter, joined by Navy Secretary Welles, described recent failures of General Banks' Red River expedition. Grant had opposed this action and was right in his expectations that the campaign would probably not succeed. I agreed to assigning General Edward Canby to assume field command of the Army at once, with Banks to assume administrative command of the Department of the Gulf. I will depend upon Banks to see that my reconstruction policies for Louisiana are carried out.

Author's notes:

At the end of the day the 27th Michigan Volunteers' Band performed for an enthusiastic crowd at the White House. They played Julia Ward Howe's song "The Battle Hymn of the Republic," and the crowd serenaded the president and his wife and son, Tad.

The White House – Tuesday, May 10, 1864

At breakfast this morning I was asked about Henry Clay by Tad, who is now studying American history. Mother told him that her father, Robert Todd, had been taught by Clay when he attended Transylvania University. It was the first university west of the Appalachian Mountains. I learned that although Clay owned a great many slaves in his lifetime, his will stipulated that upon his death, all of his slaves were to be freed. To my mind, Henry Clay was one of the greatest public servants in American history. Had he been elected president this dreadful Civil War might have been avoided, or surely delayed. Clay stood for Union. His life was one of personal tragedy. He and his wife, Lucretia, had 11 children, and seven of them died. His son Theodore had to be placed in a mental hospital. His son Henry, to whom he was closest, had been a brilliant scholar at West Point. Upon fulfilling his Army obligations, he had begun a promising career in law and politics. When the war with Mexico began, he raised a regiment of Kentucky volunteers and joined the forces of Zachary Taylor. He was killed at Buena Vista. Henry Clay had opposed the war knowing that disposing of any territory taken from Mexico would spark more debate over the expansion of slavery.

Author's notes:

Clay's Whig Party collapsed after his death in 1852. Mississippi Senator Henry S. Foote stated his opinion that "had there been one such man in Congress as Henry Clay in 1860 to 1861 there would, I feel sure, have been no Civil War." Lincoln said of Clay, "He was my ideal of a great man." Some historians have argued that Clay's victory in the 1844 election would have prevented both the Mexican American War and the American Civil War. In 1957 a Senate committee selected Clay as one of the five greatest U.S. senators, along with Webster, Calhoun, La Follette and Robert Taft. In 2015, political scientist Michael Miller and historian Ken Owen ranked Clay as one of the four most influential politicians who never served as president, alongside Alexander Hamilton, William Jennings Bryan and John C. Calhoun.

The White House – Thursday, May 12, 1864

Friday and Saturday of last week a small but decisive battle was fought in Chesterfield County, Virginia, between about 8,000 soldiers under General Benjamin Butler's Army of the James and Confederate troops under Brigadier General Johnson Hagood. What looked like a Confederate victory on day one, turned into a Union win on day two. On May 6, Hagood's men stopped initial Federal probes at Port Walthall Junction. But on May 7, a Union division drove Hagood's and Brigadier General Bushrod Johnson's brigades from the Railroad junction. This allowed Federal troops to cut the Richmond – Petersburg railroad at this strategically important location. Confederate defenders retired behind Swift Run Creek and awaited reinforcements.

Author's notes:

Bushrod Johnson was born in Ohio in 1817 and graduated from the U.S. Military Academy. He was raised a Quaker and worked on the Underground Railroad with his uncle. He fought in the Seminole War in Florida and in the Mexican American War. When the Civil War broke out he sided with the South. He saw action at Fort Donelson, Shiloh, Perryville, Stones River, Chickamauga, Knoxville, Bermuda Hundred, Swift Creek, Battle of the Crater, Siege of Petersburg, Battle of White Oak Road, Five Forks and Sayler's Creek. After the war he returned to teaching. He became a professor and co-chancellor (1870) of the University of Nashville with former Confederate General Edmund Kirby Smith. He retired in 1875 to a farm in Brighton, Illinois, where he died in 1880 at age 63.

The White House – Friday, May 13, 1864

I forwarded to the Senate correspondence related to a controversy between Chile and Bolivia. It seems that Bolivia has declared war upon Chile for having appropriated some three degrees latitude of territory comprising the desert of Atacama. Secretary Seward and I have recommended that the nation of Spain should be requested to arbitrate the issue. We have enough on our plate right now to justify our not getting involved in a faraway dispute among Spanish-speaking peoples with whom we have had good relations for generations.

I had a pleasant visit from James Brackenridge, a retired lawyer who practiced near my home when I was about 20 years old. I recognized him the minute he opened the door to my office. I used to attend court and watch cases in which Brackenridge was defense counsel. He later moved from Illinois to Texas and is now back in Illinois. I vividly recall attending a murder trail in which he was the defendant's lawyer. I told him then that I had listened to his jury speech and believed it was the best speech, up to that time, I had ever heard. I said that if I could ever make as good a speech as that, my soul would be satisfied. I confessed that during the trial I'd formed a fixed determination to study the law and make it my profession. He must have thought I was crazy. As he was leaving, he told me that he and his family would be supporting my re-election in November. We shook hands warmly.

Author's notes:

From May 7 to May 13 the Battle of Rocky Face Ridge was fought in Whitfield County, Georgia, during the Atlanta Campaign. General Joseph Johnson's Confederate Army was forced to evacuate their strong position due to a flanking movement by the Union forces under General William T. Sherman. Johnson retired south toward Resaca on May 12. Casualties were 837 for the Union and 600 for the Confederates. In 2016, the Civil War Trust and its partners acquired 301 acres of the Rocky Face Ridge Battlefield, including surviving earthworks and the remains of a continuous entrenchment more than 2,000 feet long. That purchase expanded the total battlefield acreage acquired and preserved by the Trust and its partners to 926 acres.

The White House – Saturday, May 14, 1864

General Halleck and staff members acquainted the Cabinet with the details of recent actions in Virginia at Swift Creek and Cloyd's Mountain on the 9th of May. Initial reports suggest that the first action was inconclusive except for damage inflicted upon railroad track and rolling stock. In the second event, Confederate Brigadier General Albert G. Jenkins was badly wounded and captured. Halleck informed us that Jenkins had an arm amputated and is not expected to survive. The battle is considered a Union victory.

Author's notes:

Brigadier General Jenkins was a a graduate of Harvard Law School and a delegate to the Democratic National Convention in Cincinnati in 1856. He served in the U.S. Congress from Virginia's 11th District from 1857 to 1861. He resigned from Congress and later served in the Confederate Congress after secession. He raised a company of partisan rangers and rose to become commander of a brigade of cavalry. He was wounded at Gettysburg and at Cloyd's Mountain. He died of his wounds on May 21, 1864 at aged 33.

The White House – Monday, May 16, 1864

I mailed a letter today to Mrs. Augustus C. French, the wife of the former governor of Illinois, which included my autograph to be used at the Mississippi Valley Sanitary Fair. It will help raise money for the relief and comfort of our brave soldiers. This is a common request and I am always pleased to accommodate with my signature. I usually sign my name "A. Lincoln," but for the fairs I sign "Abraham Lincoln."

The Cabinet discussed recent military actions at Chester Station, Cove Mountain and Yellow Tavern in Virginia. We were informed that General J.E.B. Stuart was shot at Yellow Tavern by a dismounted private in the 5th Michigan Cavalry from less than 30 yards. He reportedly died on May 12th in Richmond. He is reputed to have been the finest cavalry officer in the Confederate Army.

Author's notes:

His friend from his close Federal Army days, Union Major General John Sedgwick, said that Stuart was the "greatest cavalry officer ever foaled in America." His aide, Major Andrew Venable, wrote of Stuart, "He told me he never expected to live through the war, and that if we were conquered, that he did not want to live." Stuart died at 7:38 P.M. on May 12 the day before his wife, Flora, reached his side. Upon hearing of Stuart's death, General Lee is reported to have said that he could hardly keep from weeping at the mere mention of Stuart's name and that Stuart had never given him a bad piece of information. Flora Stuart wore the black of mourning for the remainder of her life, and never remarried. She is buried alongside her husband and their daughter, Little Flora, in Hollywood Cemetery in Richmond, Virginia.

The White House – Tuesday, May 17, 1864

A very long Cabinet meeting was held today. Events in Spotsylvania are of great concern to all of us. Halleck and his staff have given us several briefings since the battle began on May 8 and the bitter fighting continues to this day. General Halleck showed me a telegraphic message that he received during the fighting from Grant. It reads, "I propose to fight it out on this line if it takes all summer." I continue to have faith in U.S. Grant.

Halleck also explained to us recent military events that have taken place in Virginia, Georgia and Louisiana at Proctor's Creek, Resaca and New Market.

Author's notes:

In the time since the Battle of the Wilderness began on May 5, Grant had about 36,000 casualties while Halleck estimated that Lee probably had over 25,000 casualties. At Spotsylvania five general officers were killed or mortally wounded during the battle: Union Major General John Sedgwick and Brigadier Generals James C. Rice and Thomas G. Stevenson; and Confederate Brigadier General Junius Daniel and Abner M. Perrin. Forty-three men received the Medal of Honor during the Battle of Spotsylvania Court House. Historians have judged the fighting inconclusive.

The White House – Wednesday, May 18, 1864

I ordered General Dix to arrest the editors of the New York World and the Journal of Commerce in New York for printing a spurious proclamation, which purported to be signed by me. I also ordered that the printing of the two newspapers be suspended. The papers published a fake story claiming that I had ordered the drafting of 400,000 men, which was not true. This can only hurt the war effort. General Dix has been asked to find out how this could have happened. I've asked Secretaries Stanton and Seward to get to the bottom of this matter.

Early in the evening I attended a lecture by Dr. J.R. Warner given in the Hall of the House of Representatives on the Battle of Gettysburg. He gave an accurate and stirring presentation of the epic battle. Many members of both houses of Congress were in attendance and gave the speaker a generous applause at the conclusion of his detailed presentation.

Author's notes:

An investigation quickly found that a fake proclamation had been composed by Joseph Howard Jr., the editor of the Brooklyn Eagle, and Francis Mallison, one of the paper's reporters. Howard was a speculator who wanted to increase the value of the gold he personally owned. Howard delivered the phony proclamation to the newspapers pretending to be a messenger from the Associated Press just before press time, which did not allow the duped editors to check the veracity of the story. The price of gold shot up 10% on the news. When the facts were made clear, the editors were released from jail and the newspapers allowed to publish.

The White House – Thursday, May 19, 1864

Yesterday I was visited by a large delegation from the Methodist Episcopal Church. I asked God's blessing on their church and all churches at this critical time in our nation's history. I asked that we bless God who at this time of great trial giveth us the churches. One member asked me to describe my own religious views. I told them about my early religious experiences as a very young boy going to the Little Pigeon Baptist Church with my mother, father and sister near Lincoln City, Indiana. When we moved to rustic New Salem, there was no church there. I told them that I still have the Bible owned by my family and read it every chance I get. I said that as a young man I had serious doubts about many aspects of my faith, but with time those doubts have been resolved. I have never denied the truth of the Scriptures and never spoken with an intentional disrespect of religion. I admitted to them that I prefer short to long sermons and that I have found during America's terrible civil strife great comfort in reading the Sermon on the Mount. I often recite the beatitudes of Christ from memory for Mary and Tad before he goes to sleep:

"Blessed are the poor in spirit, for theirs is the kingdom of heaven. Blessed are those who mourn, for they will be comforted. Blessed are the meek, for they will inherit the earth. Blessed are those who hunger and thirst for righteousness, for they will be filled. Blessed are the merciful, for they will be shown mercy. Blessed are the pure in heart, for they will see God. Blessed are the peacemakers, for they will be called children of God. Blessed are those who are persecuted because of righteousness, for theirs is the kingdom of heaven. Blessed are you when people insult you and falsely say all kinds of evil against you because of me. Rejoice and be glad, because great is your reward in heaven, for in the same way they persecuted the prophets who were before you."

Author's notes:

The Bible used for Lincoln's 1861 inauguration is an Oxford University Press edition published in 1853. It has 1,280 pages and is small in size, measuring 4 inches wide by 1.75 inches thick. It is bound in burgundy red velvet with gilt edges. When that event took place, his personal Bible had not arrived from Springfield, Illinois. In 1928, Mary Eunice Harland, the widow of his oldest son, Robert Todd Lincoln, donated the inaugural Bible to the Library of Congress. It contained markers at the 31st chapter of Deuteronomy and the fourth chapter of the Book of Hosea. President Barack Obama chose that same Bible to use at his historic inaugurations of 2009 and 2013

The White House – Friday, May 20, 1864

Secretary Welles and his staff presented information to the full Cabinet about the Confederate warship Alabama, and the extensive damage it has been causing to American and neutral ships that it has intercepted and destroyed. She is commanded by a former U.S. Navy commander, now CSA Captain Raphael Semmes. The Alabama is his second Confederate command. His first warship was the CSA Sumter, which was ultimately sold after six months of service at Charleston harbor as a merchant ship. The Sumter's new owner changed its name to the Gibraltar and made one or two voyages as a blockade runner. It is believed to have been lost in the North Sea. Captain Semmes' current warship, the Alabama, which was built in Great Britain at Laird Shipyard, is larger, faster and much better-armed than the Sumter. She has a crew of over 100 men. Secretary Seward informs Secretary Welles whenever one of our foreign offices learns of the Alabama's entering a foreign port where we have representatives stationed. Yet despite receipt of this intelligence, we have yet to engage her in battle. She is elusive and very successful in sinking or burning our merchant ships and whalers.

Author's notes:

During the six months that the Sumter cruised, she captured 17 ships as follows: Golden Rocket, Cuba Machias, Ben. Dunning, Albert Adams, Naiad, Louisa Kilham, West Wind, Abby Bradford, Joseph Maxwell, Joseph Parke, D. Trowbridge, Montmorency, Arcade, Vigilant, Eben Dodge, Neapolitan, and Investigator. While this was going on the U.S. Navy assigned six ships of war to be constantly searching for the Sumter, which weakened the federal blockade of the Southern coast.

The White House – Saturday, May 21, 1864

I have lifted the publication ban on the New York World and the Journal of Commerce having determined that the editors of those papers acted in good faith. They were deceived and published a fake presidential proclamation in total innocence. I consider both papers to be loyal to the Union and regret the situation arose as it did. I believe in freedom of the press.

I declined an invitation to go to St. Louis to attend the Mississippi Valley Sanitary Fair. The amount of good done by these fairs is far beyond calculation.

An act to provide temporary government for the Montana Territory having been passed, I instructed Attorney General Bates and Secretary Seward to brief applications for offices in so far as they are related to their departments.

I telegraphed Miss Christiana Sack of Baltimore that I cannot postpone the execution of her brother, Henry Sack, who is a convicted spy, purely based on her telegram claiming that he is innocent. However, I did authorize that she be authorized to see him. I will see to it that he will not be hung but will instead probably be sentenced to imprisonment at hard labor for the duration of the war. She should therefore pray for an early end to the conflict! I've asked Hay to follow this matter closely and to keep me informed of the ultimate outcome of the case.

Author's notes:

On this day the bloody Battle of Spotsylvania ended.

The White House – Monday, May 23, 1864

Yesterday, General Halleck and members of his staff came by in the afternoon and presented to me and Secretaries Stanton and Welles a comprehensive review of recent military actions at Adairsville in Georgia, Yellow Bayou in Louisiana and Ware Bottom Church in Virginia.

In Georgia, the Confederate forces under General Joseph E. Johnston failed to destroy part of the Union force approaching Atlanta under Sherman. The battle consisted of a series of skirmishes throughout May 17. This delaying action allowed Johnston to move south toward Cassville. Sherman then sent the Army of the Ohio with one corps of the Army of the Cumberland in pursuit of the retreating Rebels. The enemy, apparently fearing that Federal soldiers were now in his rear, fell back and rejoined General Polk, failing to spring the trap Johnston had prepared for Sherman's Army. Sherman continues his steady move to Atlanta. It is my sense that our strategy of keeping the enemy engaged in as many places at once as is humanly possible is the only way to wear him down. Our advantage in superior numbers must in the end triumph.

At Yellow Bayou in Avoyelles Parish, Louisiana, Union forces under General Joseph Mower attacked the Rebels and drove them back to their main line. The Confederates then counterattacked, forcing our men to retreat, until they finally repulsed the attack. A see-saw action lasted a few hours, until the ground cover caught fire and both sides were forced to withdraw. We had 360 casualties.

At Ware Bottom Church, General Benjamin Butler suffered a defeat at the hands of General P.G.T. Beauregard. Butler's troops are continuing to man their Bermuda Hundred defenses.

Author's notes:

The Ware Bottom Church, one of the oldest in Virginia, was unfortunately destroyed during fighting on June 18, when it became the source of annoyance for Parker's Virginia Battery, only a few hundred yards from the church. Federal sharpshooters had been using the church to harass the gunners. The Civil War Trust and its partners have acquired and preserved 22 acres of the battlefield.

The White House – Tuesday, May 24, 1864

I telegraphed Governor John Brough of Ohio today and advised him that General Grant had informed me and the Cabinet that "Everything looks exceedingly favorable to us." John is so large that when he ran the railroad in Madison, Indiana, the railroad company named one of its largest engines "John Brough" in his honor. In June of last year, he was elected governor on a pro-Union ticket. He was neither a Republican nor a Democrat. He defeated Copperhead leader Clement Vallandigham. When I learned that he had won I sent him a telegraphic message that read, "Glory to God in the Highest. Ohio has saved the nation." Since his election he has been incredibly supportive of our war policies. His efforts have raised more than 34,000 troops, thus exceeding his quota.

Author's notes:

John Brough died on August 29, 1865. He had fallen in the State House yard, bruising his hand and badly spraining his ankle. Using a cane caused inflammation over time and gangrene eventually set in.

The White House – Wednesday, May 25, 1864

I wrote a short note to General Meade requesting his authorization to allow Mr. J. C. Swift to follow the Army and pick up rags and cast-off clothing dropped by Grant's troops. He offers to pay $200 a month to the Sanitary Commission for this exclusive permission. I also wrote to Secretary Stanton requesting that Stephen C. Campbell, now held as a prisoner of war at Johnson's Island, be discharged upon taking the oath. The man voluntarily quit the Rebel Army and is subject to epileptic fits.

Members of the Pittsburgh Sanitary Fair have asked me to send them my autograph to be used as a fund-raising item at their next event. I will do so tomorrow.

Late tonight at the telegraph office I received initial reports of a battle fought at Wilson's Wharf near Charles City, Virginia, on the James River. The Rebels were led by General Fitzhugh Lee. It was the first combat encounter between Lee's forces with African American soldiers, known as United States Colored Troops. Brigadier General Edward A. Wild's Union forces were supported by the U.S.S. George Washington and the U.S.S. Dawn. The Confederates withdrew to Charles City Court House.

Author's notes:

About 200 Confederate troops were killed or wounded. Federal forces losses were six killed and 40 wounded.

The White House – Thursday, May 26, 1864

Attorney General Bates and Senator Sumner joined me in a lengthy discussion of equitable pay for colored union chaplains. It is my view that black and white soldiers, sailors and black and white chaplains all deserve equal pay.

At 11:30 this morning Secretary of State Seward joined Baron Fredrich von Gerolt at lunch with Mother and me. We always enjoy meeting with Gerolt. He has been in America for about 25 years representing the kingdom of Prussia and speaks perfect English. By education he is an expert in mining and geology. He has spent a great deal of time in Mexico and has published geological maps that are highly regarded. We discussed recent political matters in Mexico, and he gave us his opinions about French ambitions in that country. It is his view that the French have enough on their plate in Europe at this time and may soon bring home its military forces from Mexico. He believes that the recent installation of Archduke Maximilian to the throne of Mexico under the aegis of the French will never prove popular with the citizens of that poor nation. I agree. I did not like to see the United States go to war with Mexico back in 1846 and I disliked seeing France behaved in ways against the spirit of the Monroe Doctrine.

Author's notes:

Maximilian and his wife, Princess Charlotte of Belgium, the daughter of Leopold I, King of the Belgians, and his wife, Louise of Orleans, lived as Austrian regents in Milan or Viceroys of Lombardy-Venetia from 1857 to 1859. In 1859 Ferdinand Maximilian was approached by Mexican monarchists to become emperor of Mexico. On October 20, 1861 in Paris, he received a letter from members of the Mexican aristocracy to take the Mexican throne. He did not accept immediately, but at the invitation of Napoleon III, after a French-staged plebiscite in Mexico that confirmed the proclamation of empire, Maximilian consented to accept the crown in October of 1863. The new emperor landed in Vera Cruz on May 29, 1864. In 1866 Napoleon III withdrew his troops from Mexico in face of Mexican resistance and U.S. opposition under the Monroe Doctrine as well as opposition from an ever-growing Prussian military. Maximilian was captured by Republican forces and sentenced to death following a court-martial. He was executed by a firing squad on June 19, 1867.

The White House – Saturday, May 28, 1864

Augustus N. Dickens of Chicago, the youngest brother of famed author Charles Dickens, came by and asked me for my autograph. Mother and I discussed his brother's writings and she served him tea and cake. He has a ready humor and is a brilliant conversationalist with the polished manners of an English gentleman. As a young man he had acted in his brother's plays in London and is now employed by the Illinois Central Land Department. I have admired Charles Dickens for many years and Tad loves to be read Dickens by his mother at bedtime. He has toured our country and a great many Americans consider him the world's greatest novelist. I have found none better. Robert's favorite book by Dickens is "A Tale of Two Cities." Mine is "Oliver Twist." Mary's is "A Christmas Carol." Tad loves them all.

Author's notes:

Augustus N. Dickens was born November 10, 1827 and died October 4, 1866. He died from tuberculosis at age 39. Charles Dickens supported both of Augustus' wives financially.

The White House – Monday, May 30, 1864

Over the weekend I met with Secretary Welles, Admiral Dahlgren and several naval staff officers to review the serious and vexing matter of the Confederate raider Alabama. No matter how hard the Navy tries, it cannot seem to locate this Rebel commerce raider, which is causing significant damage to our merchant shipping, thus resulting in high insurance rates for those in maritime trade. Captain Raphael Semmes has been incredibly successful in avoiding our warships who search for him but never locate his ship. It has been reported sighted in the North Atlantic, the South Atlantic and as far away as Cape Town, South Africa, and even in the East Indies. Welles advises that in 1862 alone, the Alabama claimed 28 prizes and last year even more.

Author's notes:

The C.S.S. Alabama burned 65 prizes valued at nearly $6,000,000. During all its raiding ventures, captured ships' crews and passengers were never harmed, only detained until they could be placed aboard a neutral ship or placed ashore in a friendly or neutral port. The U.S. government pursued the "Alabama Claims" against Great Britain for the losses caused by the Alabama and other raiders that had been built and fitted out in Britain. Upon completion of her seven expeditionary raids, Alabama had been at sea for 534 days out of 657, never visiting a single Confederate port. She boarded nearly 450 vessels and took more than 2,000 prisoners without a single loss of life from either prisoners or her own crew. A joint arbitration commission awarded the United States $15.5 million in damages. In 1851, Captain Semmes, when serving as a U.S. Navy officer, had observed: Commerce raiders are little better than licensed pirates; and it behooves all civilized nations to suppress the practice altogether.

The White House – Tuesday, May 31, 1864

A beautiful day – Mother says that she believes we will have even nicer weather throughout June. I received a very moving letter today from John H. Bryant of Princeton, Illinois, asking me to attend a meeting of friends of the late Owen Lovejoy, the representative from Illinois' 5th District, who died suddenly after a short illness. Owen Lovejoy was a unique man, a radical Republican and an avid abolitionist with whom I had a long and warm relationship. His many good friends wish to honor him with a monument and ask that I write in support of this idea. I am fully in favor of a monument to Owen's memory. Recently Owen had been speaking in the House about ultimate reconstruction after the war. He shared my viewpoint that there are not "rebel states," but only "states that rebels have taken possession of and overthrown the legitimate governments for the time being…and that as soon as we get in possession of them we will breathe into them the spirit of republican life – a free soul again." He and I both want to dispossess the ship of State of her piratical crew and to put into their place loyal men to sail her as our forefathers sailed the old Union. He had been tireless in urging reconciliation after hostilities cease. I saw him just before he left for Maine in February to seek a cure for his declining health. Sadly, he died in February in Brooklyn, New York.

Author's notes:

Lincoln wrote to the monument committee, "My personal acquaintance with him commenced only about ten years ago, since when it has been quite intimate; and every step in it has been one of increasing respect and esteem, ending, with his life, in no less than affection on my part. Throughout my heavy and perplexing responsibilities here, to the day of his death, it would scarcely wrong any other to say, he was my most generous friend.

The White House – Wednesday, June 1, 1864

I responded to a resolution from a committee of Baptists from Springfield, Massachusetts, who are members of the American Baptist Home Mission Society. I wrote to them thanking them for their support of the Union and liberty. I noted that in the South many so-called preachers had appealed to the Christian world to aid them in doing to a whole race of men as they would have no men do unto themselves. To my way of thinking, they condemned and insulted God and His church, far more than did Satan when he tempted the Savior with the kingdoms of the earth. The devil's attempt was no falser, and far less hypocritical. But let me forbear, remembering it is also written, "Judge not, lest ye be judged."

I contributed my autograph to benefit the good ladies running the Sanitary Fair in Philadelphia.

Author's notes:

On this day Lincoln received in coin, $883.30 being the interest due him on $16,200 in 7.3% bonds in custody of the U.S. Treasurer. He congratulated José M. Medina on election to the presidency of the Republic of Honduras.

The White House – Thursday, June 2, 1864

General Sherman has reported that he suffered approximately 1,600 casualties in Paulding County, Georgia, at the hands of forces under General Joseph E. Johnston as he continues his drive to Atlanta. Major General Joseph Hooker's XX Corp led the two-day Federal attack upon Johnston's troops. According to General Halleck, challenging terrain made it difficult to coordinate the attack effectively. In this action, Confederate artillery was particularly effective against us. Today we are informed that Sherman is continuing his efforts in the area of Pickett's Mill.

This evening Mother attended the opera, accompanied by Postmaster Blair and his daughter. When she returned home, she told me that the singer was not up to her high expectations and that they did not enjoy the performance. That is one reason why I prefer plays to operas. In the latter, if the lead singer fails the whole evening is shot. With plays, usually the company of actors will not fail to please. I guess there are more good actors than singers.

Senator Oliver Browning came by and we discussed arrangements that will allow Charles Jonas, the son of my dying friend, Abraham Jonas, to receive three week's parole to visit his father. Abraham has been a lifelong good friend. It broke his heart when his son joined the Confederate Army. The good news is that Charles is now in Union captivity and was not killed in action. His family will be thrilled that he will be with his father at this sad time.

Author's notes:

In 1865 Johnston returned to command the few remaining Southern forces in North Carolina. He surrendered his armies to Sherman at Bennett Place near Durham, North Carolina, on April 26, 1865, 11 days after the assassination of President Lincoln. Ulysses S. Grant and William T. Sherman both praised his actions in the war and became friends with Johnston afterward. He was elected as a Democrat in Virginia's 3rd District in the U.S. House of Representatives, serving a single term. His grandmother, Mary Valentine Johnston, was a niece of Patrick Henry. His father served under Light-Horse Harry Lee in the Revolutionary War. His brother, Charles Clement Johnston, served as a congressman, and his nephew, John Warfield Johnston, was a U.S. senator. Both represented Virginia. Johnston graduated from the U.S. Military Academy in 1825, ranking 13th of 46 cadets. He served in the Mexican American and Seminole Wars.

The White House – Friday, June 3, 1864

I mailed a check for $3.53 on the Springfield Marine Bank to pay the taxes on land owned in Council Bluffs, Iowa. I declined an invitation from Frederick Conkling and 19 others, that I received yesterday, to attend a meeting in Union Square in Manhattan on the 4th to honor General Grant and the noble armies under his command. I regret not being able to go in large part because General Scott will be in attendance. Scott's sound advice I always welcome. It has been way too long since we've spoken. Late in the day I did a little politicking, when I met with groups of delegates en route to the National Union Convention in Baltimore. Many hands were shaken. Many promises were made by the delegates to vote for the Old Rail Splitter!

Author's notes:

Lincoln wrote to Frederick Conkling and others, "I approve whatever may tend to strengthen and sustain Gen. Grant and the noble armies now under his direction. My previous high estimate of Gen. Grant has been maintained and heightened by what has occurred in the remarkable campaign he is now conducting; while the magnitude and difficulty of the task before him does not prove less than I expected. He and his brave soldiers are now in the midst of their great trial, and I trust that at your meeting you will shape your good words that they may turn men and guns moving to his and their support."

The White House – Saturday, June 4, 1864

More delegates to the national convention in Baltimore stopped by the White House today to pay their respects and pledge their loyalty. Many have asked me if I had a specific man to recommend for vice president, and I have repeatedly said that I did not.

General Halleck and his staff presented information to me and the Cabinet about a battle waged in Paulding County, Georgia, on the 27th of May involving the IV Corps of Federal forces under the command of General Oliver O. Howard. His men, at the command of General Sherman attacked the right flank of the forces of Confederate General Patrick Cleburne, under orders of General Joe Johnston. Our forces were unsuccessful in their efforts and incurred casualties of over 1,600. It seems that the closer we get to Atlanta the harder this nut will be to crack. This battle lasted only 45 minutes, yet half of Hazen's brigade were killed or wounded in only 30 minutes of fierce fighting.

Author's notes:

Pickett's Mill Battlefield Historic Site is now preserved as a Georgia state park and includes roads used by Union and Confederate troops, earthwork battlements and an 1800-era pioneer cabin. The area's ravine is a site where hundreds of soldiers died.

The White House – Monday, June 6, 1864

A telegram confirmed late this evening that our soldiers achieved another important victory on May 28 in Dallas, Georgia, at a cost of 2,400 casualties. Troops under command of Major General John A. Logan of the Army of the Tennessee defeated forces of significantly less size under Confederate Lieutenant General Hardee. Fighting was heavy at two different points, but the Rebels were repulsed and experienced high casualties. Sherman, in overall command, is determined to keep the pressure on Joe Johnston as the hard fighting in this area has repeatedly demonstrated.

John Nicolay has sent several telegraphic messages from the convention to Hay keeping us aware of events unfolding there. I have stressed to the delegates that I do not wish to pick the vice president but have stressed that the border states must be considered when the selecting is done. I also have recommended that the party plank include language calling for a Constitutional amendment outlawing slavery forever in the United States.

Author's notes:

Lincoln wrote to the convention, "Such an amendment of the Constitution as it is now proposed became a fitting, and necessary conclusion to the final success of the Union cause. Such alone can meet and cover all cavils. Now the unconditional Union men, North and South, perceive its importance, and embrace it. In the joint names of Liberty and Union let us labor to give it legal form, and practical effects".

The White House – Tuesday, June 7, 1864

Early this morning, the full Cabinet was given a summary of recent military actions in Virginia. Specifically, we were shown maps and General Halleck described the events that took place at Haw's Shop, Totopotomoy Creek and Old Church. All are considered victories. Halleck estimates that as many as 80,000 soldiers on both sides may have been engaged in the various actions. Union losses are just under 1,000 casualties. Hopefully, we will soon realize a meaningful result from all this bloodshed. The ultimate outcome now rests in the hands of the two senior generals, Lee and Grant. They are now at each other's throats with Lee forced to defend Richmond to the death. Halleck has warned that although we have more troops engaged, those of Lee are more seasoned and they are defending their homeland. Unpredictable factors that must be put into the equation.

Author's notes:

On this date, Frederick C. Meyer, chairman, Baltimore Convention, telegraphs Lincoln, "The Convention has been called to order, everything is progressing." Lincoln interviewed Burton C. Cook, chairman of the Illinois delegation. In Philadelphia, the Great Central Fair of the U.S. Sanitary Commission opened. Marshall Lamon wired Lincoln from the convention site, "Enthusiastic unanimity beyond my wildest expectations. Nomination to be made tomorrow."

The White House – Thursday, June 9, 1864

Yesterday was a red-letter day…the National Union Convention nominated me for president. Early in the morning I was on the telegraph with General Grant, who has been under extreme pressure as the battles being fought outside of Richmond are taking huge tolls in dead and wounded on both sides of the struggle. At 4:30 P.M. I learned from the Convention that it had nominated Military Governor of Tennessee Andrew Johnson for vice president. He has demonstrated his loyalty to the Union and is well-regarded by the delegates. Last evening, I went alone to Grover's Theatre. As I entered my box the audience stood and gave me three cheers. It was heart-warming.

Today, I met and spent several hours with Elisha H. Allen, envoy and minister from Hawaii. I would love to visit the island someday. It sounds like a paradise. Allen is a very interesting man and an accomplished attorney. He served from 1841 to 1843 in the House of Representatives from Maine's 8th District as a Whig, losing his election to now Vice President Hannibal Hamlin in 1843. Hamlin has only good things to say about Allen. From 1850 to 1853 he was the U.S. consul in Hawaii under President Fillmore. In 1853 he became a citizen of the kingdom of Hawaii and was appointed its minister of finance and later became chief justice of its Supreme Court. He is now minister plenipotentiary from the kingdom to the United States.

Author's notes:

Elisha Hunt Allen served as minister plenipotentiary from the kingdom from 1856 until his death in 1883. When in Washington, he discussed with Lincoln a trade treaty with Hawaii. During the Civil War sugar shipments from the American South were interrupted, increasing the demand from Hawaii. In 1875 he negotiated a reciprocity treaty with the United States, which was signed by President Grant. It removed tariffs on sugar and gave the United States the use of Pearl Harbor, which was not a popular concession with the native Hawaiians. Allen represented Hawaii during the terms of presidents Pierce, Buchanan, Lincoln, Johnson, Grant, Hayes, Garfield and Arthur.

The White House – Friday, June 10, 1864

Late yesterday, I received an enthusiastic delegation from the National Union League of Philadelphia. I replied to their resolutions congratulating me upon receiving the party's nomination by telling them the story of the old Dutch farmer, who said, "It was not best to swap horses when crossing streams." Later a great many attendees to the Baltimore Convention came by, led by Governor Dennison of Ohio. We met in the East Room, where I was joined by Mary and Tad. Later the Cabinet joined us. The Ohio delegates brought Captain Menter's American Coronet Band with them and the delegates serenaded us with rousing songs, including some suggested by Mother and Tad. I then asked them to give me a rendition of "Dixie," one of my favorite tunes. I hope one day soon it will again be sung in every state in a reunited nation. It was a fine ending to a long and busy day.

Early this morning I got John Hay out of his bed and handed him a note to hand deliver to General Rosecrans in St. Louis concerning a reported conspiracy to overthrow the government. Hay's official rank now is major, assistant adjutant general. The matter concerns an organization calling itself the Order of American Knights believed to be led by Clement L. Vallandigham and Charles Hunt, Belgian consul at St. Louis.

Author's notes:

On June 10 Lincoln thanked Rev. Julian M. Sturtevant and members of the Triennial Convention of the Congregational Church for its resolutions urging the appointment of a day of national fasting and prayer, including protests against atrocities committed on colored troops, and that measures be taken to protect them.

The White House – Saturday, June 11, 1864

I told Mother that I had a very bad dream last night. In it, General Grant was badly wounded, and I was informed by Stanton that he was not expected to live. At that point in the dream I awoke in a sweat and had trouble getting back to sleep. It was just too realistic. Once awake I kept thinking about General Grant and how the hopes of the nation rest upon his success in the field. Mother believes that dreams are precursors to future events. I pray this one is not. I've been told by men who have served with him that the general is fearless and is often found in the very thick of battle. That means he is at far greater risk than need be, but he believes in leading from the front when required. I should not have mentioned the dream to Mother, for it will frighten her and depress her.

At two o'clock the Cabinet adjourned its meeting to receive members of the 130th Ohio Regiment. I addressed them with thanks for their coming to help us from Ohio at this fearsome time.

Author's notes:

The 130th Ohio was made up of 100-day volunteers, having in its ranks lawyers, clergymen, some of the best men in the state. They volunteered to go to the front at a time when the Army was experiencing unusually high casualty rates in Virginia and Georgia.

The White House – Monday, June 13, 1864

Over the weekend I asked John Hay and William Stoddard to find as many written records and reports of public utterances of Jefferson Davis before he became president of the Confederacy and since, and to prepare a report for me on his public positions taken over the many years that he has held elected or appointed offices. I am particularly interested in his views on the U.S. Constitution and slavery. John Nicolay is starting a trip west because of poor health.

When this war is over many will want to hang Davis from the nearest tree. My view is that all the leaders of the secession must sooner or later re-enter the life of the nation as brothers in a reunited nation. I am not one for vengeance for past wrongs. Revenge has never been a human trait that I have admired. Sir Francis Bacon in his essays wrote that "Revenge is a kind of wild justice, which the more man's nature runs to it, the more ought law to weed it out." I fully agree with the sentiments of Bacon. When I spoke to Mother about revenge, she reminded me of "The Merchant of Venice" and Shakespeare's line about Jews, "If you prick us, do we not bleed? If you tickle us, do we not laugh? If you poison us, do we not die? And if you wrong us, shall we not revenge?"

Author's notes:

The president notified officials of the Great Central Fair in Philadelphia that he and Mrs. Lincoln would leave Washington by special train for Philadelphia on Wednesday afternoon, June 16, and remain in Philadelphia till Thursday afternoon, June 17.

The White House – Tuesday, June 14, 1864

The full Cabinet met with General Halleck and staff members to review the recent military situation in Virginia. After the meeting, I predicted that the war in Virginia should be over by the end of this year. I made that statement based upon the latest information communicated to me by General Grant in the field. His belief is that by united efforts on several fronts simultaneously, the great power of the Federal forces must ultimately succeed. The Cabinet asked many questions about our strategies at the recent battles waged at Cold Harbor, Piedmont, Petersburg and Trevilian Station.

Author's notes:

The Union Army, in attempting a futile assault at Cold Harbor, lost 10,000 to 13,000 men over a period of 12 days. The battle brought the toll in Union casualties since the beginning of May to a total of over more than 52,000, compared to 33,000 for Lee's forces. Grant commented after the war, "I have always regretted that the last assault at Cold Harbor was ever made. There, no advantage was gained to compensate for the heavy loss we sustained."

On June 15, Lincoln telegraphed Grant, "I have just read your dispatch of 1 P.M. yesterday. I begin to see it. You will succeed." The president spent June 16 and June 17 in Philadelphia, returning to Washington on a special train at 8 A.M. on the 17th.

The White House – Saturday, June 18, 1864

I telegraphed Mother, who will be staying at the Fifth Avenue Hotel in Manhattan, where I expect she will be doing some shopping while in the city. I advised Mary that Tad has arrived home safely from New York. Her efforts to add beauty to the White House never cease and are greatly appreciated by me and by our guests who can see the many improvements she has made since our arrival in Washington. I may visit General Grant in the field soon, and plan to take Tad with me when I do so.

Several staff officers from Halleck's office came to a Cabinet meeting this morning to give us a description of a recent engagement that occurred in Harrison County, Kentucky, on the 11th and 12th of this month. The action took place in and around the town of Cynthiana. It resulted in a victory of Federal troops over Rebel cavalry units under General John Morgan. Having no artillery in which to drive Union soldiers from their defensive positions, Morgan set fire to the town, burning 37 buildings. Many Rebels were killed or captured. Morgan escaped.

Author's notes:

On June 10, Confederate Major General N.B. Forrest's 2nd Tennessee Cavalry routed a Union force nearly three times as large at Brice's Crossroads in Mississippi. The battlefield at Brice's Crossroads is considered one of the best preserved of the American Civil War. The National Park Service erected and maintains monuments and interpretive panels on a small 1-acre plot at the crossroads. Over 1,420 acres have been preserved.

The White House – Friday, June 24, 1864

Tad and I have been with General Grant. We left Washington with Assistant Secretary of the Navy Gustavus Fox aboard the U.S.S. Baltimore on the James River. Grant's headquarters are at City Point, Virginia. Tuesday, when we met with the general, I was not feeling well, having an upset stomach. I was offered Champagne and refused it, saying that many fellows get seasick ashore from drinking the stuff. When reviewing the troops at Petersburg, I was given General Grant's horse, "Cincinnati," and he rode a fine spirited horse called "Jeff Davis." Grant is a fine horseman, and I am told he was the best rider in his class at West Point. A highlight of our visit was to see Negro troops marching under the command of General Edward Hinks. They cheered me loudly and I returned their cheers with a salute. Tad joined me in waving to the soldiers.

On Wednesday, we sailed up the James River to inspect that portion of our lines and to visit the flagship of Acting Rear Admiral Samuel Lee. At Bermuda Hundred we picked up General Benjamin Butler and then sailed up as far as it was considered safe. The differences between the belligerents becomes more and more stark when one realizes that we have an active, powerful navy and they are limited to almost no warships at all. I have been mightily impressed by all that I have seen on this trip. There is a unity of spirit that is heartening.

Yesterday, Tad and I left the area near Fort Darling, Virginia, with Assistant Secretary Fox and arrived back in Washington at 5 P.M. I am a bit sunburned but refreshed and cheered by all I have seen and heard. I telegraphed Mother that we have been with General Grant, and that it was very warm. I reported I am tired and that all is well with Tad and me.

Author's notes:

Orville Browning's diary of June 26 records, "During the past week, the president visited Grant's army. He told me last night that Grant said, when he left him, that "You, Mr. President, need be under no apprehension. You will never hear of me farther from Richmond than now, till I have taken it. I am just as sure of going to Richmond as I am of any future event. It may take a long summer day, but I will go in." Grant told him that in the Wilderness he had completely routed Lee but did not know it at the time – and that, "had he known it, he could have ruined him, and ended the campaign."

The White House – Saturday, June 25, 1864

This morning I interviewed General Quincy Adams Gillmore. Halleck told me that Gillmore was first in his class at West Point in 1849. He is now considered the foremost siege officer in the Army, having demonstrated in 1862 at Fort Pulaski in Chatham County, Georgia, that brick fortifications are obsolete when attacked by powerful rifled naval cannon. He told me that the fort was begun in 1829, had been worked on by Robert E. Lee, then a recent graduate of West Point. Gillmore said that it was constructed over 18 years, using 25 million bricks. Walls were 11-feet thick and believed to be impenetrable.

Author's notes:

Under Gillmore's orders, more than 5,000 artillery shells fell on Fort Pulaski during a short siege from a range of 1,700 yards. After Gillmore's success at Fort Pulaski, brick and stone fortifications like it were considered obsolete.

On July 18, 1863, during the siege of Charleston, South Carolina, General Gillmore launched a major attack on Fort Wagner. The troops who assaulted the fort were comprised primarily of the 54th Massachusetts Regiment, which included only African Americans in its complement.

Fort Pulaski National Monument is located on Cockspur Island between Savannah and Tybee Island, Georgia. It covers 5,623 acres. The fort covers 260 acres. The monument includes most of Cockspur Island (containing the fort) and all adjacent McQueens Island. The fort was also used as a Confederate prisoner-of-war camp.

The White House – Monday, June 27, 1864

I spent some time this morning with Secretary Welles. We discussed the removal of Isaac Henderson as Navy agent in New York City. This is one of those matters where one must try and judge who is telling the truth in a situation where the man in question has many friends and many enemies. In the final resolution I have deferred to Welles to settle things with justice.

I accepted the nomination of the National Union Convention for the Presidency of the United States for four years from the fourth of March next, which I received today. I did so by writing to William Dennison and others of the Convention Committee. I advised them that the platform resolutions are accepted by me as written. I was particularly pleased that the convention did not forget the soldiers and sailors whose sacrifices will long be remembered by a grateful country.

Author's notes:

The committee's letter read, "The National Union Convention, which assembled in Baltimore on the 7th of June 1864 has instructed us to inform you that you were nominated with enthusiastic unanimity for the Presidency of the United States for four years from the fourth of March next."

The letter ends, "Your character and career prove your unswerving fidelity to the cardinal principles of American Liberty and of the American Constitution. In the name of that Liberty and Constitution, Sir, we earnestly request our acceptance of this nomination; reverently commending our beloved country, and you its chief magistrate, with its brave sons who on sea and land are faithfully defending the good old American cause of equal rights, to the blessing of Almighty God."

The White House – Tuesday, June 28, 1864

I was feeling unwell today, but still managed to conduct a Cabinet meeting at which minor matters were discussed and handled. Secretary Chase reviewed with us the relative strengths of the Union and the Confederate states at the time of secession and as of today. He pointed out that at the beginning of the conflict the Rebels' land area covered 727,000 square miles and was populated by little over 9,000,000 people, white and black, with taxable property aggregating about $3.5 billion, not counting "slave property." The Union commanded some 941,000 square miles, not counting territories, claimed by both sides, but largely controlled by our forces. Our 22 states had a population of more than 22,000,000, mostly white, and a taxable property estimated at more than $6.75 billion. Since then we have conquered more of more of its land and freed its slaves, thus the Confederacy is a much smaller and weaker confederation. That is why I continue to believe that time is on our side.

Author's notes:

In 1863, Jefferson Davis issued an address to the people of the Confederate States, urging them to produce more food. In it he noted, "We began this struggle without a single gun afloat while the resources of our enemy enabled them to gather fleets which consisted of 427 vessels, measuring 340,036 tons and carrying 3,268 guns."

The White House – Wednesday, June 29, 1864

Treasury Secretary Chase submitted his resignation today. This is not the first time he has done so. He is an incredibly brilliant man and an incredibly ambitious one. In his mind I am certain he feels far more qualified to be president, and that has not helped matters in our relationship. For his significant contributions to our government I have only the highest admiration. I told Hay that I could not stand the constant irritations from the man any longer. We were not comfortable in meeting each other and that meant that one of us had to go. He lost. He shall be replaced by a good man, I am sure of that.

I shall be glad when Mother returns from New York. I miss her company, as does Tad.

I directed General Steele to give the new government of Arkansas the same support and protection that you would if the senators and representatives sent from that state had been admitted to the Congress.

Author's notes:

Lincoln wrote to Chase: "Your resignation ...is accepted. Of all I said in commendation of your ability and fidelity, I have nothing to unsay; and yet you and I have reached a point of mutual embarrassment in our official relation which it seems cannot be overcome, or longer sustained, consistently with the public service. Your Obt. Servt. A Lincoln."

In December, Lincoln named Chase chief justice of the Supreme Court of the United States. Hay wrote, "No other man than Lincoln would have had.... the degree of magnanimity to thus forgive and exalt a rival who had so deeply and unjustifiably intrigued against him. It is another illustration of the greatness of the President, in this age of little men."

The White House – Thursday, June 30, 1864

The Cabinet met for the first time without Secretary Chase being a member. There was shock that I had accepted his resignation in the Cabinet and in the press. I had planned to nominate former Governor David Tod of Ohio to fill his shoes. I think that no governor has helped me more and troubled me less than has Tod. He enthusiastically endorsed the Emancipation Proclamation. But after inviting Tod to join the Cabinet, he telegraphed me to decline the Treasury post for reasons of poor health. My inclination is to offer the job to Senator William Pitt Fessenden of Maine, who has headed the Finance Committee in the Senate.

Author's notes:

David Tod, knowing he was not radical enough for Republicans in the U.S. Senate and in fragile health, declined Lincoln's invitation to become Treasury secretary. He died of a stroke in 1868 at the age of 63, leaving a widow and seven children.

Senator Fessenden initially refused the nomination, but at last accepted in obedience to universal public pressure. He began his service as Treasury secretary on July 5, 1864. He resigned his position as secretary, leaving on March 3, 1865, to return to the Senate, to which he had now for the third time been elected.

The White House – Friday, July 1, 1864

I forwarded the nomination to the Senate of Senator Fessenden as secretary of the Treasury. It was confirmed upon arrival. I expect to have a meeting with the new secretary tomorrow morning to discuss many Treasury matters including personnel.

Author's notes:

Lincoln advised Secretary Fessenden on July 4th that he would keep no person in office in his department against the secretary's express will. He agreed that the new Treasury secretary, when filling vacancy, will strive to give his willing assent to Lincoln's wishes in cases when the president lets him know that he has such wishes. The secretary is to have complete control of his department. The president advised him that nothing would be done particularly affecting any department without consultation with the head of that department.

The White House – Saturday, July 2, 1864

Today the family will begin its summer stays at the Soldiers' Home. Mother prefers it to the White House. Tad is happy anywhere! I spent considerable time with new Secretary of the Treasury Fessenden today going over his new responsibilities. Gold is now at $225 an ounce and the paper dollar is only worth about 34 cents. Fessenden believes that we can put on the market a loan in the form of bonds bearing an interest rate of 7.30 percent, in denominations as low as $50.00 so that people of moderate means can afford to buy them. War takes money; so I am counting on him to find a way to raise the amounts we require. I like the way Fessenden thinks. There is nothing rash or radical about him. He is a thoughtful moderate.

Author's notes:

The seven-thirty loan became a triumphant financial success. Fessenden later recommended measures, adopted by Congress, which permitted the subsequent consolidation and funding of the government loans into 4 percent and 4.5 percent bonds.

During the impeachment trial of President Andrew Johnson in 1868, Senator Fessenden broke party ranks, along with six other Republican senators, and in a courageous act of political suicide, voted for acquittal. As a result, a vote of 35-19 in favor of removing the president failed by a single vote of reaching a two-thirds majority.

The White House – Monday, July 4th, Independence Day

Tad is excited because this evening on the White House lawn there will be a fireworks display, and the Marine Band will provide a concert for the public. I wonder how the Rebels celebrate the Fourth of July. In 1776 all the Colonies, North and South, were united when they declared American Independence and freedom from Great Britain.

I spent time at the Capitol this morning signing bills and conferring with members of Congress in the President's Room. I spent much of my time with Senator Zachariah Chandler of Michigan. I told him that I had legal and moral doubts about the Wade-Davis Bill. He angrily walked out of our meeting. Obviously, I failed to please him with my thinking. He represents an attitude of punitive reconstruction that I oppose strongly. My thinking is that a peace after the hostilities that is oppressive upon the losers can only hamper the nation in the long run as it seeks to put aside the hatreds that have flowed from secession and war.

Author's notes:

The Wade-Davis Bill created a framework for reconstruction and the readmittance of the Confederate states to the union. In December of 1863 Lincoln proposed a reconstruction program that would allow Confederate states to establish new governments after 10 percent of their male populations took loyalty oaths and the states recognized the "permanent freedom of slaves." Senator Chandler and other senators thought Lincoln's 10 percent plan too mild. In February 1864, Senator Benjamin Wade and Representative Henry Winter Davis proposed a more stringent plan. Their bill required 50 percent of a state's white males to take a loyalty oath in order to be readmitted into the Union. In addition, states were required to give blacks the right to vote.

Lincoln chose not to sign the bill, killing it with a pocket veto. After his assassination in 1865, Congress imposed the harsher requirements first proposed in the Wade-Davis Bill.

The White House – Tuesday, July 5, 1864

Last evening was a very patriotic night as hundreds attended the White House fireworks display and band music. I had them play the "Battle Hymn" and a rendition of "Dixie." Several hundred troops from Indiana and Michigan were in the crowd, and they sang loudly and with gusto. Mother enjoyed it tremendously, as did the audience.

Today I held our first Cabinet meeting in which Senator Fessenden attended filling the place formerly held by Secretary Chase. I have been fortunate to have had the professional wisdom of Chase, albeit he was always difficult to deal with on a personal level. Fessenden said little today but did come up to me after the meeting to reassure me that he was committed to solving our immediate financial needs. I am impressed by his attention to matters of importance and determination to establish priorities. I admire people who stick to solving problems, and we do have a serious money problem right now that can use a great deal of help.

Secretary Halleck and his staff joined the meeting after lunch and presented to the Cabinet a comprehensive review of military matters during the last weeks of June, including fighting occurring in the states of Virginia and Georgia. Emphasis was given to the fierce fighting at the second battle at Petersburg, Virginia. There, Lee repulsed Grant at the back door to Richmond. At Kennesaw Mountain in Georgia, the Confederates had a victory when Johnston repulsed Sherman's forces.

Author's notes:

Having achieved no gains from four bloody days of assault at Petersburg, Union General Meade ordered his forces to dig in. Union casualties at Petersburg were 11,386, (1,688 killed, 8,513 wounded, 1,185 missing or captured). Grant's opportunity to take Petersburg easily had been lost, but Lee, who arrived around noon on June 18, was unable to prevent the larger Union Army from laying siege to the city. The siege would last until April of 1865.

During the battle on June 18, 900 men of the 1st Maine Heavy Artillery Regiment, which had been converted from essentially garrison duty manning artillery to be infantrymen at the start of the Overland Campaign, lost 632 men in an assault, the heaviest single-battle loss of any Union regiment during the entire war.

The White House – Thursday, July 7, 1864

Yesterday I was visited by five young men who are studying to become lawyers in Boston. They were interested in learning how I became an attorney. I admitted to them that I had never spent one day in a law school but was self-taught. I told them that John Todd Stuart, a Springfield attorney, encouraged me to study law and kindly lent me lawbooks to study. I had read Blackstone's Commentaries, Chitty's Pleadings, Greenleaf's Evidence and Story's Equity and Equity Pleadings repeatedly. I guess I did that for three years before I was admitted to the bar of the State of Illinois. I wrote my first legal document for a friend on November 12, 1831 and got a license to practice law in 1836. On March 1, 1837, my name was entered on the list of lawyers in the Illinois Supreme Court. On April 15, 1837 I moved to Springfield to practice law with John Stuart. On October 12, 1838, I successfully represented accused murderer Henry Truett in People v. Truett. I informed them that when I return to Illinois after completing my presidential duties I intend to again practice law in Springfield with William Herndon, my friend and partner for many happy years.

Author's notes:

On September 23, 1839, Lincoln started practicing law on the Illinois Eighth Judicial Circuit. On June 18, 1840, he argued his first of many cases before the Illinois Supreme Court. April 14, 1841, he ended partnership with John Stuart and became Stephen T. Logan's partner. March 1, 1842, he was admitted to practice law in the U.S. District Court. In December 1844, he dissolved partnership with Stephen Logan; and accepted William H. Herndon as junior partner. October 16, 1847, he appeared for plaintiff in a fugitive slave case (Bryant t al. v. Matson). March 7, 1849 admitted to practice law before the U.S. Supreme Court and gave his only oral argument there. February 28, 1854, he represented railroad before Illinois Supreme Court (Illinois Central RR v. County of McLean). September 19 – 26, 1855 attends trial in Cincinnati, Ohio (McCormick v. Manny) but Edwin Stanton prevented his participation. December 1, 1856, he helped prosecute murder case in which defendant pleaded insanity (People v. Wyant). May 7, 1858, he used almanac to clear Duff Armstrong of murder charge (People v. Armstrong).

The White House Friday, July 8, 1864

Yesterday I issued a Proclamation of a Day of Prayer at the request of the Senate and the House of Representatives. The date will be the first Thursday in August.

I reviewed 35 court-martial cases. This is always a trying experience as the awesome power to save or take life and death is held in my pen. My instincts are to favor life over death. I also discussed the Baltimore convention with F.B. Carpenter and John Hay. Carpenter is working away at his painting of the Emancipation Proclamation. He enjoys talking about politics and is very well-informed on the issues of the day. Congressman William Kelley of Pennsylvania joined our discussion. Kelley has a great sense of humor and always has a good Pat and Mike joke to share.

Later Generals Hitchcock and Halleck conferred about Rebel troops threatening Washington. They are under the command of Confederate General Jubal A. Early. Grant is not concerned about Early's forces. He believes Early has been ordered to threaten Washington so that we will shift troops away from our efforts outside of Richmond. Grant believes we have enough forces to defend Washington while continuing to threaten Richmond.

Author's notes:

Lincoln issued passes for James R. Gillmore and Colonel James Jaquess to go South to meet with Jefferson Davis in Richmond. Lincoln authorized the men to meet with Davis to see if there might be a peace offer from the Confederate leader. He advised Grant that the men were meeting with Jefferson Davis as private citizens and did not speak for the United States government.

The White House – Saturday, July 9, 1864

I answered Editor Horace Greely's suggestion that the United States send officials to meet with Confederate representatives in Canada. I am convinced that Jefferson Davis has no intention of agreeing to peace terms that demand the end of the Confederacy. I advised Greely that if he can find any authorized person anywhere professing to have any proposition from Davis in writing, for peace say to him that he may come to me anytime. Davis must accept the full restoration of the Union and the abandonment of slavery.

I telegraphed John W. Garrett, president of the B & O Railroad, asking what he has heard about a battle fought at Monocacy today. The situation is unclear. Apparently Rebel troops under General Jubal Early have crossed the Potomac River at Shepherdstown into Maryland coming from the Shenandoah Valley from Lynchburg.

Grant has telegraphed that he has embarked troops of the VI Corps on transports at City Point to the Washington area.

Late in the day I reviewed 31 court-martial cases.

Author's notes:

On July 9th a Union force under Major General Lew Wallace attempted to arrest Lieutenant General Jubal Early's invading Confederate divisions along the Monocacy River, just east of Frederick, Maryland. Wallace's forces were defeated. His loss at Monocacy bought time for veteran Union troops sent by Grant to arrive in time to bolster the defenses of Washington. Early's advance reached the outskirts of Washington on July 11th. Monocacy was called "The Battle that Saved Washington."

The White House – Monday, July 11, 1864

Yesterday, General James Hardie and I visited several forts surrounding Washington with a mounted escort. In the evening our family left the Soldiers' Home and spent the night here in the White House at the recommendation of Secretary Stanton. He thought that we would be safer here.

At 9 A.M. I rode out to the front in the direction of Tennalytown. Mrs. Lincoln accompanied me to Fort Stevens. We were able to see our troops skirmishing with those of the enemy in front of the fort. Later we went to the wharf to greet troops sent up the Potomac by General Grant as valuable reinforcements. I thanked the men for their service. They gave me a rousing cheer, which was gratefully accepted.

Author's notes:

On this date President Lincoln ordered militia members and volunteers of Washington into the service of the United States for a period of 60 days due to the present military threat to the capital.

The White House – Tuesday, July 12, 1864

The Cabinet met and much of our discussion centered around the current threat to the city of Washington occasioned by incursions by troops of General Early. I plan to again visit the troops who are guarding the city and watch as they repulse the invaders. Grant believes that the purpose of the attacks by the Rebels on Washington may be attributed to Robert E. Lee and Jefferson Davis' need to cause Union troops to leave the significantly threatened Richmond area to respond to Early's attacks here.

In the Cabinet meeting, Secretary Blair raised the issue of the fate of President Davis and other Rebel leaders once hostilities are ended. My personal preference would be that Davis and his senior government and military officials would simply disappear from sight, never to be seen again. That of course is a naïve approach to a complex issue. My instincts are to see the Rebels surrender and return to their homes as soon as possible from privates to the president himself. I want no imprisonment of Confederate officials or senior military people. No revenge. No hatred. I want a peaceful reunion and a return to normalcy. The sooner the better for the good of all.

Author's notes:

After Lincoln's assassination, Jefferson Davis was captured and held in federal military imprisonment for over two years. Initially he was shackled in irons. He asked to be tried but a trial never took place. Instead, on February 15, 1869, the district attorney, by leave of the court, formally announced that he would not prosecute Jefferson Davis on behalf of the United States. The case was then marked "dismissed," and the bondsman declared forever released.

Davis' lawyer, Daniel O'Connor, wrote how he would have defended Davis had a trial occurred. "With so admirably prepared and so overwhelmingly conclusive a brief (as Rawle's View of the Constitution), my task would have been indeed easy." If the case had come to trial, the defense would have offered in evidence the textbook on Constitutional Law (Rawle's View of the Constitution) from which Davis had been instructed at West Point by the authority of the U.S. government, and in which the right of secession is maintained as one of the Constitutional rights of a state. His lawyers were content to argue that "admitting everything you say in the indictment is true, no offence under the law had been committed." Thus, Davis could not be convicted of treason. No evidence was ever found connecting Davis to the assassination of Abraham Lincoln.

The White House – Thursday, July 14, 1864

Yesterday, Attorney General Edward Bates came by and presented his views on the Baltimore Convention. He is genuinely optimistic about our chances in November. Bates has a keen mind and good insights into matters of party politics.

Tonight, the family will be returning to the Soldiers' Home – the threat from invasion by Jubal Early's troops is no longer considered the serious threat that it posed just hours ago.

I presented to General John Todd an inscribed copy of Herman Haupt's latest book, "Military Bridges," which was just published. Haupt is a remarkable individual and an engineering genius. His significant contributions to the war effort by overseeing our railroads and bridges is beyond calculation. I regret that he left the Army but know that we will forever be in his debt for what he accomplished in keeping our railroads running and our bridges standing.

Author's notes:

On May 28, 1862, Lincoln visited a site where Haupt had constructed a railroad bridge. He said, "That man Haupt has built a bridge four hundred feet long and one hundred feet high, across Potomac Creek, on which loaded trains are passing every hour, and upon my word, gentlemen, there is nothing in it but cornstalks and beanpoles."

The White House – Friday, July 15, 1864

I wrote again to Editor Horace Greeley, this time advising him that John Hay has been sent to him with an answer to his letter to me of the 13th. I advised him that I had not expected a letter from him, but that he would instead bring to me a man, or men, who could speak for Jefferson Davis on the matter of peace negotiations. I gave Hay a letter to hand-deliver to Greeley, which he may show to the Confederate representatives. It promises four men safe-conduct passage to Washington for purposes of peace discussions with me.

Author's notes:

The safe-conduct issued by Hay read, "The President of the United States directs that the four persons whose names follow, to wit: Hon. Clement C. Clay, Jacob Thompson, Prof. James B. Holcombe, George N. Sanders shall have safe conduct to the City of Washington in company of the Hon. Horace Greeley, and shall be exempt from arrest or annoyance of any kind by any officer of the United States during their journey to the said City of Washington. By order of the President. John Hay, Major & A.G.G.

The president's position regarding peace was delivered to persons in Canada purporting to represent the Confederate states: "Any proposition, which embraces the restoration of peace, the integrity of the whole Union, and the abandonment of slavery, and which comes by and with an authority that can control the armies now at war against the United States will be received and considered by the Executive government of the United States, and will be met by liberal terms on other substantial and collateral points; and the bearer, or bearers thereof shall have safe-conduct both ways."

The White House – Saturday, July 16, 1864

Today Tad and I took a long carriage ride and, in the evening, we attended a concert on the lawn by the Marine Band.

At 3 P.M. I signed a Proclamation for 500,000 volunteers according to the Act of July 4, 1864 with the understanding that if the number of volunteers fails to meet that object, then persons may be drafted for one year to fill such quotas or any part thereof which may be unfilled.

Tomorrow Governor Curtin of Pennsylvania will visit with me and Cabinet members to discuss the 2nd Pennsylvanian Heavy Artillery.

Author's notes:

President Lincoln received a letter accompanied by a suit of clothing, which read, "Among the contributions to the clothing department of the Great Central Fair, for the benefit of the United States Sanitary Commission, there was presented by Messrs. Rockhill and Wilson, an elegant suit of garments made to your measure. The fair Treasury having been fully compensated; I am desired by the donors to forward the same to you. I am happy honored Sir, to be the medium of the presentation. T.J. Leberman." The president replied to Mr. Leberman, "The suit of garments sent by you, on behalf of Messrs. Rockhill and Wilson, came duly to hand; and for which you and they will please accept my thanks. Yours truly, A. Lincoln."

The White House – Monday, July 18, 1864

Newspaperman James Gilmore reported to me the results of his recent meeting with Jefferson Davis and Judah Benjamin in Richmond, when accompanied by Colonel James Jaquess of the 73rd Illinois. They reiterated my positions; namely, reunion, emancipation and amnesty. Davis responded angrily that amnesty applies to "criminals." He stated that the South was fighting for Independence and stated that, "The Union may emancipate every Negro in the Confederacy, but we will be free." He said, "We will govern ourselves…if we have to see every Southern plantation sacked, and every Southern city in flames." I told Gilmore that I approved of his publishing his findings in The Atlantic Monthly and The New York Times. I did so because it shows that Davis will listen to no proposals that do not embrace disunion. This will show our people that efforts being made in the North by the Peace Party delude our people into a belief that peace is now possible without disunion. Davis' words are peculiarly timely and valuable. Thurlow Weed continues to say that the people are "mad for peace." I agree. But at what price?

Author's notes:

On this date President Lincoln officially issued a call for 500,000 volunteers. He converted $26,181.40 into U.S. government bonds.

The White House – Tuesday, July 19, 1864

Postmaster General Montgomery Blair showed me a collection of Rebel postage stamps, most of them featuring the image of Jefferson Davis. When hostilities broke out the Southern post offices held large quantities of U.S. stamps. The federal government then declared that all existing U.S. stamps would be demonetized (declared invalid) as of June 1, 1861, and that all U.S. postal operations in the seceded states would cease on that day. As a result, a Confederate Post Office Department was founded in February of 1861. John Henninger Reagan was appointed postmaster general of the Confederate Post Office, which operates out of our old offices and with many of our postmasters still sorting and delivering the mail. According to Blair, many of the U.S. Post Office's best managers followed Reagan into the Confederacy at the time. Reagan was initially hamstrung by shortages of ink, paper and printing companies equipped to produce enough quantities of postage stamps. When the June 1, deadline approached, and mail service ended between the Union and the Southern states in rebellion, some Southern postmasters hand-stamped the word "Paid" on envelopes while others in major cities like New Orleans produced provisional stamps to keep the mail moving within their region. Within 20 weeks, the Confederate Post Office began to provide stamps to its post offices. After August 26, 1861 northern mail was no longer delivered to Southern addresses but could only be delivered under a flag of truce. I informed Blair that I wished that my picture would not be printed on postage stamps. I prefer that our stamps continue to honor George Washington, Thomas Jefferson and Benjamin Franklin as they have since 1847.

Author's notes:

A light blue colored 5-cent stamp picturing Jefferson Davis, with the copy "Postage Five Cents – Confederate States of America," was issued on October 16, 1861. It was produced by the Richmond firm Hoyer and Ludwig using stone lithography. For most Southerners, this was the first time they saw what their new president looked like. It was also the first time that a living president appeared on a stamp used in the United States. Later the Confederate Post Office issued stamps picturing Andrew Jackson, Thomas Jefferson, James Calhoun and George Washington. Upon the death of Lincoln, the U.S. Post Office issued a black 15-cent mourning stamp based on a photo taken of Lincoln by C.S. German in 1861, shortly after he was inaugurated.

The White House – Thursday, July 21, 1864

Yesterday, General Halleck and members of his staff acquainted the Cabinet with details known of military actions at the Battle of Monocacy in Maryland and at Fort Stevens in the District of Columbia. At Fort Stevens I personally viewed the action from the ramparts and came under Confederate fire. Halleck also described a Union victory at the Battle of Tupelo in Mississippi. It is reported that in the fighting there on the 15th that Rebel cavalry leader Nathan Bedford Forrest was seriously wounded in action. Our troops were unsuccessful on July 18 and July 19 at Cool Spring, Virginia.

Late in the afternoon yesterday I had a telegram from General Grant proposing that we issue a call for 300,000 more troops. I was pleased to reply to Grant that we had anticipated his needs and had issued a call for 500,000 on the 18th of July.

Today, I asked the Treasury Department to find a place for Mrs. Ann Sprig. She was my landlady years ago when I was serving as a member of the House of Representatives. She is now very needy and can use a job and the income. When I boarded with her, I always found her to be unfailingly pleasant and dependable in all things.

Author's notes:

Late in the day the full Cabinet viewed the painting of the Emancipation Proclamation by F.B. Carpenter.

The White House – Friday, July 22, 1864

Today, I reviewed with the Cabinet my recent correspondence with Horace Greely concerning a possible meeting in Canada at Niagara Falls of Editor Greeley with persons believed to be representatives of Jefferson Davis. The intention of the meeting was to gain knowledge of the current thinking of Davis insofar as a possible peace settlement might occur. It is my belief that Davis will only consent to a peaceful settlement of differences with the United States upon terms that cannot be accepted by this government. A key component of my communication with the South was that slavery had to be abandoned as a necessary element of any peace that restored the Union.

Author's notes:

Lincoln believed that to "jettison emancipation as a condition would ruin the Union cause." He asked, "Why would they (former slaves) give their lives for us, with full notice of our purpose to betray them?" Lincoln informed two Wisconsin Republicans that a hundred thousand or more black soldiers and sailors were fighting for the Union. "If they stake their lives for us, they must be prompted by the strongest motive – even the promise of freedom. And the promise being made must be kept. To jettison emancipation as a condition in such a public way would ruin the Union cause itself. All colored men in the service would instantly desert us. And rightfully too."

The White House – Saturday, July 23, 1864

Telegraphed reports tell us of a Union victory at Rutherford's Farm in Frederick County near Winchester, Virginia, on the 20th of the month. Our forces were well led by Major General William Averell. The Confederates, part of troops under Lieutenant Jubal Early and commanded by Major General Stephen Ramseur, suffered about double our casualties. I have been told that Private John Shanes, of Company K, 14th West Virginia Infantry, has been recommended for the Medal of Honor for charging upon a Confederate fieldpiece in advance of his comrades, and by his individual courage and exertions silenced the piece. I have asked General Halleck to bring this exceptional soldier to the White House when practical, so that I may meet him and thank him personally for his bravery when pinning the medal upon him.

Author's notes:

President Lincoln signed a bill providing for a Medal of Honor for the Navy on December 21, 1861, to be bestowed upon such petty officers, seamen, landsmen and Marines as shall distinguish themselves by their gallantry and other seamanlike qualities during the present war. Legislation to include the Army was signed into law on July 12, 1862. During the Civil War 1,522 were awarded. At least 32 were awarded to African Americans. One medal for Andrew Jackson Smith from that war was not awarded until 2001, 137 years after the action in which it was earned. President Barack Obama awarded the medal to Union Army First Lieutenant Alonzo Cushing for his actions at the Battle of Gettysburg, a delay of 151 years.

The White House – Monday, July 25, 1864

Today, I sent a "thank you" letter to the loyal ladies of Trenton, New Jersey, who were kind enough to present me with a beautiful hand-carved cane at the recent Sanitary Fair in Philadelphia. Its wood comes from a ceremonial arch that had been constructed in their city in 1789 to welcome America's first president to their city. It commemorated America's victory at Yorktown. Having anything connected with the life of George Washington is a signal honor. I can only imagine how our first president must have felt when he saw that arch constructed in his honor. They say that when General Washington rode under it, the ladies of Trenton scattered flowers under it to celebrate his great victory over Cornwallis and the British Army, which ended the Revolutionary War. If I were not superstitious, I would have General Meigs start designing a grand arch to be placed over Pennsylvania Avenue for that inevitable time when our triumphant troops will return in glory after this bloody struggle ends.

Author's notes:

The Grand Review of the Armies was a military parade in the national capital on May 23 and 24, 1865. Elements of the Union Army paraded through the streets of Washington, D.C., to receive accolades from crowds and reviewing politicians, including President Andrew Johnson, a month after the assassination of President Lincoln. They marched up Pennsylvania Avenue heading northwest from the Capitol toward the White House at 15th Street N.W. by the U.S. Treasury Department building. Attending were Ulysses S. Grant, General-in-Chief, General George Gordon Meade, and General William T. Sherman.

The White House – Tuesday, July 26, 1864

Secretary Stanton and General Halleck presented to the Cabinet a review of our forces' important successes at the Battle of Peachtree Creek, as the troops of General Sherman beat back Confederate attacks north of Atlanta. We are informed that Confederate General Joe Johnston was removed from command of the Rebel forces on July 17th and replaced by General John B. Hood of Texas. According to Halleck, Hood has a reputation for aggressiveness and recklessness, whereas Johnston is known to be more cautious and conservative in action. Captured prisoners tell us that Hood took command on July 19th, the day before the battle began. The morning of the 20th our forces crossed Peachtree Creek and began taking defensive positions. Hood committed two of his three corps to the attack. The Southerners suffered heavy losses. Hood withdrew into the defenses of Atlanta, having failed to break Union lines. Estimated casualties were 1,750 on our side and perhaps as high as 2,500 on the Rebel side. In the battle three Medals of Honor have been recommended, to be awarded to Lieutenant Colonel Douglas Hapeman of the 104th Illinois Infantry, First Lieutenant Frank Baldwin of the 19th Michigan Infantry, and Private Denis Buckley of the 136th New York Infantry.

Author's notes:

A message received several days after the battle by General Halleck at headquarters in Washington from Major General J.D. Cox read, "Few battlefields of the war have been strewn so thickly with dead and wounded as they lay that evening around Collier's Mill." In the action General George H. Thomas commanded the Army of the Cumberland. Confederate General John B. Hood commanded the Army of the Tennessee.

The White House – Wednesday, July 27, 1864

Late yesterday we received word of a battle fought on July 24th at Kernstown in Virginia, outside of Winchester, Virginia, where another battle had been waged in 1862. Commanding the Army of West Virginia was Brigadier General George Crook. General Jubal Early commanded the Army of the Valley. Mistakenly thinking that Early was leaving the area, we withdrew the VI and XIX Corps from the valley to return to the aid of Grant's siege of Petersburg on July 20th. Crook believed that Early's infantry had left the valley and sent only two of his divisions to meet his attack. On the 24th Early marched his army north against Crook, and heavy skirmishing took place. Crook soon concluded that we were heavily outnumbered. In the confusion of battle our boys panicked and were driven from the Shenandoah Valley.

I appointed Richard W. Thompson, former Congressman of Indiana as commissioner to examine the Union Pacific Railroads.

Author's notes:

General Early went on to burn Chambersburg, Pennsylvania, in retribution for the Union forces burning of civilian homes and farms earlier in the campaign. On July 30th Grant appointed Major General Philip Sheridan as commander of Union forces, turning the tide once and for all against Confederates in the Shenandoah Valley. The Confederate victory at Kernstown marked the high-water point for the Confederates in the Valley in 1864. Early had been successful in attacking the Baltimore and Ohio Railroad in Maryland and West Virginia. In the battle Union losses were 1,200 and Confederate losses 600.

Richard Thompson was appointed Secretary of the Navy by President Rutherford B. Hayes. He served from 1877 to 1880. He died February 9, 1890.

The White House – Thursday, July 28, 1864

Tad asked me about comets this morning at breakfast. I told him that when he was five years old his mother and I had viewed Donati's Comet, which had been discovered by an Italian astronomer early in 1858. At the time people stayed up late night after night to catch glimpses of it. It had a long bright tail. On the eve of my third debate with Stephen Douglas, Mother and I watched the heavenly event from the hotel porch in Jonesboro, Illinois. Hundreds of townspeople had come out to watch the rare event. Comet watchers were disappointed when they read in the Ashtabula Weekly Telegraph that the comet's tail was not expected to be fully visible in time to be seen during the annual township fair but that viewers would have to wait until late October to enjoy the full spectacle.

I telegraphed John W. Forney and Morton McMichael, editors of the Philadelphia North American newspaper, to please come to the White House tomorrow. Forney has been ill and is about to sail for Europe on the Scotia for health reasons. Both men have been loyal supporters of the war effort, and of my candidacy for re-election.

I've asked General Grant to meet me at Fortress Monroe, Virginia, Saturday at 8 P.M. I am anxious to learn first-hand how matters are going in his campaign. I have been thinking we may gain much by combining the departments of Susquehanna, Washington, Middle Virginia and West Virginia under the command of General Meade.

Author's notes:

The North American, a daily newspaper in Philadelphia, was first published in 1839. The paper was a staunch supporter of Abraham Lincoln and developed to become a supporter of the Republican Party. Morton McMichael's two sons assumed control of the paper in his final years, his son Clayton assuming chief editorial duties. In 1899, the paper was acquired by Thomas B. Wanamaker. In 1925 Cyrus Curtis, owner of the Public Ledger, acquired the newspaper from Wanamaker's estate.

The president's plans changed, and he notified General Grant that he would meet him on Sunday, July 31st, at 10 A.M. at Fortress Monroe.

The White House – Friday, July 29, 1864

Today I wrote a thank-you note to Mrs. Anne Williamson, age 81, of Edinburgh, Scotland. She had very kindly sent me a shepherd's checked plaid scarf. I told her I thought it was a particularly pretty and a very useful present. But still more important to me were the good wishes offered to me and to our country, which prompted her to send it. With a war being waged and the tugs of traditional friendships sometimes sorely tried, it was nice to be reminded that the people of Scotland and England remain friendly to their American cousins. Mother was particularly pleased to see and feel the lady's gift. I shall wear it this winter. I plan to show it to the British ambassador the next time Seward brings him to the White House. I want him to realize how appreciative I am of Mrs. Williamson's thoughtfulness.

Author's notes:

Mrs. Williamson's letter to Lincoln read: "My Lord President: As one deeply interested in your present struggle, I trust the Lord will bless all your endeavors for the peace of your country and the freedom of the slave. As this letter is written by an old lady of 81, she hopes you will overlook its imperfections; and, with good wishes to you, and your family..."

Confederate forces under General Richard S. Ewell won a victory at the First Battle of Deep Bottom in Henrico County, Virginia, on July 27th to July 29th as part of the siege of Petersburg. Union forces under Generals Winfield Hancock and Philip Sheridan suffered 488 casualties. Confederate casualties numbered 679.

On July 28th, Union forces won a victory when Confederate attacks on the Union Army northwest of Atlanta failed to gain the element of surprise, finding entrenched federal soldiers in their path during the Battle of Ezra Church in Fulton County, Georgia. Federal troops under Generals Sherman and Howard numbered 13,266. Confederate forces under Generals John Hood and Stephen D. Lee numbered 18,450. Federal losses were 642 casualties; Rebel casualties totaled 3,000. Sherman's strategy was to destroy all railroad lines in his path. By the 24th of July, the Macon & Western Railroad was the only one leading into Atlanta left to destroy.

The White House – Monday, August 1, 1864

I have been away visiting General Grant, his staff and our troops at Fortress Monroe, Virginia since Saturday, July 30th. Mrs. Lincoln and some of her lady friends joined our party. Grant met with me and with Gideon Welles and Assistant Navy Secretary Gustavus Fox aboard the U.S.S. Baltimore at a conference which began at 10 A.M Sunday. We had a most rewarding meeting with Grant, in which we discussed a recent catastrophe in which a tunnel exploded at Petersburg, Virginia killing and wounding 5,300 of our men, who were trapped in a crater caused by the blast. Afterward, we returned to Washington at 3 P.M. yesterday, after having sailed to Norfolk, Virginia. It has been good being with Grant and learning how he thinks and handles matters. I know that since he has assumed command I sleep better at night. He provides a welcome and calming influence, which has long been needed.

Before I went to bed last night, I read a few lines from Shakespeare – (Henry V, IV.) They were: "No not all these, thrice-gorgeous ceremony, not all these, laid in bed majestical, can sleep so soundly as the wretched slave, who with a body filled and vacant mind gets him to rest, crammed with distressful bread." How I envy the ability of the bard to provide words which one can never forget, and which always inspire. King Henry also provides me with, "We few, we band of brothers, for he today that sheds his blood with me, shall be my brother."

Our ship arrived back at the Navy Yard early this morning. We had good sailing weather with calm seas. No one was seasick. Mother is a particularly good sailor!

Author's notes:

General Grant later wrote of the crater incident that it was "the saddest affair I have witnessed in this war."

162

The White House – Tuesday, August 2, 1864

This morning Secretary Welles and his staff presented to the Cabinet a report on the meeting in the English Channel of the U.S.S. Kearsarge and the Rebel raider, the C.S.A. Alabama, under Captain Raphael Semmes, which occurred on June 19th. According to information gleaned from sailors rescued from the sinking Alabama, Semmes' ship, which had been at sea for 22 months without once putting into a Southern port, had defective powder. It also had no armor over its hull. At the start of the battle a 110-pound projectile from the Alabama lodged in the Kearsarge's stern post but did not explode, presumably because of a defective fuse. Almost immediately in the action, a shot from the Kearsarge destroyed the Alabama's steering apparatus and the ship had to be steered with tackles. Shells from Captain Winslow's powerful Dahlgrens smashed into the Alabama below the waterline and she began to sink. Semmes was saved, as were many crewmen by a nearby yacht owned by a wealthy Briton who had observed the action and took survivors to Southampton. According to our minister, Charles Francis Adams, Semmes was lionized in the British press. British admirers replaced Semmes' sword, which was lost in action, and he was wined and dined by the aristocracy. He blamed the loss of the Alabama on the protective iron chains that protected the hull of the Kearsarge, and upon his poor powder. Welles pointed out that the Navy Department has estimated that Semmes managed over his wartime cruise to have burned 54 Federal merchantmen, bonded 10 others and sank the U.S.S. Hatteras. Welles believes that Semmes will find his way back to the Confederacy and again cause the United States trouble.

Author's notes:

Captain Raphael Semmes returned to Richmond and was promoted to rear admiral and put in charge of the James River fleet of Rebel gunboats. When Richmond fell, he was named a brigadier general and became the only Confederate officer to hold the dual ranks of admiral and general. In 1865 he was arrested and imprisoned for violations of the rules of war. After two months in prison, the government concluded it had no case and he was released. Semmes returned to Mobile to practice law and write his memoirs. His book, "Memoirs of Service Afloat During the War Between the States," was the first important Confederate memoir to appear after the war. The first seven chapters are an eloquent defense of the right of secession. Semmes was a remarkable skipper. He kept his two wooden vessels at sea for almost three years without an overhaul and without losing a crewman or prisoner to disease. He was the first commerce raider to operate in the age of steam and was perhaps the best of all time.

The White House – Wednesday, August 3, 1864

Today was a day of international diplomacy, with letters signed to four world leaders. First, to Charles XV, king of Sweden and Norway, upon the marriage of Prince Nicolas Auguste to Princess Therese Amelie Caroline Josephine Antoinette of Saxe Altenbourg in April. Second, to Francis Joseph I, Emperor of Austria, on the death of Archduchess Hildegarde, wife of his beloved cousin, Archduke Albrecht. Third, to William I, king of Prussia, upon the birth by Princess Antonie, sister of His majesty the king of Portugal, of a prince named Guillaume Auguste Charles Joseph Ferdinand Pierre Benoit. Fourth, to Leopold, king of the Belgians, upon the birth in May of a princess, Stephanie Clotilde Louise Herminie Marie Charlotte, daughter of the Duchess of Brabant, his daughter-in-law.

At the Office of U.S. Military Telegraph I sent a cypher to General Grant advising him that if the strategy is of putting our Army south of the enemy, or of following him to the death in any direction, that I repeat, will never be done nor attempted unless you watch it every day and force it. Two hours later, Grant advised that he would be here within two hours to meet with General David Hunter, who has ordered the removal of certain secessionist citizens from Frederick, Maryland, including James M. Schley and his family and relatives. Hunter has had his ups and downs. He has managed to please many and offend few. Unfortunately, he has not won the respect of General Grant, who is now the final arbiter of matters concerning his future in the Army.

Author's notes:

On August 1, 1864, General Grant placed Major General Philip Sheridan in command of the effort to destroy Jubal Early's Army. The Shenandoah, Maryland and Washington, D.C., fell under General Hunter's military department, but Grant had no intention of allowing Hunter any direct command on paper while Sheridan did the active field campaigning. He advised Hunter he could retain command on paper while Sheridan did the active field campaigning. Hunter declined the offer. Grant relieved Hunter of his post. In 1865 Hunter was promoted to brevet major general. He served in the honor guard at the funeral of Abraham Lincoln and accompanied his body back to Springfield. He was president of the military commission trying the conspirators of Lincoln's assassination from May 8 to July 15, 1865. He retired from the Army in July 1866.

The White House – Friday, August 5, 1864

Today the Cabinet met with General Grant, who came to Washington from City Point late yesterday. He and Secretary Stanton brought us all up to date on present doings related to Army actions in and around the Capital. Later I interviewed General Sheridan who will be meeting with Grant at Monocacy Junction this afternoon. I received my salary warrant for $1,981.67. Uncle Sam removed $101.66 due to the income tax, which was enacted on June 30 of this year to help pay down the war debt.

Editor Horace Greeley had written to John Hay asking permission to publish letters written by me to Greeley about the Niagara Falls matter in which Southerners in Canada purporting to represent Jefferson Davis were proposing a peace agreement. I have assented to the publication. Davis believes that secession is legal, and that the Confederacy is a legitimate nation. I and our government strongly disagree and therefore a "peace negotiation" is an impossibility, except to accept the surrender of all Rebel forces in the field and at sea.

Author's notes:

On August 6 President Lincoln telegraphed Horace Greeley, "Yours to Major Hay about publication of our correspondence received. With the suppression of a few passages in your letters, in regard to which I think you and I would not disagree, I should be glad of the publication. Please come over and see me. A Lincoln."

The White House – Saturday, August 6, 1864

Secretary Welles came by with Secretary Stanton at noon today to discuss various pressing military matters and to recommend that Colonel Griffin A. Stedman, who is reportedly dying from wounds received in action in battle outside of Petersburg, Virginia, be promoted to brigadier general. The promotion was recommended by General Edward Ord. I told them that I shall be glad to have this done and asked that the colonel be told at once of my decision. Stedman was from Connecticut and was a prominent attorney in that state before enlisting. I plan to write to his bereaved family this weekend. He was a well-liked and admired officer noted for his bravery in battle.

Late in the afternoon, Colonel Samuel M. Bowman spent time with me and General Halleck. He described his efforts to muster more Negro troops in Maryland. He is the chief mustering officer in the state for that purpose. His efforts have proved very effective. He says that his biggest problem is finding Negroes interested in volunteering. Most of them do not know how to read and thus advertising in newspapers does not work. I suggested that he print handbills for colored neighborhoods and send soldiers into those neighborhoods to distribute messages to people of any color who can read so they in turn can communicate our message. I authorized him to hire people to do this for the cause. He will try it and says he will get back to me in two months advising of his success.

Author's notes:

Free black men were permitted to enlist in the Union Army late in 1862. They had served in the American Revolution and the War of 1812 but were not permitted to enlist in the Mexican War. Frederick Douglass and other black leaders encouraged black men to enlist as a way to ensure eventual full citizenship. By the time the war ended some 179,000 black men had served in over 160 units of the Union Army, representing 10 percent of its total. The number included Northern free African Americans and runaway slaves who enlisted to fight. Nearly 20,000 more served in the Navy. Nearly 40,000 died, three-fourths of them due to disease or infections.

Black Union soldiers did not receive equal pay or equal treatment. They were paid $10 a month, with $3 deducted from that pay for clothing – white soldiers received $13 a month with no clothing deduction – until June 1864, when Congress granted retroactive equal pay.

The White House – Monday, August 8, 1864

At the Cabinet meeting it was confirmed by Secretary Stanton that Colonel Stedman had died. A fine soldier. Later in the day Secretary Seward brought Count Edward Piper, who represents Norway and Sweden. He is a highly regarded member of the diplomatic corps. The last time we met he presented me with a portfolio of fine engravings from Oslo, which he asked to be given to Mrs. Lincoln. She loves them as does Tad, who has an appreciation for good art. The subjects of the engravings are birds, that are native to his homeland.

I wrote a telegraphic message to General Stephen Burbridge at Lexington, Kentucky, to clarify my views related to Mary's half-sister, Mrs. Emily T. Helm, the widow of Confederate General Ben Helm. She had visited Mother when on a recent trip from Georgia back to Kentucky. I had given her a paper to protect her from the fact that she is Helm's widow. I learned that Burbridge had sought her arrested for disloyal acts since her return to Kentucky. I informed him that Emily is to be treated as any other citizen. Her husband was a good friend of mine, who I had hoped might be willing to serve in the Union Army, but like so many Southerners, he felt obligated to serve his state rather than the nation.

I sent a letter to a group of Shakers from Maine who had sent me a very comfortable chair they had made especially for me. I now sit upon it in my office. They are good peace-loving citizens.

Author's notes:

General Ben Helm was killed at the Battle of Chickamauga in September of 1863. In June of 1895, Emily Helm addressed an open letter to Century Magazine, in which she averred, "This dispatch (Lincoln's telegram) is a surprise to me, since I was never arrested and never had any trouble with the United States authorities."

The Shakers were pacifists and did not believe it was acceptable to kill or harm others, even in time of war. Both Union and Confederate soldiers found their way to the Shaker communities. Shakers tended to sympathize with the Union, but they did provide care and feed for both Union and Confederate soldiers. President Lincoln exempted Shaker males from military service, and they became some of the first conscientious objectors in American history. Today there are no active Shaker communities in the United States.

The White House – Tuesday, August 9, 1864

A long Cabinet meeting. I advised the members that I have authorized Editor Horace Greeley to publish all letters related to the Niagara Falls correspondence between him and me. I sent to Greeley copies of our correspondence for this use. I wrote to General Nathaniel Banks having just seen the new Constitution adopted by the Convention of Louisiana. I trust it may soon be ratified by the people of that state. Governor Michael Hahn of Louisiana, who arrived in Washington three days ago, brought a copy of the document for us to review.

Author's notes:

On September 5, 1864, the Constitution of Louisiana was submitted to the people of the state, at an election held in all the parishes within Federal lines for that purpose and for the election of members of Congress and the State Legislature. The Constitution was ratified by a large majority. General Banks advised Lincoln, "Your policy here will be adopted in other states and work out in the end the reestablishment of the Union, into whosoever hands its administration may fall."

The White House – Wednesday, August 10, 1864

Several members of the War Department attended a meeting here to review recent military actions since late July. Included in the presentations were the battles of Ezra Church in Georgia, Kildeer Mountain in the Dakota Territory and Folck's Mill in Maryland, with more information provided about the tragic Battle of the Crater in Virginia. Later in the day, Secretary Welles and his staff brought the Cabinet up to date on the Battle of Mobile Bay, a significant naval victory in which Admiral Farragut took this important Southern port. This naval victory, together with that of the U.S.S. Kearsarge over the C.S.A. Alabama, can only strengthen our image abroad, particularly in Britain and France.

Author's notes:

Mobile Bay was protected by three fortresses, a small Confederate fleet and a large minefield. Admiral David Farragut's bold attack secured Union control over the Gulf of Mexico. Northern newspapers heralded news of the victory by broadcasting news of Farragut's alleged battle cry, "Damn the torpedoes, full speed ahead!" while commanding his ships to proceed through the minefield. News of the victory was a powerful boost to civilian morale and strengthened Lincoln's chances during the election campaign of 1864.

On September 2, 1864, President Lincoln issued an order for Celebration of Victories at Mobile, Alabama. Included in the celebration was the firing of 100 guns at the Arsenal and Navy Yard on Thursday, September 6.

On September 3, 1864, an Order of Thanks was issued to Admiral David Farragut and Major General Edward Canby for the skill and harmony with which the recent operations in Mobile Bay Harbor, and against Fort Powell, Fort Gaines and Fort Morgan, were planned and carried to execution.

The White House – Thursday, August 11, 1864

I invited General Carl Schurz and his wife, Margarethe, to the White House to lunch with Mary and me. He and his wife are marvelous people. The ladies are good friends and share many common interests, particularly the education of young children. We discussed among other things his views on Spain, where he had served for a short time as U.S. minister. When in Spain he had succeeded in quietly dissuading Spain from supporting the Confederacy. He is highly supportive of General Grant's leadership and optimistic about my chances of being re-elected this November. He tells me that after the war he may publish a newspaper in St. Louis. He says he does not intend to return to a career as a lawyer. I confessed that my ambition after the war is to return to the practice of law in Springfield.

Author's notes:

After the war Schurz established a newspaper in St. Louis and won election to the U.S. Senate, becoming the first German-born American elected to that body. Breaking with the Republican Party when Grant was president, he helped establish the Liberal Republican Party, which advocated civil service reform and opposed Grant's efforts to protect African American civil rights in the South during reconstruction. In 1874 Schurz lost his re-election bid and resumed his career as a newspaper editor. In 1876 President Rutherford B. Hayes appointed Schurz as his secretary of the Interior. Schurz moved to New York City after Hayes left office and served as editor of the New York Post and The Nation. He later became a writer for Harper's Weekly. He died in New York City in 1906.

The White House – Friday, August 12, 1864

Early this morning, I must have had 25 cavalrymen accompanying me as I rode to the White House from the Soldiers' Home. I think the Army is overdoing it as to my safety, but Stanton fears that an assassin could easily have killed me under previous arrangements, which he thinks were far too lax. I will defer to his judgment in the matter.

Author's notes:

On this date, the poet Walt Whitman wrote in his notebook, "I see the President almost every day, as I happen to live where he passes to or from his lodgings out of town. I saw him this morning about 8:30 coming into business, riding on Vermont Avenue, near L Street. He always has a company of twenty-five or thirty cavalry, with sabers drawn and held upright over their shoulders."

Walt Whitman was born in 1819 and died in 1892. The Civil War was the central event of his life. Whitman worked for the government and volunteered his services helping to nurse wounded soldiers. As the war progressed Whitman came to love Lincoln, though the two men never met. Before the war Lincoln had read his most famous poem from "Leaves of Grass". "Oh Captain! My Captain!" became one of his most famous works, one that he would read at the end of his famous lecture about the Lincoln assassination. After famed actor Robin Williams' death in August 2014, fans of his work used social media to pay tribute to him with photo and video re-enactments of the Dead Poets Society "O Captain! My Captain!" scene. The poem was included in the fourth printing of "Leaves of Grass" published in 1867.

The White House – Saturday, August 13, 1864

At yesterday's Cabinet meeting all but Stanton and Fessenden attended. Fessenden has made himself of great value to our deliberations since joining our group. His predecessor was a brilliant man but lacked any sense of modesty. Fessenden is willing to allow others to take the bows. Thurlow Weed came down from New York City with a gloomy view of the upcoming elections. I have asked Colonel Eaton to visit General Grant and to ascertain his interest in becoming a presidential candidate. John Hay is leaving for a five or six week visit to his family. He shall be missed as he is my number one aide. Among other places he will be visiting will be Keokuk, Iowa.

This evening Mother and I had General and Mrs. Robert Anderson as our guests for dinner. The Sewards and the Welleses joined the party. Anderson is a remarkable man who is rightly regarded as the first hero of the war when he defended the flag flying over Fort Sumter. I reminded him that during the Black Hawk War, as a colonel of Illinois volunteers he had mustered me in twice. He has not been in good health yet seemed remarkably fit when he was here. I treasure his friendship.

Author's notes:

After Robert E. Lee's surrender at Appomattox, at the behest of Secretary of War Stanton, Anderson returned to Charleston in uniform four years after lowering the 33-star flag in surrender. Anderson raised it in triumph over the recaptured and badly battered fort. Within hours of the ceremony on April 14, 1865, John Wilkes Booth assassinated President Lincoln. After the war, Anderson became a companion of the Military Order of the Loyal Legion of the United States. In 1869 he discussed the future of the Army with Sylvanus Thayer. Afterward, they helped establish the Military Academy's Association of Graduates. Anderson died in Nice, France, on October 26, 1871, while seeking a cure for his ailments. He is interred at West Point Cemetery. He served in the Army from 1825 to 1863, retiring with the rank of major general. His father, Richard Clough Anderson (1750 to 1826), served in the Continental Army as an aide-de-camp of the Marquis de Lafayette and was a charter member of the Society of Cincinnati. His mother, Sarah Marshall, was a cousin of John Marshall, the fourth chief justice of the Supreme Court.

The White House – Monday, August 15, 1864

Frederick Douglass has answered a letter from me and advises that he will be here on Friday to discuss several matters of concern. I have great admiration for Douglass and value his opinions on matters of which he has special knowledge. We have significantly increased the number of Negroes serving in the Army and Navy and his advice about their service is welcomed by me. He has done much to personally encourage black men to enlist in the Army and the Navy and has explained to me the justice of black soldiers and sailors being paid the same wages as white men. I have assured him this will be my policy as will the policy of appointing qualified black men to officer status when appropriate. I consider Douglass a trusted friend and a man who has significantly helped the war effort.

Author's notes:

Douglass pointed out to Lincoln that black soldiers, all of whom were relegated to segregated units under white officers, had no hope of being promoted to officer status, no matter how meritorious their service. Lincoln told him that "he would sign any commission to colored soldiers, whom his secretary of war should commend to him." By the end of the war about 110 black officers were commissioned. When equal pay was finally agreed upon it was made retroactive to Negroes. When Douglass met Lincoln for the first time, Douglass said, "I was treated by him with dignity just as you have seen one gentleman receive another. I was never more quickly and completely put at ease in the presence of a great man. Mr. Lincoln listened with great earnest attention and with very apparent sympathy, and replied to each point his own peculiar, forcible way."

After President Lincoln's death, Mary Lincoln presented Frederick Douglass with a handsome gold-tipped cane that had been owned by the president. Douglass wrote to her,"Dear Madam, Allow me to thank you, as I certainly do thank you most sincerely for your thoughtful kindness in making me the owner of a cane which was formerly the property and the favorite walking staff of your late lamented husband the honored and venerated President of the United States. I assure you, that this inestimable memento of his Excellency will be retained in my possession while I live – an object of sacred interest – a token not merely of the kind consideration in which I have reason to know that the President was pleased to hold me personally, but as an indication of the humane interest in the welfare of my whole race. With proper sentiment of Respect and Esteem, I am, Dear Madam, your obedient servant. Frederick Douglass."

The White House – Wednesday, August 17, 1864

Yesterday, the Cabinet learned details of two recent military actions: the Battle of Utoy Creek in Georgia, outside of Atlanta, and the Battle of Moorefield; fought in West Virginia. Utoy Creek was fought from August 4th to 7th and was inconclusive. Moorefield was a Union victory. Sherman has partially surrounded Atlanta, with forces there now under the command of Confederate General John Bell Hood. Sherman's goal is to attack the railroad lines, thus destroying the enemy's supplies. Sherman had ordered this attack twice before. Atlanta is a tough nut to crack. General John Schofield's XXIII Corps was transferred from his left to his right flank. The rebels strengthened their position with an abatis, which slowed our forces' attack on the 6th. We suffered over 850 casualties. Sherman reports that he will not be discouraged and will take Atlanta, of that he is certain.

At Moorefield in Hardy County, West Virginia, Union cavalry under Brigadier General William Averell defeated forces led by Brigadier General John McCausland on August 7. The enemy had recently burned the town of Chambersburg in Pennsylvania. The fighting took place along the South Branch of the Potomac River, north of Moorefield. Averell estimates that his cavalry units numbered 3,000 to the enemy's 1,760. He reports 42 casualties to the enemys' losses of 488. Our cavalry included units from West Virginia, New York, Ohio and Pennsylvania.

Today, I telegraphed General Grant this message: "I have seen your dispatch, expressing your unwillingness to break your hold where you are. Neither am I willing. Hold on with a bull-dog gripe, and chew and choke, as much as possible." Although we've suffered tremendous losses it is my view that we are far better able to accept such losses than is our enemy. We have the greater population and we now see that the South is losing former slaves who continue to come over to our side, preferring freedom to slavery. The wheels of war turn slowly, but they do turn. To my mind they turn to victory. May it be sooner rather than later.

Author's notes:

The Confederate forces at Moorefield were no match for the Union cavalry, which was armed with sabers, 6-shot revolvers and 7-shot repeating rifles. Averell's victory inflicted permanent damage on the Confederate cavalry, and it was never again the dominant force it once was in the Shenandoah Valley.

The White House – Thursday, August 18, 1864

I wired General Ethan Allen Hitchcock this morning agreeing to his proposal that Confederate Major Thomas D. Armesy, who was arrested April 18th near Clarksburg, Virginia, and who is now under conviction and imprisonment as a spy, may be exchanged for Major Nathan Goff, Jr. a Union prisoner of war held in Richmond, Virginia. Armesy was arrested and tried on the charge of recruiting men within our lines for the purpose of joining the Rebel Army. He has been sentenced to 15 years of hard labor in prison at Fort Warren, Boston Harbor. Goff wrote to Senator Waitman T. Willey from Libby Prison in Richmond on May 16, advising that he is being held in close confinement for amnesty. It is an acceptable exchange.

Today I spoke to the 164th Ohio Regiment assembled here at the White House lawn. I thanked them for their service as a One Hundred Day regiment of militia called up to defend Washington, D.C. They will return to their homes in Ohio tomorrow with the nation's thanks.

Author's notes:

On this date Lincoln met with Leonard Swett, a longtime friend, lawyer and political leader from Illinois. Swett notified Lincoln that it was his belief that Lincoln could not be re-elected and urged him to withdraw from the presidential race. Lincoln refused his friend's advice.

175

The White House – Friday, August 19, 1864

I reviewed 15 to 20 court-martial cases this morning. Most were minor matters, but they almost required as much time as major cases. I signed a proclamation which states that the port of Newport in the state of Vermont shall be entitled to all the privileges in regard to the exportation of merchandise in bond to the British North American Provinces, adjoining the United States. One of the benefits of a good relationship with Canada is that the United States is not required to consider military threats from the North at this time in our history. Seward tells me that 4th Viscount Lord Monck has long been concerned about Southern violations of neutrality since Confederate agents had appeared in Canada. Monk is pro-North rather than neutral, according to Seward, and has been doing his utmost to discourage the Confederacy from sending agents to Canada. Last year he foiled a Southern plot to attack the Federal prisoner of war camp on Johnson's Island in Lake Erie off Sandusky, Ohio.

Frederick Douglass and I had a good discussion about many matters of concern to him, including pay for Negro sailors and soldiers, including the commissioning of black officers. I thanked him for his many efforts to convince qualified former slaves and freedmen to enlist in our armed forces and he promises to do even more in this regard.

Author's notes:

On this date, President Lincoln spent an hour in discussions about the upcoming election with the former governor of Wisconsin, and currently the first assistant postmaster general, Alexander W. Randall, and Judge Joseph T. Mills.

The White House – Saturday, August 20, 1864

Last night I dreamed a familiar dream of mine; in it I am defending Jesus Christ in his trial before a Jewish court and before his appearance before Pontius Pilate and a Roman tribunal. I don't think I have had this particular dream since very soon after the war began. My thought is that when I am no longer president, I might like to write a book about the trials of Christ and how he was treated illegally according to both Roman and Jewish law of the time. How he must have suffered, particularly when he was deserted by Peter in his greatest hour of need. In Jewish law of that time, the proceedings against Jesus were illegal because they were conducted on a day preceding a Jewish Sabbath, on a feast day (the Feast of the Unleavened Bread) and on the eve of Passover, all of which is recorded in all the Gospels). It was Thursday night. Jewish reckoning of the day began at sundown one day and terminated at the beginning of sundown the next day. The Jewish day was not 24 hours. It was that period that varies each day. It was the night of April 6th or the 14th of Nisan according to the Jewish calendar. The Feast of the Unleavened Bread, which lasted for seven days, had begun. The Mishnah tells us that the court couldn't be held on the Sabbath or Holy Day. And, if it was a capital trial, which had to run two days if it were to result in a conviction, it couldn't start on a day before either the Sabbath or feast day either because it would be required to run over into the next day. There could be no adjournment for a day under Jewish law. Jews paid strict attention to the law as it was recorded in the Talmud prohibiting labor on the Sabbath. And the proceedings had to be recorded by the court officers in connection with the voting. Under Rabbinical Law, even writing on the Sabbath day was work and a violation of the Mosaic Code to keep the Sabbath day holy. It is my intention one day when I have the time to invite several Rabbis and Jewish attorneys to the White House to discuss my limited understanding of Jewish law.

Author's notes:

Abraham Lincoln kept a Bible in his bedroom and another copy in his office. He often read the Bible and could recite verses from it by memory. As the war continued his Biblical references became more frequent.

The White House – Monday, August 22, 1864

Yesterday, I established an Ordnance Board, with General Quincy A. Gillmore to be president; competent ordnance officers are to be appointed to the board by the secretaries of War and Navy. It is to meet in Bridgeport, Connecticut, on September 1, to test a 7-inch wrought-iron cannon manufactured by the Ames Company. I have high hopes for the gun.

Today, I talked to members of the 166th Ohio Regiment upon the completion of their 100 days of volunteer service and thanked them for their service to the nation. Tomorrow, I will make similar remarks to members of the 147th Ohio Regiment, including Colonel Benjamin Rosson, its commanding officer. Secretary Stanton will join me at both talks. My theme will be that this great nation is well-worth fighting for.

Author's notes:

The 7-inch wrought-iron cannon of the Ames Company was test-fired 700 times and was judged by the Ordnance Board to be satisfactory for purchase by both the Army and Navy.

The White House – Tuesday, August 23, 1864

My talk to the 147th Ohio Regiment this morning was well-received. They'll soon be home with their loved ones with the thanks of the nation. Later, I presented to the members of the Cabinet a memorandum concerning the probable failure of re-election. I asked each member to sign the back of the document (without reading it), which I intend to keep until election day. In the memo I confess that I expect to lose and will be required to cooperate with the incoming president-elect so as to preserve the Union between election day and the day of inauguration. I mentioned that if we lose, I fear the person elected cannot possibly save the nation. I believe that General McClellan will not continue our present policies, which I believe are working. The public is wild for peace and the Peace Candidate may win by promising peace through negotiation vs. peace won on the battlefields.

Author's notes:

Lincoln's Memorandum Concerning the Probable Failure of Re-election read:
"This morning and for some days past, it seems exceedingly probable that this
Administration will not be re-elected. Then it will be my duty to co-operate with
the President elect, as to save the Union between the election and the inauguration;
as he will have secured his election on such ground that he cannot possibly save it
afterwards. A. Lincoln."

GIVEN MEMORIAL LIBRARY
150 Cherokee Rd PO Box 159
Pinehurst, NC 28370
910-295-6022

The White House – Thursday, August 25, 1864

Yesterday, the Cabinet listened to detailed presentations from General Halleck and members of his staff concerning recent battles fought in Georgia, Virginia, Tennessee and West Virginia. The periods covered were August 14 to August 21. At Dalton, Georgia, Globe Tavern, Virginia, and Memphis, Tennessee, Union forces prevailed. At Deep Bottom, Virginia, and Lovejoy's Station, Georgia the Confederates were more successful. At Guard Hill and Summit Point, Virginia the results were inconclusive. Perhaps the most significant battle was the one waged at Globe Tavern, where Confederate forces lost control of the railroads at Petersburg. Reports from General Sherman indicate that he expects to take Atlanta within the next 10 days. Sherman never issues wishful messages. I hope he is right about Atlanta. It is a key city in the struggle to seriously damage the Southern war effort.

Today, I again received a letter from a young man asking my advice about pursuing a career in the law. This boy, Joshua Smith, lives in Bangor, Maine. I told him as I have told others that the best mode is very simple, though it is laborious and tedious work. The way I did it was to get the required books and read and study them carefully. I began my reading with Blackstone's Commentaries, and after digesting it two or three times I took up Chitty's Pleadings, Greenleaf's Evidence and Story's equity, etc., in succession. There are no shortcuts in the law. Work, work, work is the main thing. I wonder if one day I may read that a Justice Smith is sitting on the Supreme Court. Every lawyer to be successful must read and digest the same books. There is no easy path I am afraid.

Author's notes:

On September 3, 1864, a telegram from General Sherman arrived in Washington announcing, "Atlanta is ours, and fairly won." The impact of the news on the nation was astounding. It reversed Northern opinion about the success or failure of the war effort overnight. Newspapers called it the greatest event of the war. A Republican newspaper summed it all up with this front-page message: "VICTORY. Is the war a failure? Old Abe's Reply to the Chicago Convention."

The White House – Friday, August 26, 1864

Yesterday, Secretary Welles, Seward, Stanton, Fessenden and Henry J. Raymond, editor of The New York Times joined me in a discussion concerning the subject of a possible peace mission being sent to Jefferson Davis. Today, I decided against sending a mission, as I believe I know in advance how Davis would react. He sees reunion as defeat. He continues to hold that the Confederacy is a legitimate government, and I do not. Only through victory of our arms in this struggle can we have peace.

Lord Lyons, the British minister, came by after lunch to bring me up to date on several matters, mostly involving the enlisting of British subjects into our Army. I admire Lyons and find him not only bright, but also fair-minded and anxious to maintain good relations between his great nation and ours. We discussed Captain Raphael Semmes of the Confederate Navy, who was rescued by a British yacht after the sinking of the commerce raider Alabama by the U.S.S. Kearsarge. Semmes may still be in England. I mentioned to Lyons that Secretary Wells had informed me that before the war, when Semmes was a serving U.S. Navy officer, he had written, "Commerce raiders are little better than licensed pirates; and it behooves all civilized nations to suppress the practice altogether." Lord Lyons said he believed that Semmes would soon be leaving England and may have already done so. My fear is that he will be given another ship by Jefferson Davis and returned to the high seas to do even greater damage to American shipping.

Author's notes:

Captain Semmes did return to the Confederacy. During his two-year career as a commerce raider Semmes claimed 65 prizes valued at nearly $6,000,000 or $96,000,000 in today's dollars. After the war the United States pursued the "Alabama Claims" in international law against Great Britain for losses caused by the Alabama and other raiders fitted out in Britain. A joint arbitration commission awarded the U.S. $15.5 million in damages.

The White House – Sunday, August 28, 1864

Yesterday, Hay brought me a sad telegram sent to me by Mary McCook Baldwin of Nashville, Tennessee. She implored me to not execute John S. Young. Mrs. McCook Baldwin is the daughter of Major and Paymaster Daniel McCook, and sister of Colonel Robert McCook of the 9th Ohio and Colonel Daniel McCook of the 51st Ohio, and Private Charles M. McCook, 2nd Ohio, all of whom have been killed in the war. She asks that the Army not execute John S. Young, the son of a former secretary of state who is under sentence of death. I have ordered that the sentence be suspended until further order. That one family should have suffered so much death in the Union cause is breathtaking and beyond understanding. May God bless her family.

Near midnight last evening, the lawyer Charles J.M. Gwinn of Baltimore visited me at the Soldiers' Home to ask for a reprieve in the case of four convicted spies. Their names are William Rodgers, John Emberet, Branton Lyons and Samuel Hearn. I telegraphed General Lewis Wallace in Baltimore that their sentences are commuted. The men are to be confined to the penitentiary at hard labor during the war. Halleck has told me that General Lew Wallace is an attorney and a gifted writer who intends to become an author after the war.

Today, Hay joined me, Secretary Stanton and a group of Army officers as we watched a demonstration of signaling in Morse Code from the tower of the Soldiers' Home to the roof of the Smithsonian Institution. It was too bad that Tad missed the event, but he and his mother are up in New England enjoying the cooler weather. I know that Tad would have enjoyed seeing the signaling done.

Author's notes:

John S. Young was the son of Dr. John S. Young, secretary of state of Tennessee, 1839 to 1847.

General Lew Wallace was named territorial governor of New Mexico after the war. When he was in Santa Fe, he wrote the manuscript for the novel Ben-Hur. In 1880 Harper and Brothers published the book, "Ben-Hur: A Tale of the Christ." It became the best-selling American novel of the 19th century. In 1881, Wallace was appointed U.S. minister to the Ottoman Empire. He remained in the post until 1885. By 1889 the book had sold 400,000 copies. At the time of "Ben-Hur's" 100th anniversary, it had never been out of print and had been adapted for stage and several motion pictures.

The White House – Monday, August 29, 1864

I interviewed Hon. Paul C. Brink of Newark, New Jersey, who believes that troop quotas have been set unfairly high for his municipality. I've asked Stanton to have an analysis of numbers made by the War Department to see if we can lower Brink's quotas.

I sent John Nicolay to New York at noon today on a political mission involving changes in Custom House officials.

I received a summary of the military events at the Battle of Smithfield Crossing in Jefferson and Berkeley counties in West Virginia earlier this month. Like so many clashes of troops, this is another that is best described as "inconclusive."

Author's notes:

This battle between two cavalry units of Confederate Lieutenant General Jubal Early and one of General Wesley Merritt's Union cavalry resulted in Merritt being initially forced back. However, a counterattack by General James B. Rickett's infantry division stopped the Confederate advance, and the results were a draw. This was the last engagement of the war to take place in West Virginia.

The Middleway Conservancy Organization commemorated the Battle of Smithfield Crossing in August 2014. To expand the community's knowledge and interest in this battle, The Conservancy hosted a living history event and re-enactments of the battle.

The White House – Tuesday, August 30, 1864

General Sherman confirmed by telegraph that Fort Morgan has been captured. The fort is located at the entrance to Mobile Bay. Stanton showed me a copy of the plans for the pentagonal bastion, which were drawn in 1817. Construction was completed in 1834. He reminded me that eight days before Alabama seceded from the Union, four companies of the Alabama National Guard captured the fort on January 3, 1861. During the Battle of Mobile Bay, Admiral Farragut was able to get past Fort Morgan and enter the Bay. He captured the Tennessee and Selma and sank the Gaines. Union land forces under Gordon Granger besieged the fort. On August 23, 1864, after first spiking the fort's guns, Confederate Major Richard L. Page surrendered.

Author's notes:

Fort Morgan was designated a National Historic Landmark in 1960. In 2007 it was listed as "one of the most endangered sites" by the Civil War Preservation Trust.

The White House – Wednesday, August 31, 1864

At noon today I telegraphed Mother, who is staying in Manchester, Vermont. I advised that I am reasonably well, and that Robert has not arrived yet. I miss her and Tad, who says he is enjoying exploring the area toward Bromley Mountain. His concerns when away are of his many pets that he has left behind.

I addressed the 148th Ohio Regiment, which is now on its way home after the completion of its service. The men are all very healthy looking and glad to be going home. I issued an order that stipulates that persons bringing out cotton from occupied areas in conformity with Treasury regulations must not be hindered by other government departments. I told the men that it was my hope that the Union flag would soon be waving over Atlanta, Georgia. The men cheered loudly when I told them that. They feel that the sooner Atlanta falls, the sooner this war will be over.

Today is one of the hottest days of the year. That is one reason why I enjoy living at the Soldiers' Home, because its hilltop location makes it several degrees cooler than the White House.

Author's notes:

Lincoln spent roughly 25 percent of his time as president at the Soldiers' Home. It was conveniently located 13 miles from the White House.

On September 3, 1864, Atlanta was occupied by Union forces under the command of Major General William Tecumseh Sherman. He wired President Lincoln, "Atlanta is ours, and fairly won."

The White House – Thursday, September 1, 1864

I received a letter from Mrs. Eliza P. Gurney, a fine Quaker lady who wrote me from her summer home near Atlantic City, New Jersey. I met her two years ago when she and three friends visited me here. She wrote advising me that the Quakers, although opposed to war, are in her words favorable to my candidacy for re-election. She wrote, "I may venture to say, that Friends are not less loyal for the lenity with which their honest convictions have been treated, and I believe there are few amongst us who would not lament to see any other than Abraham Lincoln fill the President's chair – at least at the next election – May our worthy Chief Magistrate yet see the day, when the Prince of Peace, the wonderful counsellor shall rule and reign over this now distracted country." I shall write to her later his week in appreciation of her kind and generous sentiments.

I conferred with Governor Hahn about the new constitution for Louisiana. I wired Postmaster General Blair, who is in Portsmouth, New Hampshire, to return as soon as possible to Washington.

Author's notes:

It was important that Blair be in Washington because Lincoln wanted First Assistant Postmaster General Alexander W. Randall to be able to leave his post in Washington so he could do some political campaigning in the West on behalf of the president. On September 3, Blair's wife, Mary E. Blair, telegraphed from Portsmouth, New Hampshire: "Mr. Blair left this morning and will be in Washington Monday."

The White House – Saturday, September 3, 1864

Yesterday I spent about an hour with George C. Haskins, the postmaster of Bennington, New York, which is in Wyoming County. He tells me that his territory encompasses 55 square miles. We talked about Horace Greeley and the political atmosphere of his area of New York. Haskins fears that General McClellan may do strongly in the November election as a Peace Democrat. Haskins has been encouraging postal workers in his area to vote for yours truly, for which I am grateful. I told Haskins that Greeley had recently tried to arrange for a peace proposal from Jefferson Davis, which Greeley thought could come to me through Confederate operatives in the Niagara Falls area of Canada. It was all a waste of time because Davis is an idealist who stubbornly clings to the idea that the Confederacy is a legitimate nation state. It is not. It is merely an idea whose time is running out as best I can tell. Unfortunately, by the time that Davis' hourglass runs out of sand, oceans of blood will have been spilled for his forsaken cause. As I explained to Haskins, the outcome is now in the trusted hands of Grant, Sherman and the other war leaders who I am counting upon to deliver victory sooner rather than later.

Today I issued an Order for Celebration of Victories at Atlanta, Georgia, and Mobile, Alabama. I also published an Order of Thanks to Admiral David Farragut and Others for their victories in Mobile Bay, and to General Sherman and Others for Courage and Perseverance in the Campaign leading to the Capture of the City of Atlanta.

Author's notes:

On September 3, 1864, Lincoln issued a proclamation of Thanksgiving and Prayer citing the operations of the United States fleet and Army in the harbor of Mobile and the reduction of Fort Powell, Fort Gaines and Fort Morgan; and the glorious achievements of the Army under Major General Sherman in the state of Georgia.

The White House – Monday, September 5, 1864

General Montgomery Meigs is a very well-read man. In addition, he is a very competent engineer. Yesterday he came by the Soldiers' Home for lunch and we discussed the ancient pyramids of Egypt, which he has studied for years. He thoughtfully brought some photographs of the pyramids with him. Tad and Mary were fascinated by Meigs' descriptions of the ancient wonders. He pointed out that the work was done roughly 2700 B.C. to 2500 B.C. Meigs believes that the Step Pyramid of Saqqara was the first monument in the world to be built entirely of stone. It rose to a height of 204 feet. The enterprise required a highly organized supply system involving quarries, mines, shipyards, storehouses, workshops and a labor force of thousands. Meigs estimates that the pyramid consisted of 600,000 tons of limestone blocks. Copper mines had to have been opened in the eastern desert to allow the production of copper chisels needed to cut such a vast quantity of stone blocks. Khufu's Great Pyramid may consist of 2.3 million blocks of stone each weighing on average more than a ton, reaching a height of 480 feet. The base extended over 13 acres and was a near-perfect square, closely aligned to the four cardinal points of the compass, with a precise orientation to true north. It is still regarded as one of the Seven Wonders of the Ancient World. Ultimately the pharaohs could no longer sustain the huge economic drain of funding such colossal monuments. I told Meigs that when this war is over, I would like to take Tad and Robert to Egypt with Mother to see the pyramids and the Great Sphinx, which Meigs says measures 200 feet long and rises to a height of 65 feet above the desert floor. I believe when finished the Washington Monument will reach 555 feet in height.

Author's notes:

On this day, Lincoln wrote to Mrs. Eliza P. Gurney in part, "The purposes of the Almighty are perfect, and must prevail, though we erring mortals may fail to accurately perceive them in advance. Surely, he intends some great good to follow this mighty convulsion, which no mortal could make, and no mortal stay. We hoped for a happy termination of this terrible war long before this; but God knows best and has ruled otherwise."

The White House – Tuesday, September 6, 1864

Today Mary gave me a small basket of ripe peaches, which I shared with the Cabinet members. They are particularly juicy and tasty this time of year. She and the wives of Cabinet members plan to take peach baskets to local military hospitals this week. After our meeting I interviewed a brave woman who served with the 34th Indiana Regiment when she was wounded. The paymaster withheld five months' pay from this courageous lady. I told her that if he didn't pay her I would. I wonder if in future wars women will be more involved than they are now. Her name is Mary E. Wise. She told me that she can hit squirrels with her rifle from 30 yards and I believe her.

I wrote to the son of my good friend John Meier. The boy sent me $5 to help the sick and wounded. He is wise beyond his years.

Author's notes:

John Meier's son was schooled in Dusseldorf, Germany. For the past 18 months he had been saving pennies, the proceeds of which he mailed to President Lincoln to "help the sick and wounded of our brave boys fighting for the glorious cause of truth and freedom as he himself was not old enough to fight." Lincoln wrote Meier, "I thank your boy, not only for myself, but also for the children of the nation, who are even more interested than those of us, of mature age, that this war shall be successful, and the Union be maintained and perpetuated."

The White House – Wednesday, September 7, 1864

At 3 P.M. today a committee of colored men from Baltimore presented me with an elegant Bible. It is inscribed "To Abraham Lincoln, President of the United States, the Friend of Universal Freedom, from the Loyal Colored People of Baltimore, as a token of respect and gratitude." I told them that I consider the Holy Bible to be the best gift God has given to man. We could never know good from wrong but for it. Earlier at our Cabinet meeting I had the members taste some hardtack crackers that had been made by the U.S. military bakery located in Jeffersonville, Indiana. Army specifications require that they be made of flour, water, and sometimes salt. They are supposed to be white, crisp, light and exhibit a flaky appearance when broken. In truth, many that reach our men are substandard and often moldy, riddled with maggots and weevils. They are typically so hard that they cannot be bitten without risk to the teeth of those who eat them. Many soldiers soak them in water, coffee or soup. Some fry them in pork fat, calling it "Skillygaleee." The samples we tasted were excellent, but one would not expect to be sent substandard crackers. I've asked our quartermaster general to see that the products are inspected more frequently before shipment to the soldiers and sailors who rely upon them for nourishment.

Author's notes:

Hardtack measured 3.5" X 2.8" X .5" and weighed 1.6 to 1.8 ounces. Each soldier was to receive 9 to 10 pieces as part of his daily "camp" ration. They were expected to keep for 3 to 12 months. Production at the Jeffersonville, Indiana bakery, between May 1863 and August 1865 used 149,429 barrels of flour, 20,491 bushels of coal and 5,990 cords of wood to produce 27,500,536 pieces of hardtack at a cost of $1,311,609.19 and a profit of $285,751.

The White House – Friday, September 9, 1864

Yesterday evening I telegraphed Mrs. Lincoln, who is staying in Manchester, Vermont, advising her that I missed her and Tad and that all is well here for the president and Tad's goat and pony.

Today I interviewed Mrs. Joshua F. Noble, whose husband, Joshua, is serving his sentence in the military prison located in the Dry Tortugas, Florida. I have asked the War Department to send me the details of the case. I am told by his wife that the soldier served a full nine months sentence for a former desertion and was then sent to the Dry Tortugas by mistake. It seems to me that this may be a case of Army red tape causing a soldier to be punished in error. I promised his wife to look into the matter personally and will do so. No man should spend one hour longer than required at Dry Tortugas.

Author's notes:

Joshua Noble, a private in Company A of the Second New Jersey Volunteers, had deserted on June 17,1861. On September 3, 1862, he re-enlisted in Company H, Thirteenth New Jersey Volunteers, where he served until transferred back to his old regiment on May 22, 1863. On June 26, 1863, he was sentenced to Dry Tortugas. Ultimately Lincoln was advised that the file of Private Noble had been lost by the War Department and the judge advocate general was not able to comment on the case.

The White House – Saturday, September 10, 1864

Tomorrow at 8 A.M. I have an appointment to meet with Democratic Congressman Fernando Wood of New York at the Soldiers' Home. The former mayor of New York City, Wood is a formidable character. He served three terms as mayor. He had recommended that New York City secede from the Union when the war broke out. He favored continued cotton trade with the South at the time. Since then he has come to see the errors of his ways and is a loyal Union supporter today. But even so, he still favors slavery and opposes the thinking behind the 13th Amendment, which will abolish slavery in the United States.

Author's notes:

Fernando Wood was married three times; his first wife was Anna Taylor of Philadelphia, whom he married in 1832. In 1841 he married Ann Dole Richardson, who died in 1859. In 1860 he married Alice Fenner Mills, who survived him. Wood was the father of 16 children, 11 of whom survived him. He was chairman of the House of Ways and Means Committee in both the 45th and 46th Congress (1877 to 1871). He served in the U.S. Congress from 1863 to 1865 and then again from 1867 until his death in Hot Springs, Arkansas, on February 14, 1881. His most notable child was son Henry Alexander Wise Wood.

The White House – Monday, September 12, 1864

Secretary Seward and I cooperated on writing a message to Emperor Napoleon III upon the birth of a son to Princess Clotilde Napoleon, a cousin of the French ruler. We have an excellent minister serving in Paris, William Lewis Dayton, who was selected by the Republican Party as its first nominee for vice president at the Philadelphia Convention, which picked John C. Frémont as its losing candidate. They were defeated by the Democratic ticket of James Buchanan and John C. Breckinridge. Dayton has done an excellent job, helping to keep the French neutral during the Civil War.

Seward had been in New York City last week where he had given a speech urging my re-election, for which I gave him my sincerest thanks. He showed me a copy of the New York Tribune, in which his speech was printed and praised editorially by Horace Greeley. New York will be an important state in the upcoming election. I can use all the help I can get there.

Mother is expected home from New England this week. I have invited Seward and Henri Mercier, the French minister to the White House, to join us at a dinner party when she returns. Mother has asked the cook to prepare bouillabaisse fish soup for the minister, his wife and several members of the French embassy. This will be the first time I have tasted what she promises will be a wonderful treat. Mother enjoys speaking French, the language she learned as a child and this will be her opportunity to shine. Tad has been taking French lessons but to date he has made little progress in mastering the language of diplomacy.

Author's notes:

Ambassador William Dayton was born February 17, 1807, in Basking Ridge, New Jersey. He died December 1, 1864, aged 57, in Paris and was buried in Riverview Cemetery, Trenton, New Jersey. The town of Dayton, New Jersey, was named in his honor. His son, William Dayton, Jr., graduated from Princeton in 1858 and served as President Chester A. Arthur's Ambassador to the Netherlands from 1882 to 1885. He died in 1897.

The White House – Tuesday, September 13, 1864

This was a perfect fall day. I went for a two-mile walk to clear my mind. When I am out of the office no one can call upon me for a favor, job or pardon! Last evening, I dreamed about the time when, as a young lad, my father hired me out for two days to do rail-splitting work for a nearby neighbor by the name of Robert Johnson. I believe he paid my father one dollar each day or $2 in total. (I saw none of that for my own pocket.) I must have been about 10 or 11 years old at the time. Johnson was a kindly man, originally from London, who had a small library in his house. He and I talked about books and he lent me his copy of "The Pilgrim's Progress" to read at home. I must have read it four or five times before I returned it to him. The full title of the book is, "The Pilgrim's Progress from This World to That Which is to Come." Johnson told me that John Bunyan, its author, was imprisoned in Bedfordshire County Prison for violations of the Conventicle Act of 1664, which prohibited holding of religious services outside the auspices of the Established Church of England. He may have started writing "The Pilgrim's Progress" while in prison again in 1675. I now have my own copy here in the White House and read it from time to time. It never grows old. I owe much to Robert Johnson for his generosity. I will never forget the day he trusted me with his precious copy of "The Pilgrim's Progress."

Author's notes:

The first copy of "The Pilgrim's Progress" was published in London in 1678. An expanded version was published in 1684. There were 11 editions of the first part in John Bunyan's lifetime, published in successive years from 1678 to 1685 and in 1688. There were two editions of the second part, published in 1684 and 1686. It has been translated into 200 languages and has never been out of print. It has also been cited as the first novel in English.

The White House – Wednesday, September 14, 1864

Last night a large crowd of people, including some soldiers and sailors, marched from a Republican political rally, held at the Mt. Vernon Hotel on 9th and Pennsylvania Avenue, to the White House to serenade me. A men's choir from my church sang the "Battle Hymn of the Republic" and an Army band performed "Dixie" (my favorite tune). My hope is that the Republican Party may be able to sponsor similar political events in large population areas to stimulate interest and enthusiasm for a big voter turnout in November.

I was invited by Isaac M. Schermerhorn of Buffalo, New York, to attend a similar political event in Buffalo. I wrote declining the offer. With a war to wage, I cannot indulge in the luxury of leaving Washington to campaign at this critical time.

We held a belated Cabinet meeting with General Halleck and his staff to review events surrounding military action in Georgia from August 31 to September 1. It was a Union victory at the Battle of Jonesborough in which the troops of Confederate General William J. Hardee's men were defeated, resulting in the fall of Atlanta. We were also brought up to date on events at Berryville, Virginia, earlier in the month. There Confederate General Jubal Early sent General Joseph Kershaw's division to attack Colonel Joseph Thorburn's left flank. The next morning, Early recognizing the strength of the Union's entrenched line, retreated behind Opequon Creek.

Author's notes:

On September 19, General Philip H. Sheridan telegraphed General Grant, "I have the honor to report that I attacked General Early over the Berryville Pike at the crossing of Opequon Creek, and after a most stubborn and sanguinary engagement… completely defeated him…driving him through Winchester, capturing about 2500 prisoners – five of artillery, nine Army flags and most of their wounded." When Lincoln received this information, he wired General Sheridan on September 20, "Have just heard of your great victory. God bless you all, officers and men. Strongly inclined to come up and see you. A. Lincoln." Several officers were killed or wounded on both sides.

The White House – Thursday, September 15, 1864

This morning Mrs. George W. McElrath came by the White House. She is the widow of Major McElrath, late of the Confederate Army. She is a lovely woman who asked for permission to return to Knoxville, Tennessee. She said that General James B. Steedman had ordered her sent away from her home. After our meeting, I telegraphed General Steedman at Chattanooga, Tennessee and advised him that I will agree to her returning to her home if he agrees. I trust he will accommodate the lady's wishes.

Author's note:

On October 27, Representative Nathaniel G. Taylor wrote to Lincoln of Mrs. McElrath's successful return to her residence in Knoxville. He advised the president that she took the Oath of Amnesty of the United States from Brigadier General Samuel B. Carter at Knoxville. Taylor reported that she said of you, "Speaking of President Lincoln, when General Carter's name was mentioned, you had remarked to her, that you did not think General Carter was any better friend of his that she was. Her family thanks you for allowing her to come home and she prays for peace."

Nathaniel G. Taylor served as a member of the U.S. House of Representatives from Tennessee from 1854 to 1855 and 1866 to 1867. He was appointed commissioner of Indian Affairs by President Andrew Johnson and served from 1867 to 1869. He was born December 29, 1819, and died April 1, 1887.

The White House – Saturday, September 17, 1864

Yesterday, Thomas Turner, chairman of the Union State Central Committee, and S.H. Melvin, commissioner of the Union League, met with me and Secretary Stanton to consider draft quotas for Illinois. They report that our goals will be met and then some. The state is mighty proud of General Grant. His determined leadership in the struggle is inspiring more voluntary enlistments in Illinois and across the nation. Grant is a remarkable man.

I conferred at lunch today with Post-Master Montgomery Blair about patronage matters and his thoughts on the presidential election. He is a wise old owl and his political instincts are always on course. He is optimistic about the election and predicts that the soldier and sailor vote will be especially high for me. He reiterated to me that he is willing to resign his post at any time that I feel it important that he does so. We both know that he has many enemies out for his scalp. My mother once said to me that "politics is like a ladder. And every step up the ladder can often be the face of a friend." Mamma knew what she was talking about!

Author's notes:

Montgomery Blair's unpopularity with the radical Republicans, Frémont's supporters in particular, is borne out by numerous letters in the Lincoln Papers, which recommended his removal. On September 23, 1864, Lincoln asked Blair to resign his Cabinet post for the good of the party. Blair immediately resigns. He wrote to Lincoln, "I cannot take leave of you without renewing the expressions of my gratitude for the uniform kindness which has marked your course towards, Yours truly. M. Blair."

On September 24, 1863, President Lincoln appointed Governor William Donovan of Ohio Post Master General of the United States. Lincoln always spelled the Cabinet position "Post-Master General." He also misspelled Fort Sumter, spelling it Fort Sumpter.

The White House – Monday, September 19, 1864

I telegraphed General Sherman, advising him that Indiana is the only important state, voting in October, whose soldiers cannot vote in the field. I asked him if there is anything that he can safely do to let her soldiers or any part of them go home and vote in Indiana's election. It is not an order, but an effort to impress upon Sherman the importance to the Army itself of doing all it safely can.

Hay has returned from his visit to New York and brought me up to date on how the press is treating me as far as the election goes. I am now thinking of sending Nicolay there to meet with Thurlow Weed and with two or three of the prominent newspaper editors, including Horace Greeley, whose ego requires constant praise and stroking.

Secretary Stanton and General Halleck met with me to discuss the issue of prisoner exchanges again. Too many good men on both sides are dying needlessly from disease and hunger in both Northern and Southern prison camps. In winter weather we can expect matters to get worse not better.

Author's notes:

On this date President Lincoln approved the exchange of Lieutenant Leopold Markbreit of the 28th Ohio Volunteers for a Rebel officer held by Federal forces. He was the half-brother of Frederick Hassaurek, the American minister to Ecuador. Markbreit was being held in Libby Prison and was reportedly weak and broken down from close confinement, and an inadequate daily diet of corn bread, boiled beans and two ounces of bacon. The prisoner exchange was affected on January 5, 1865.

The White House – Tuesday, September 20, 1864

As I sit here writing there are loud blasts of thunder coming from the West. I expect heavy showers very soon. When it rains, I often think of the troops in the field laboring in the mud over difficult roadways. I do not believe the public has any idea of the physical challenges their sons and fathers must meet to move ever forward against our determined enemy.

Earlier in the day, I met with Judge William Tod Otto regarding the sale of public lands in Kansas. Otto is a good friend of mine and has been so for many years. He headed the Indiana delegation to the 1860 Republican Convention that nominated me for the presidency and helped in delivering Indiana, a key state in that election. He has been an important member of the Interior Department since appointed assistant secretary last year.

Author's notes:

Judge Otto studied law at the University of Pennsylvania and practiced law in Brownstown, Indiana. He was among those surrounding Lincoln's bedside when he died after being shot by John Wilkes Booth. He went on to serve as a diplomat, helping arbitrate claims against Spain, and was also a delegate to the Universal Postal Union Congress in Lisbon, Portugal, in 1875. He was named reporter of decisions of the U.S. Supreme Court in 1875, a position he held until 1883. He was born January 19, 1816 and died November 7, 1905.

The White House – Wednesday, September 21, 1864

I was visited today by M.M. Broadwell of New York City. He is a prominent merchant who wishes to provide blankets and other clothing to prisoners of war, both Federal and Confederate. I advised him that although his is a noble deed, I cannot guarantee delivery of such items to our own soldiers now being held by the Rebels. I am not opposed to his providing goods for Rebel prisoners in our hands. He has asked to go to Richmond to talk with senior Confederate officials in hopes of getting them to cooperate in the mission. I thanked him for his generosity and authorized that he be given a pass to go to Richmond. Colonel William Hoffman, who is in charge of prisoners, has been notified of these arrangements. Before the war broke out Broadwell had close relations with many Southern businessmen and believes he will be well-received in the Confederate capital. I trust he may, for his is a good cause. One of the great vexations of this struggle is that men imprisoned suffer greatly and for long periods of time.

Secretary Seward came by to discuss the political picture in New York. He is concerned that recent heavy casualty figures may be encouraging potential voters to favor those candidates who call for peace at any price. Victories are the surest antidote for voter gloom.

Author's notes:

On this date President Lincoln wrote to Major General R.S. Canby vouching for General Baily, of Rapides Parish, Louisiana, who had written appealing for food from the Army to be distributed on behalf of the people in his region, who were mostly Union people in danger of starvation. Lincoln urged that the loyal Unionists be given food to help them survive. He asked that the government "do for them the best you can, consistently with the interests of the public service." On December 19th General Canby advised Lincoln that he recommended not providing food to the destitute people of Alexandria, Louisiana. He argued that it would only prolong the war.

The White House – Friday, September 23, 1864

At yesterday's Cabinet meeting I learned that General Frémont has withdrawn from the presidential race. That is very good news because in some quarters, he still holds strong popular appeal. Secretary Seward pointed out that when the general learned that the Democratic National Party's convention's platform was "Union with Slavery," he had to reject its nomination. General Frémont has always been strongly anti-slavery. He is a very complicated individual, but at heart he supports the national war effort, which includes freeing the slaves and not keeping them in bondage. His dropping out of the presidential contest was the subject of most our meeting.

After the meeting, I interviewed Michigan's Senator Zachariah Chandler and State Senator David Jerome regarding support for me in their state. Both men were optimistic, referring to our recent taking of Atlanta and how that victory has energized the party. They both anticipate large turnouts in their state. I got similar positive reactions later in the day from Senator Benjamin Wade of Ohio and Congressman Henry Davis of Maryland, both of whom mentioned Sherman's Atlanta victory as the main reason for their expectations of an electoral triumph in November.

Today I advised the Cabinet of Post-Master General Blair's resignation letter and my acceptance of it. His wisdom will be missed in our future deliberations.

Author's notes:

The results of the 1864 presidential election were: 212 electoral votes cast for Lincoln and 21 cast for General McClellan. Only 117 votes were needed to win.

The White House – Saturday, September 24, 1864

This morning I telegraphed former Governor William Dennison of Ohio to come immediately to Washington to assume his office as Post-Master General. He has been confirmed by the Senate.

I issued a comprehensive executive order "Relative to the Purchase of Products of Insurrectionary States" today. It details with great specificity how goods may be bought as authorized by Congress. It affects trade transactions occurring in New Orleans, Memphis, Nashville, Pensacola, Port Royal, Beaufort and Norfolk by appointed agents and regulations under which products may be legally purchased. No military or naval officer, except as are appointed for that purpose, shall engage in trade or traffic in the products of insurrectionary states, or furnish transportation thereof under pain of being deemed guilty of unlawful trading with the enemy and punished accordingly.

Hay read me a letter sent from New York by Nicolay, who has been meeting with editors in New York City and talking to various political leaders in that city. I have instructed Nicolay to stay a while longer and to keep me posted on what he learns.

Author's notes:

John Nicolay returned to Washington on the 26th of September after attending a meeting in New York with Thurlow Weed and other major political leaders in New York City.

The White House – Monday, September 26, 1864

The subject of General McClellan came up yesterday afternoon when I met with Henry Hoffman, collector of customs for Baltimore and chairman of the Maryland Unconditional Union Central Committee. I told Hoffman that in my view McClellan was about as fine a general as one could find were the job to be only the preparation and training of men for combat. When in that role he was exceptionally capable. However, when it came to serious fighting with our determined enemy with verve and dispatch, I found him seriously wanting and after many trials and errors I had to end our relationship. Now, ironically, I may soon find myself again meeting with him here in the White House. But that will only take place if the former general and now candidate wins the November election. He is a man of strong ambitions. He is beloved by many in the Army.

Author's notes:

General McClellan formally resigned his commission on November 8, 1864. He ran for president as the Democratic Party's candidate with George Pendleton as his running mate for vice president. McClellan ran opposed to "death, debt and destruction with no end in sight." The delegates to the Democratic Party adopted proposals for a cease-fire and a negotiated settlement with the Confederacy to end the Civil War. After he won his party's nomination McClellan repudiated its platform and vowed to continue the war effort and to do a better job with this than Lincoln. Lincoln asked his Cabinet to cooperate with McClellan if he won the election. With a voter turnout of 78 percent, incumbent Lincoln won with 55 percent of the popular vote and 90 percent of the electoral votes. Lincoln received 78 percent of the soldier and sailor vote.

The White House – Tuesday, September 27, 1864

It is good to have Nicolay back with us. A telegram was sent to General Rosecrans reminding him that wherever the law allows soldiers to vote in Missouri, their officers must allow it. He answered it promptly, advising that he is following orders and allowing votes to be taken by our men, and that those who have participated in the rebellion are not allowed to vote.

I exchanged telegraphic messages with General Grant about William H. Kent, a war correspondent for The New York Tribune, who appealed to me about his having been excluded from General Meade and Hancock's command. At the same time another reporter, William Swinton of The New York Times, was also removed from the Army's command but later allowed to return. Grant advised me that Kent had submitted false and injurious reports about Hancock's command and that Grant recommends that Kent not be allowed to return. I believe we need to maintain a liberal policy regarding the press, but that does not extend to misbehavior as reported by Grant. Therefore, Kent will not be granted a pass to return. Because he works for Horace Greeley, I may will expect to hear from his boss about this matter shortly.

Author's notes:

Lincoln rarely withdrew passes from war correspondents, but in all cases, he deferred to the recommendations of the general in command of the relevant war zone before making a final decision.

The White House – Wednesday, September 28, 1864

Secretary Stanton and General Halleck with two staff members discussed with the Cabinet the events of September 21 to 22 at Fisher's Hill and Cedar Creek, Virginia. Despite its very strong defense position, the Confederate forces under General Jubal Early were bested by almost 30,000 men under General Philip H. Sheridan. Halleck has estimated that the Army of the Shenandoah outnumbered Early's Army of the Valley by over 3 to 1. Four Army enlisted men and one officer were recommended for the Medal of Honor for their actions at Fisher's Hill. After the battle the Rebels fell back to Waynesboro, Virginia. Union casualties totaled 528, Confederate casualties are estimated to have exceeded 1,200.

Author's notes:

The men cited for bravery: Private James Connors, 43rd New York Infantry, Private John Creed, 23rd Illinois Infantry, Private George C. Moore, 11th West Virginia Infantry, Sergeant Sylvester D. Rhodes, 61st Pennsylvania Infantry and First Lieutenant Edward N. Whittier, 5th Battery Main Light Artillery. The Civil War Trust has acquired and preserved 362 acres of the Battlefield at Fisher's Hill. It is marked by trails and interpretive signs.

The White House – Friday, September 30, 1864

Today a delegation of 15 Quakers from the Western part of Pennsylvania visited me early in the afternoon. I told them that it is my belief that some of my ancestors may have belonged to their faith. I have great respect for and interest in their highly respectable religious community. If all men and women belonged to it there would be no war going on right now. They have a quiet humor of their own and possess a wisdom that must come from so much time spent in prayer and contemplation. I do not believe that they are, as many believe, more honest than those of other faiths. I do believe man should honor the Sabbath and regret that during the war I have consistently failed to do so. But when I can, I do like to take Tad and Mother to church. Ironically, a great many battles, particularly early in the war, were fought on a Sunday, or on what my dear mother and stepmother always called, the Lord's Day. I've often been asked by Quakers and people of other faiths not to fight on Sundays. I've usually told them that they might wish to speak to Jefferson Davis or Robert E. Lee about that, as well as to me. I believe wars are waged when needed by events, and surely not by the church calendar. To me, war is man's greatest sin. It remains a fearful violation of the laws of God and man. It is a time when mercy and religion are cast to the winds, and thus, the sanctity of a day Christians naturally wish to honor will in wartime be dishonored.

The Cabinet met and we discussed the admission of Nevada into the Union.

Author's notes:

On March 2, 1861, the Nevada Territory separated from the Utah Territory and adopted its current name, shortened from Sierra Nevada (Spanish for snow-covered mountain range).

Eight days before the 1864 presidential election, Nevada became the 36th state in the union. Its population was little more than 10,000. Rather than sending the full text of the state constitution to Washington by Pony Express, it was sent to Washington by telegraph at a cost of $3,416.77 – the costliest telegraph then on file for a single dispatch. On October 31, 1864, the response came: "The pain is over, the child was born, Nevada is this day admitted into the Union." Nevada is one of only two states to significantly expand its borders after admission to the Union. The other is Missouri, which acquired additional territory in 1837 due to the Platte Purchase.

The White House – Saturday, October 1, 1864

Early this morning, Mother, Tad and I walked to the site of the unfinished Washington Monument. I like to visit the memorial and reflect upon the life of our first president. I get inspiration from just thinking about the man and how he set the standards and practices for our Republican government which continue to this day. He was a remarkable patriot and leader. His modesty and patience deserve emulation. Tad asked me if I thought the nation would build a monument to honor me and I told him that there was only one Washington, and that I did not expect another large edifice would ever be built in Washington to honor a president, and certainly not this one. It is interesting to reflect that the nation elected Washington, born of one of the nation's richest men, and me, born one of the nation's poorest. As a young boy I read Parson Mason Locke Weems' book, "The Life of Washington". It had a profound effect upon me. Hay believes that Weems invented many of the episodes in his famous book, particularly the Cherry Tree anecdote, but I prefer to accept them as written. I think such tales inspire young people and are of real value. The "I shall not tell a lie," myth or fact, is worth preserving.

Author's notes:

The Washington Monument was not completed until 1885 and was officially dedicated on February 21, 1885. It sits on 106 acres, is 555 feet tall and is the world's tallest obelisk. The cornerstone was laid on July 4, 1848. When Lincoln was in the White House the Washington Monument was only about 80% completed. Construction was halted during the Civil War. The Jefferson Memorial was not constructed until the presidency of Franklin Delano Roosevelt.

The Lincoln Memorial was dedicated on May 22, 1922. Abraham Lincoln's son Robert Todd Lincoln attended the ceremonies. The seated Lincoln statue was created by sculptor Daniel Chester French (1850 to 1931). Planners chose the words of the Gettysburg Address and First Inaugural Address to surround the statue. It was carved from 28 blocks of marble.

The White House – Monday, October 3, 1864

General Halleck presented to the Cabinet a recapitulation of military events in Missouri, which occurred on the 26th and 27th of September in Iron County at Fort Davidson. Here 1,500 of our troops under Brigadier General Thomas Ewing, deputy commander of the District of St. Louis, were attacked by approximately 12,000 Confederate mounted infantry under Major General Sterling Price's Army of Missouri. Because the fort had a good defensive position and was strongly built, it was able to resist the enemy attack, which began on September 26. Ewing rejected several demands to surrender. The defenders were able to resist repeated attacks in which the enemy suffered considerable losses. That night our soldiers were able to silently exit the fort after midnight and withdraw directly between two Rebel encampments without being detected. They left a slow-burning fuse to their powder magazine, which detonated in a huge blast well after they had gone. Price had lost 10% of his Army and realized his reduced force could now not take St. Louis, his original object. We are informed that Price is now headed for Jefferson City.

Author's notes:

Thomas Ewing was the brother-in-law of General William T. Sherman.
General Ewing received a personal letter from President Lincoln thanking him for his efforts at Fort Davidson.

At the subsequent Battle of Mine Creek, the largest cavalry action of the Civil War was fought in Kansas, Price's Army was virtually destroyed as an effective unit. It limped back into Arkansas, having lost over 50% of its men who began the campaign in September. Today the battle area is operated by the Missouri State Parks system as the "Fort Davidson State Historic Site." The earthworks of the fort are still intact, surrounding a huge hole that was caused by the powder explosion. One of the rifle pits was used for a mass grave, now marked with a granite monument. The 41-acre site is listed on the U.S. National Register of Historic Places.

The White House – Tuesday, October 4, 1864

Yesterday I interviewed Morris Hallowell of Philadelphia, a highly respected cotton dealer who was accompanied by J.W. Forney. After our meeting I advised Secretary of the Treasury Fessenden to assist Hallowell in getting certain cotton out of Arkansas. Hallowell, a Quaker and a fine businessman, has 3,600 bales of cotton. I told Fessenden that I would like to see these allowed out of the state under authority of the government. My sense is this is a meritorious cotton case, and this action will be to the common good and will thus allow Hallowell's debtors in Arkansas to pay him what he is owed.

Today I asked John Nicolay to make a special trip to St. Louis and report back to me the political and military situation there. I am particularly interested in learning the election sympathies of Union men. I met with Secretary Wells, Seward and Stanton to discuss the exchange of naval prisoners. This is to be done under the aegis of General Grant and by General Butler. There are only few men involved. The exchanges will take place through Army lines within Butler's area of responsibility. After the meeting we telegraphed Captain Melancthon Smith to turn the prisoners over to General Grant for his disposal.

Author's notes:

John Weiss Forney was a longtime personal and political friend of Lincoln. On February 22, 1862, he became the first secretary of the U.S. Senate to read aloud, to a joint session of Congress, George Washington's Farewell Address, a reading that became traditional after 1888.

The White House – Thursday, October 6, 1864

This was a particularly happy day for me because one of my best and oldest friends, Judge Ebenezer Peck, came by to visit with me and to say "Hello" to Mother. Ebenezer is now serving as an associate justice of the U.S. Court of Claims. I will forever be in Peck's debt, because it was only through the actions of him and O.M. Hatch, Norman B. Judd, Jackson Grimshaw and others who urged me to become the Illinois candidate for president that I am here today. At a meeting we attended in early 1860, they urged me to allow my name to be announced and placed in the field of candidates. Peck reminded me that I had said to them, "I beg that you will not give it further mention. Seriously, I do not think I am fit for the presidency." They all said they had a personal preference for me to run. It was the first concerted effort on my behalf by my friends to see me elected.

Later I met with Colonel Benjamin H. Bristow and others from Christian County, Kentucky. We discussed the political climate in their state. All seemed optimistic about our chances in November.

Author's notes:

President Lincoln appointed Ebenezer Peck to the Court of Claims, where he served from March of 1863 to May of 1878.

Benjamin Helm Bristow served as the first solicitor general of the United States from 1870 to 1872 under President Ulysses Grant. He was the 30th U.S. secretary of the Treasury from 1874 to 1876. He received national fame for breaking up and prosecuting the Whiskey Ring, a corrupt tax evasion profiteering ring that depleted the national treasury. In 1876 he made an unsuccessful attempt at gaining the Republican nomination for president, running as a reformer. During the Civil War he mustered the 25th Kentucky Infantry and was its lieutenant colonel. He fought under General Grant and served bravely at Fort Henry, Fort Donelson and Shiloh, where he was seriously wounded. In July 1863, Colonel Bristow and the Kentucky 8th Cavalry assisted in the capture of John Hunt Morgan during his July 1863 raid through Indiana and Ohio. He died in New York City on June 22, 1896, age 64.

The White House – Friday, October 7, 1864

Secretary Seward escorted Theophilus Plate, consul for the Free Hanseatic City of Hamburg at Philadelphia, and Joseph Benziger, consul of the Swiss Confederation for Ohio, Indiana and Kentucky, to meet with me and give me their thoughts on relations with the United States. In both instances the Emancipation Proclamation was discussed. They said that in their countries the reaction was strongly popular. Neither felt that their citizens felt any sympathy for the Southern cause, which was very good to hear.

An hour later, Colonel Allen called and presented Mother and me with a leather -bound album, which is a gift from Hungarian Count Móric Sándor. It contains beautiful illustrations of Sándor Palace and the city of Budapest, Hungary, where it is located. The building was begun about 1803 and belonged to Archduke Albrecht, the imperial governor of Hungary, until the failed Hungarian Revolution of 1848. Count Vincent Sandor commissioned it, and it was named after him. He was a philosopher and aristocrat in the Austro-Hungarian Empire. It is my personal wish that once I retire from politics, I may take Mary, Tad and Robert to tour the capitals of Europe, including Vienna and Budapest.

Author's notes:

On this date, President Lincoln appointed these men directors of the Union Pacific Railroad and Telegraph line from the Missouri River to the Pacific Ocean: Jesse Williams of Indiana, George Ashmun of Massachusetts, Charles Sherman of Ohio, Springer Harbaugh of Pennsylvania and Timothy Carter of Illinois. They would be the government's directors on a railroad that had received significant federal funds, and which was deemed vital to the war effort.

All 19 Hungarian prime ministers lived in the Sándor Palace. The building was destroyed during World War II and rebuilt after the Hungarian Revolution of 1989. The interior was renovated in 2002, and the building has been restored to its former glory.

The White House – Saturday, October 8, 1864

Yesterday, Mrs. Anna Byers-Jennings, along with my good friends Illinois Congressman T.J. Turner and Colonel Hancock of Chicago, came to the White House to discuss the release of Daniel Hayden of Missouri. Mrs. Byers-Jennings dined with us this evening. Based upon what she has told me I will ask Secretary Stanton to provide me with information concerning the status of the pending case of Hayden.

Today, Secretary Stanton and I attended the funeral of First Lieutenant John Rodgers Meigs, the son of Quartermaster General Montgomery C. Meigs. He was killed in action just days ago at Swift Run Gap in Virginia as part of a three-man patrol. He was interred at Oak Hill Cemetery in Georgetown with full military honors. Meigs is one of the finest officers in the Army; a brilliant engineer who has been a tireless worker for victory. Losing his son is a terrible blow for him and his family.

Author's notes:

Montgomery Meigs played a critical role in developing Arlington Cemetery during the Civil War and afterward.

The White House – Monday, October 10, 1864

After church on Sunday Mother and I were besieged by visitors during the afternoon. This morning Congressman William Kelley spent two hours with me. I think he talked about himself 95% of the time! Secretary Welles then fortuitously came by so I was able to show Kelley to the door. He was still talking to the minute I shut the door. Welles and I discussed bounties due Marines. Welles is an excellent Cabinet member. Unlike Kelley, he gets to the point, is well-prepared and his recommendations are always well-thought-out. I interviewed Charles Jones, chairman of the Union State Central Committee of New York, about getting out seamen's and sailors' votes. Jones is very well-informed and confidently predicts a high turnout in his state among his members.

Author's notes:

On this date the president provided testimony to a board of Army officers considering a claim for property damage as a result of the shelling of some houses in front of Fort Stevens on July 12, 1864. The president informed the board that he had been present during the shelling and gave his approbation to its being done. The committee found that the claims for damages to the homes was not to be considered the taking of private property, and that claims for such losses and damage by war was not the taking of private property.

The White House – Tuesday, October 11, 1864

I sent a telegraphic message to son Robert at Harvard letting him know that we are a little uneasy about his health. I asked him to telegraph how he is feeling and to consider coming here for a few days if his studies will allow. After meeting with Secretaries Seward and Fessenden I decided to issue an order suspending clearance of a warship built in New York for the Japanese government, thus forbidding that it be allowed to sail for Japan. This action has been recommended because we have received reports of a revolution in Japan and uncertainty about the stability of its government. Japan ordered two warships built in America, the Fusigama and the Funayma Solace. This government welcomes construction orders like these for our shipyards, but must consider the political picture in Japan at the same time. Hopefully, we may learn news soon from Japan clarifying the situation there. We would like to see the ships released as soon as possible while continuing to maintain good diplomatic relations with the country. The British and French ambassadors have informed Seward that both nations along with the Netherlands have experienced recent strong anti-foreign sentiment in Japan related to favorable commercial concessions granted by Japan to the United States, which were not granted to them.

Author's notes:

On this date, Secretary Stanton and General Halleck reviewed with the president recent military victories at Chaffin's Farm in New Market Heights, Virginia, and at Peebles Farm near Petersburg, Virginia.

The White House – Wednesday, October 12, 1864

At 8 P.M. last evening John Hay and I went to the telegraph office at the War Department to receive state election returns. During a lull in the receptions I read to Hay and the operators two chapters of the Nasby Letters, the humorous writings of Reverend Petroleum V. Nasby, the pen name of David Ross Locke. I regret that I have never met this creative writer. Hay tells me that Locke was apprenticed at age 12 to the Democrat, a newspaper in Cortland County, New York. He is now the editor and owner of The Jeffersonian in Findlay, Ohio, where he began writing his humorous Nasby Letters. I often read his Letters to the Cabinet in order to lighten the mood when matters may be dark, as they often are these days. I must write a letter to him, thanking him for all he has done for the war effort. I will tell him that I would gladly change places with him if he would transfer his rare talents to me!

Author's notes:

Several collections of the Nasby Letters came out in book form, some illustrated by Locke's good friend and political ally, Thomas Nast.

The White House – Friday, October 14, 1864

Yesterday I informed the Cabinet that I am in no rush to replace Chief Justice Roger Taney, who died on the 12th. Our fifth chief justice lived to be 87 years of age and had served on the Supreme Court since March 28, 1836. Tomorrow I plan to attend his funeral service with Secretary Seward, Attorney General Bates and Postmaster General Dennison, which will be at the Taney residence on Indiana Avenue near Second Street at 6 A.M. I will be in the procession to the railway station, where the funeral party will then depart in two passenger cars for Frederick, Maryland, where burial will take place at 11:30 in the morning. I will not go to the interment. We rarely spoke and had very different views of the Constitution. He opposed my suspension of Habeas Corpus early in the war and opposed me in the Prize Cases, which arose after Union ships blockading the Confederacy seized ships that conducted trade with Confederate ports. His dissenting view was that I overstepped my authority by ordering a blockade without the express consent of Congress. I remember appearing before Chief Justice Taney when, as a young lawyer, I was admitted to practice before the U.S. Supreme Court. When he swore me in as president, I thought he looked frail, but his voice was strong as he delivered the Constitutional oath.

Author's notes:

Roger Taney served as chief justice for 28 years and 198 days, the second longest tenure of any chief justice. He died nearly penniless. Lincoln made no public statement in response to his death. Lincoln appointed Salmon P. Chase, a strongly anti-slavery Republican from Ohio, to succeed Taney. Taney served as attorney general of Maryland, secretary of the Treasury, United States attorney general and secretary of war. He has been remembered for his decision in the Dred Scott v. Sandford case of 1836 when he ruled that African Americans could not be considered citizens and that Congress could not prohibit slavery in the territories of the United States. The Dred Scott decision is widely considered to be one of the worst Supreme Court decisions ever made, though some scholars hold other aspects of Taney's tenure in high regard.

On August 17, 2017, the 145-year-old statue of Chief Justice Roger Taney was removed from the State House of Maryland by Republican Governor Larry Hogan and quietly moved to Baltimore.

The White House – Saturday, October 15, 1864

Today I made my semi-annual $9.00 contribution to Illinois State University's scholarship fund. One of the founders of the institution is my good friend Jesse Fell. He has spoken to me often about his plan to plant thousands of trees on the campus, which is now barren land. Jesse would like to see every type of tree that will flourish there planted for beautification and because he wants the school to include in its curriculum the study of botany and forestry. Jesse has always had a big place in his heart for trees. Jesse sent me a letter last year in which he quoted Alexander Pope, who wrote, "Tis education forms the common mind: Just as the twig is bent, the tree's inclined." I gave the letter to Tad and Mother to read because they are very fond of Jesse.

I often wish that I could have attended such an institution when I was a young man. George Washington had favored the creation of a national university, but one was never established in his lifetime or since. Thomas Jefferson, who had attended the prestigious College of William and Mary, was personally the moving force behind the creation of the University of Virginia. He believed that it was his greatest single contribution to his state. When this war ends, I would like to visit the place. How sad he would be to realize that a great many graduates of that fine college have perished in this terrible war. It is vital to America's future well-being that the victors see to it that such a calamity never happens again.

I was proud to sign the Morrill Act on July 2, 1862, which provides each state with 30,000 acres of Federal land for each member in their Congressional delegation. The land is to be sold and proceeds used to fund public colleges that focus on agriculture and the mechanical arts.

Author's notes;

Founded in 1857, Illinois State University obtained expert advice from a professional landscape gardener named William Saunders at the recommendation of Jesse Fell. Fell began serving on the university's board in 1866. In 1867 he introduced legislation that led to the planting of trees on campus. He obtained $3,000 from the Illinois State Legislature for campus landscaping and had the land plowed for tree planting. He personally selected the trees for planting. The first tree was planted in 1868. A total of 1,740 trees were planted that year and another 107 were planted the next year. He resigned from the board in 1872. Today, Fell Arboretum is a public feature that is managed by the School of Biological Sciences. Biology, Horticulture, Botany and Agriculture are studied there.

Alexander Pope's poem is from Moral Essays (1720 – 1735). Epistle I, To Lord Cobham, (1734) line 9.

Sixty-nine colleges were funded by the Morrill Act's land grants, including Cornell University, The Massachusetts Institute of Technology, and the University of Wisconsin at Madison. Vermont Congressman Justin Smith Morrill was born in 1810 and died in 1898.

Monday, October 17, 1864

Yesterday after church I advised Congressman Moorhead of Pennsylvania that I could not stay the execution of Peter Gilner, which he had requested, without more information, which I have asked the Army to provide. Today the adjutant general provided me with a review of Gilner's case and I have therefore notified the proper authorities that Private Gilner is to be released from imprisonment and discharged from the service. Orville Browning came by to urge that Secretary Stanton be named chief justice. I told him that Attorney General Bates had already asked for the job, but I am keeping my options open a bit longer. I prefer to wait until after the election to announce my decision. My sense is that Stanton is too valuable now, as secretary of war, to move him to the court. After the war is won, that would be another matter entirely. Congressman Elihu Washburne of Illinois sent me a long letter that should be bordered in black. In it he is very pessimistic about the coming presidential election. He thinks that the party, by putting Andrew Johnson on the ticket, made a great mistake. He preferred that I keep Hannibal Hamlin on as vice president. That decision was a purely pragmatic political one. The party believes that having a former Southern senator from Tennessee, who remained loyal to the Union on the ticket, may have stronger appeal to Democratic voters. Personally, I consider Hamlin much the better man on many counts.

Author's notes:

Andrew Johnson became the first president to be impeached. He was a racist demagogue who survived his impeachment trial in the U.S. Senate. 35 Senators voted "guilty "and 19 voted "to acquit." He served out his presidential term to be followed in office by President Ulysses S. Grant. Johnson is the only former president to run for the Senate and be elected. He took office on March 4,1875 and died July 31, 1875. He was 66 years of age.

The White House – Tuesday, October 18, 1864

I spent an hour today with William O. Barrett, a close associate of James Gordon Bennett, founder of the New York Herald. We discussed New York City and State politics, campaign expenses and the possibility of James Gordon Bennett being appointed ambassador to France after the November election. At the beginning of the war Bennett's son was a naval volunteer. He is now an executive at the New York Herald.

John Nicolay, who has been in St. Louis, will be going to Chicago to test the political waters there for me.

Author's notes:

In 1861, James Gordon Bennett, Jr. was commissioned a third lieutenant in the Revenue Marine Service and volunteered his newly built schooner yacht, Henrietta, to patrol Long Island waters until February 1862, when she was sent to Port Royal, South Carolina. On March 3, 1862, Bennett commanded the Henrietta as part of the Union fleet which captured Fernandina, Florida. He returned to civilian life in May 1862. In 1880, he established international editions of his newspaper in Paris and London; their successor is the New York Times' International Edition, previously known as the International Herald-Tribune.

On March 6, 1865, James Gordon Bennett, Sr. informed President Lincoln, "I have received your kind note in which you propose to appoint me Minister Plenipotentiary to France. It expresses for me the high consideration which the President has acted by proposing so distinguished an honor. Accept my sincere thanks for that honor. I am sorry however to say that at my age I am afraid of assuming the labors and responsibilities of such an important position. Besides, in the present relations of France and the United States, I am of the decided opinion that I can be of more service to the country in the present position I occupy."

The White House – Thursday, October 20, 1864

Yesterday, Henry Willis, chairman of the loyal citizens of Maryland and a resident of Washington, led a large and enthusiastic group who marched to the White House to serenade me at 8 P.M. Tad joined me at the upper window to watch them. At their head was a large band from Emory Hospital. They played the Battle Hymn of the Republic and other patriotic numbers. Many of the marchers were carrying large signs reading "The Union Forever" and others supporting the election of Lincoln and Johnson. I responded to the crowd, giving special attention to praising our soldiers and sailors and to the great sacrifices they have made to preserve our nation and our liberties. I told them that I shall remain president until March 4th and between now and then I shall do my utmost that whoever is to hold the helm for the next voyage, shall start with the best possible chance to save the ship. I stressed that if the voters deliberately resolve to have immediate peace, even at the loss of their country, and their liberty, I know not the power or right to resist them. I am resolved to stand by them.

I wrote to Queen Isabel II of Spain today, congratulating her upon the marriage of her niece, HRH Dona Maria Isabel Francisca de Asis, to HRH the Count of Paris Louis Phillippe of Orleans. I invited Gabriel Garcia Assura, the Spanish minister to the United States, to visit with Secretary Seward and me. He speaks excellent English and told me that has been in Washington for almost eight years. He has done a very fine job representing his nation. Spain has remained neutral and not recognized the Confederate States.

Author's notes:

On this date President Lincoln issued a Proclamation of Thanksgiving, setting apart the last Thursday in November as a Day of Thanksgiving to be observed by all citizens wherever they may be then "as a day of Thanksgiving and Praise to Almighty God the beneficent Creator and Ruler of the Universe."

The White House – Friday, October 21, 1864

Early this morning I visited Arlington Cemetery with Secretary Stanton, General Halleck and Quartermaster General Montgomery Meigs, whose son was recently killed in battle. The first military burial was made here on May 13th of this year when the Army interred William Henry Christman. Meigs explained to us that the property was owned by Robert E. Lee's family, and Arlington House mansion was built by George Washington Parke Custis, grandson of Martha Washington and the adopted son of George Washington. Construction of Arlington House is believed to have begun in 1802. It was ultimately named for the Village of Arlington, Gloucestershire, England, where Custis' family was originally from.

In my diary entry of November 23, 1861, I wrote that "Mt. Vernon is the home of our opponent, Gen. Robert E. Lee." That was an incorrect entry. As Meigs clarified for me, Mount Vernon was the home of George Washington. The home of Robert E. Lee is known as the Arlington Mansion or Arlington House. And it is on Lee's property that Arlington Cemetery is now being established for the burial of our war dead. I may have been confused because the land the mansion sits upon was originally called "Mount Washington." It is property that Custis' father, John Parke Custis had purchased in 1778. John Parke Custis died in 1781 at Yorktown after the British surrender. Custis decided to build his home on the property following the death of Martha Washington and three years after the death of George Washington.

Author's notes:

Today, Arlington House is known as the Robert E. Lee Memorial. It overlooks the Potomac River and the National Mall in Washington, D.C. During the Civil War the grounds of the mansion were selected as the site of Arlington National Cemetery, in part to ensure that Lee would never again be able to return to his home. The United States has since designated the mansion as a National Memorial administered by the National Park Service. The cemetery is controlled by the U.S. Army.

The White House – Saturday, October 22, 1864

I wrote to Major General Philip H. Sheridan today advising him of my heartfelt thanks and that of the nation for his cavalry's successful operations this month in the Shenandoah Valley, with special praise for the splendid achievements of October 19th at the Battle of Cedar Creek, when his forces drove the Confederates away, after his stunning ride from Winchester, Virginia, to rally his defeated forces. When this war began, I believe the Rebels had far better cavalry units than we did. Not anymore. Sheridan has set the new standard. It is attributable to excellent leadership and superior horses.

Stanton and Halleck provided the Cabinet and me with a comprehensive summary of recent engagements in Missouri and Virginia. There is no doubt that within a year we should be able to put an end to the secession. October has been a good month for our forces. Momentum is on our side.

Tomorrow I will be meeting with Jewish gentlemen who claim to represent the Israelites of New York City.

Author's notes:

When the war began, cavalry horses cost the Union Army an average of $119 a head. By 1864 prices had reached $190. The recommended daily feed was 10 pounds of hay and 14 pounds of grain.

Monday, October 24, 1864

I learned more today from some visiting history scholars from Harvard University about the first member of my family to enter the United States. He was Samuel Lincoln (1622 to 1690,) a poor weaver's apprentice from Hingham, a village in Norfolk County, England, which is in East Anglia. Samuel settled in Hingham, Massachusetts, in 1637. It was originally called Bare Cove. From there the Lincoln family spread southward to Virginia, where my father, Thomas was born in 1778. He told me that his father, who was a farmer, moved to Kentucky when Thomas, was 4 years old. Thomas's father was killed by Indians. Thomas never went to school but learned to be a carpenter. I remember he was strong, heavy-built and worked hard at carpentry so that he could earn enough to buy farmland. Unfortunately, most of the land he purchased proved to have inadequate soil to grow good crops.

I've talked to Senator Sumner several times about Hingham, a community located on Boston Harbor that he is very familiar with. Charles Sumner is a graduate of Harvard. The students showed me on a map that the Plymouth County community was originally in Suffolk County. The land on which Hingham was settled was deeded to the English by the Wampanoag Sachem Wompatuck in 1655. The eastern part of the town became Cohasset in 1770. Hingham was born of religious dissent. The first to come were devout and strict Puritans, including my ancestor. I wonder why he left Boston for the South. Had he remained I might have grown up in Massachusetts, gone to Harvard like Sumner and run for the U.S. Senate, too. Ironically, my son Robert is the first in the family to go to Harvard. I am proud of him.

Author's notes:

A statue of Abraham Lincoln adorns the area adjacent to downtown Hingham Square.

The White House – Wednesday, October 26, 1864

Yesterday was a very busy day here. I ordered the stay of execution of Young C. Edmonson. He has had a good battle record but like many men he broke under fire and put others in his company at risk. Very young men are often apt to flee the field of fire, even men who the day before might have been cited for bravery. Apparently, Sergeant Edmonson is just such a man. I deem he may still serve our nation better alive than dead.

Reports from Missouri tell of a Union victory on the 23rd at a decisive battle fought at Westport. General Samuel Curtis reports that his Army of 22,000 roundly defeated Confederate forces under the command of General Sterling Price. Curtis believes the Rebels were outnumbered three to one. They are in full retreat.

This morning I ordered the discharge of Big Eagle. He has been imprisoned in Davenport, Iowa, along with other members of his tribe. The order was sent to General Alfred Sully. It is vitally important that we keep our relations with the Indians as positive as possible. Let us only fight one war at a time. I have received several letters from people of good reputation on behalf of this Indian leader. I believe that Big Eagle can do better for us than harm when he is free among his tribesmen.

Author's notes:

On this date Lincoln wrote to Mrs. George W. Swift of Falmouth, Massachusetts, "Your complimentary little poem asking for my autograph was duly received. I thank you for it, and cheerfully comply with your request. Yours truly. A. Lincoln."

The Battle of Westport ended the last major Confederate offensive west of the Mississippi River, and for the remainder of the war the U.S. Army maintained solid control over most of Missouri. Over30,000 men were engaged, making it one of the largest fought west of the Mississippi River.

The White House – Thursday, October 27, 1864

Secretary Welles and Admiral Dahlgren presented to the Cabinet a report concerning the doings of the Confederate raider Florida. The Rebel ship is believed to have burned or sunk 11 American ships in the Atlantic since sailing from the French port of Brest on February 10th of this year. Earlier in the war she had destroyed 37 Yankee merchantmen and bonded nine more. It is believed that the raider sailed from Tenerife in the Canary Islands early this month. No one knows where she is headed. We have been informed by our officials in England that the ship was built by the British firm William C. Miller and Sons of Toxteth, Liverpool, and purchased by the Confederacy from Fawcett, Preston & Co., also of Liverpool, who provided her steam engines. She carries sail on three masts and reportedly can attain speeds of 12 knots under sail. She has a crew of 146 men and is armed with 9 cannons. Welles admits that the Navy has no information where she is at this moment, but it continues to seek information of her presence in some foreign port.

Author's notes:

Unbeknown to Lincoln, at this time the Florida had been captured by the U.S.S. sloop-of-war Wachusett while anchored in the Brazilian port of Bahia. On October 7, 1864, while her captain was ashore with half her crew, the Florida was caught defenseless in an illegal night attack by Commander Napoleon Collins of the U.S.S. Wachusett. Towed to sea, she was sent to the United States as a prize, despite the empire of Brazil's protests at the violation of its sovereignty. Commander Collins was court-martialed and convicted of violating Brazilian territorial rights, but the verdict was set aside by Navy Secretary Welles. Collins won fame and was promoted for his daring capture of the raider. On November 28, 1864, the Florida sank under dubious circumstances after colliding with the U.S. Army Transport, USAT Alliance, a troop ferry. It could therefore not be delivered to Brazil in satisfaction of the final court order and could not rejoin the ranks of the Confederate States Navy. On September 14, 1872, the United States was awarded $15,500,000 in damages for actual losses of ships and cargoes and interest, on account of the Alabama and Florida and her tenders, and the Shenandoah after she left Melbourne. The findings resulted from the Treaty of Washington, which appointed a Tribunal of Arbitration, which met at Geneva, Switzerland.

The president was officially informed by Secretary of State William Seward of the capture of the Confederate raider Florida at Bahia, Brazil on November 11, 1864.

The White House – Friday, October 28, 1864

Today was "Ladies Day" at the Executive Mansion! First, Mrs. Margaret C. Price requested that her son, a prisoner of war, be released from Camp Chase in Ohio. I told her that I would agree to her request and so informed Albert Hodges. Right after she left the office, Mrs. George W. Bowen came by to ask the discharge of her husband, now a prisoner of war at Camp Chase, and I told her I would do so. I informed John A. Prall of Paris, Kentucky. John is a member of the Kentucky Senate and was a delegate to the Baltimore Convention. He knows the Bowen family. At three o'clock six devout Quaker ladies presented me with a beautifully illustrated Bible and wished me well in the coming election. They also gave me a red, white and blue quilt, which they made especially for Mother. I know that she will cherish it.

I wrote to Mr. S. Austin Allibone, Esq., thanking him for sending me a copy of the October 26th edition of the Boston Advertiser, which contains Edward Everett's speech of October 19th on "The duty of supporting the government in the present crisis of affairs." I must remember to write a thank you letter to Everett for his kind words.

At the Cabinet meeting the election and minor matters were discussed.

Author's notes:

On this date Secretary Welles complained to Lincoln that "All ships are tied up at Hampton Roads, consequently the blockade of Southern ports is being neglected."

The White House – Friday, October 28, 1864

Hannibal Hamlin returned to the capitol recently after serving this summer as a volunteer in Company A of the Maine National Guard, a militia unit he joined in 1860. His rank was that of a private when he entered in July, and he was a corporal when he mustered out in mid-September. He did not have to muster but told me that he preferred to do so, and I thanked him for his willingness to serve. He set an excellent example by doing the duty that is expected of any citizen regardless of rank. He reported to Fort McClary, taking part in routine duties including guard duty and even taking over as company cook. On reflection, I believe that I failed to utilize the considerable talents of Hamlin as I might have. It has been a long-standing tradition to treat the vice president as more a member of the legislative branch than that of the executive. That is because his constitutional duty is to preside over the Senate and vote in case of ties. I believe future presidents might benefit more from their vice presidents if they found specific assignments to match their talents. When we talked politics recently, he told me that he might consider running for the U.S. Senate in 1868. If he does it would be of great benefit to the nation. I have enjoyed working with him and regret that I failed to employ his talents to greater purpose.

Author's notes:

After leaving the vice presidency, Hamlin served briefly as collector of the Port of Boston, appointed by President Andrew Johnson. He resigned over Johnson's Reconstruction policies. He returned to the U.S. Senate in 1869 to serve two more six-year terms before declining to run for re-election in 1880 because of an ailing heart. President James Garfield named Hamlin U.S ambassador to Spain in 1881, a post he held until October 17, 1882. His mansion located in Bangor, Maine was posted to the National Register of Historic Places in 1979. Located at 15 15th Street it incorporates Victorian, Italianate and Mansard-style architecture. He died July 4, 1891, age 81.

The White House – Saturday, October 29, 1864

Today a remarkable black woman visited me. Her name is Sojourner Truth, a Negro woman who is an evangelist and a former slave who escaped from slavery about 25 years ago. She is now a famous lecturer about the evils of slavery. She gave me a printed copy of her speech, "Ain't I a Woman?" which she first delivered at the Woman's Rights Convention of 1851. Before the war she was active in the Underground Railroad, helping blacks escape to freedom. As a child she could only speak Dutch and was unable to read or write since slaves were not taught how to. She is the first African American woman to win a trial against a white man. The trial was about her getting her son Peter back. I would estimate her age to be about 65 years old. I introduced her to Mother, who spent about an hour and a half with her and served her tea. Mother was very impressed by her intelligence and commitment to women's rights.

Author's notes:

Sojourner Truth's name was Isabella Baumfree. She was born into slavery around 1797 in Swarterkill, New York. Her family's slave owner was Colonel Hardenbergh. Out of 13 children, she was the youngest. In 1815 she dated a fellow slave named Thomas. Together they had three children. Her family was separated in 1806. In 1826 she escaped to freedom with her infant daughter. She changed her name in 1843 from Isabella Baumfree to Sojourner Truth. During the Civil War she lectured about the right to vote for women. She spent the last years of her life in Battle Creek, Michigan, where she died on November 26, 1883.

The White House – Monday, October 31, 1864

The Cabinet was given a presentation by General Halleck and several members of his staff this morning in which we learned details of battles waged successfully in Linn County, Kansas, six days ago. General Albert Pleasonton's cavalry attacked and pursued cavalry forces of Confederate General Sterling Price there. Halleck estimates we had less than half the number of men as the Rebels but still prevailed. When I learned the name of the site of the first engagement – Marais des Cygnes - I was surprised to learn that no one knew what those French words meant. Later in the day Mother said they mean "Swamp of the Swans." It was there that Pleasonton caught up with the Rebels in three interconnected fights all waged the same day, October 25th. Later in the day we attacked retreating Southern cavalrymen at Mine Creek, which resulted in the capture of two Confederate generals, the death of a third and capture of hundreds of Rebels, including a large supply train. The final battle occurred at Marmiton River. Pleasonton believes Sterling's forces are now in full retreat heading toward Arkansas.

Author's notes:

The Battle of Mine Creek would turn out to be one of the largest cavalry engagements of the entire Civil War. After escaping at Marmiton River, which was blocking their escape plan, the Confederates ultimately found their way back to Arkansas. General Sterling had suffered a large loss of men during the month he had spent in Missouri and Kansas. Price's mission to overtake Missouri for the Confederacy had not only failed, but resulted in a large loss of men, 500 wagons of supplies and cannon. The engagement is also called the Battle of Osage or the Battle of Trading Post.

The White House – Tuesday, November 1, 1864

Yesterday I issued a proclamation admitting Nevada into the Union in accordance with an Act of Congress, which was approved on March 21, 1864. Citizens of the new state may now legally vote in the November election. Secretary Seward in the presence of Attorney General Bates read to the Cabinet a dispatch announcing the success of the new Maryland Constitution.

The government has established a domestic money order system, which can greatly assist efforts to strengthen the nation's economy. Safe and easy access to cash will be a boon to business and agriculture. In the past anyone sending cash in an envelope risked the letter being opened and the cash stolen. This has happened to soldiers and sailors sending home greenbacks in the U.S mail. Now Dr. C.F. McDonald will head up the newly created Postal Money Order Bureau in Washington. The center of the new system will be in New York City. The money taken for orders at all the country offices will be sent to New York, and postmasters all over the nation will draw on the New York office for the funds needed to meet their payments. Mr. John N. Norton, recently of the Dead Letter Office, will be in charge of the money order office in New York. 147 post offices in various parts of the country will be authorized to transact money order business initially, and this number will rapidly increase when the system has been tested by experience. This was the brainchild of Montgomery Blair when he was postmaster general. A money order system has been successfully operating in a similar fashion in Great Britain for many years.

Author's notes:

On this date Hon. Albert Hobbs of Malone, New York, telegraphed the president asking that his relative, Private Nathan Wilcox of the 22nd Massachusetts Volunteers, under sentence of death for desertion be granted clemency. The next day President Lincoln telegraphed General Ulysses Grant to "Suspend until further notice the execution of Nathan Wilcox of the 22nd Mass. Regt. Said to be at the Repair Depot City Point." The suspension of execution was at once ordered.

The White House – Wednesday, November 2, 1864

The Cabinet was presented with a review of recent military actions within the states of Alabama, Virginia and Missouri by General Halleck and staff. Of greatest interest to me was the Battle of Fair Oaks and Darbytown Road in Henrico County, Virginia, on the 27th and 28th of October. The X Corps and the XVIII Corps under Major General Benjamin Butler attacked the Richmond defenses along Darbytown Road. The XVIII marched north to Fair Oaks, where it was soundly repulsed by Major General Charles Field's Confederate Division. The Rebels counterattacked, taking some 600 of our men prisoners. The Richmond defenses remain intact. Union casualties for the two days were 1,600. Halleck estimates that Confederate casualties were probably less than 100. We were told by Secretary Stanton that the general in command of the Confederates was Lieutenant General James Longstreet, a man never to be underestimated. He has a reputation for solid thinking and caution. It is believed that when Lee ordered Pickett's charge at Gettysburg, Longstreet had strongly recommended against it, but was overruled by Lee.

New York City commissioners, accompanied by Secretary Stanton, came by for a chat at 1 P.M. They are optimistic about the upcoming election in their city. An hour later the Reverend G.H. Blakeslee, Methodist minister at Binghamton, and the Reverend E.W. Breckinridge visited me and asked me to autograph their Bibles, which I gladly did. I received another request from Mrs. Emily Todd Helm asking for the privilege of going south to sell her cotton. Mother is very concerned about Emily's well-being. Since the death in battle of her husband she has been in great distress, financial and emotional.

Author's notes:

After the war, Longstreet and his family settled in New Orleans. He joined the Republican Party during the Reconstruction era and endorsed Ulysses S. Grant for president and attended his inauguration. Grant appointed him surveyor of customs for New Orleans. In 1875 he left New Orleans for Gainesville, Georgia. In 1880 President Rutherford B. Hayes appointed him ambassador to the Ottoman Empire. From 1897 to 1904, under Presidents William McKinley and Theodore Roosevelt, he was U.S. commissioner of railroads. He died on January 2, 1904, one of the few Civil War generals to live into the 20th century.

The White House – Friday, November 4, 1864

Dr. Isachar Zacharie, my foot doctor from New York City, visited me yesterday. He treated my wrist successfully two years ago. He came down this time from New York at the suggestion of Seward to fill me in on the prospects of getting most of the Jewish vote in the city and state. He has spoken to many of his co-religionists, including many leaders of their community, and reports that my popularity among his clansmen is particularly strong. They support the Union and my candidacy overwhelmingly. He told me that when he arrived in America in 1845 from England, he was penniless. He told me that at the entrance to the tomb of Ankmahor, a king of ancient Egypt, there is a bas-relief depicting foot doctors. He has treated the feet of Stanton and Seward, both of whom swear by him,

I approved the location of the first one hundred miles of the Union and Pacific Railroad from Omaha, Nebraska. When completed this will be one of America's great engineering achievements. Soon our citizens will be able to cross the continent in days and not in weeks and months in safety and comfort. The railroad will change the economic future of the nation.

Author's notes:

The New York Herald wrote of Dr. Zacharie, "Dr. Zacharie trimmed the feet of President Lincoln and all of his Cabinet. He is a wit, gourmet and eccentric, with a splendid Roman nose, fashionable whiskers and an eloquent tongue, a dazzling diamond breast-pin, great skill in his profession, ingratiating address, a perfect knowledge of his business, and a plentiful supply of social moral courage." After the war Zacharie submitted a bill to the War Department for $45,000 for having treated 15,000 Union soldiers. The claim was denied. Soon after that he departed for England, where he passed away in 1897.

The White House – Saturday, November 5, 1864

Mother, Tad and I discussed the books I favored growing up that I read as a young man. I regret that the war has curtailed my reading greatly. I still can never get enough of Robert Burns. Some of his poems that I read and reread are: Cotter's Saturday Night, Epistle to a Young Friend, Holy Willie's Prayer, Tam O'Shanter and Willie Wastle. I also find much in Byron – The Bride of Abydos, Childe Harold's Pilgrimage, Darkness, The Destruction of Sennacherib, The Devil's Drive, Don Juan, The Girl of Cadiz, Mazeppa and To Inez. I once said that of my early life it can all be condensed into a single sentence, and that sentence will be found in Gray's Elegy: "The short and simple annals of the poor." That was how I viewed my life as a young man and still do. My life was enriched by the fact that neighbors who owned books were willing to lend them to me to read. We had no library. The fact that I can now take out books from the Library of Congress is a great help to me as president. The nation should begin an effort to see to it that in every community access to books is the rule and not the exception.

Author's notes:

One of the men who provided expertise to the federal telegraphic services during the war was Andrew Carnegie. He was assigned by Thomas Scott, vice president of the Pennsylvania Railroad, to oversee the Union's initial telegraphic services. The U.S. Telegraph Corps (USMTC) was initially organized for the purpose of securing the lines around the capital. After he became the wealthiest man in America, Carnegie decided to build libraries in the United States and around the world. His first library was built in his hometown of Dunfermline, Scotland. A total of 2,509 Carnegie Libraries were built between 1883 and 1929. 1,689 were built in the United States, 609 in the United Kingdom and Ireland, 125 in Canada, and others in Australia, South Africa, New Zealand, Serbia, Belgium, France, the Caribbean, Mauritius, Malaysia and Fiji. The first library he built in America was in Braddock, Pennsylvania.

The White House – Monday, November 7, 1864

Sunday after church I sent a telegraphic message to Admiral David Farragut at Mobile Bay to be forwarded from Hilton Head by first opportunity, which read, "Do not, on any account, or on any showing of authority whatever, from whomsoever purporting to come, allow the blockade of Mobile to be violated." I sent a message to General Butler to avoid any clash between U.S. forces and those of the State Militia during the election in New York City.

This evening Mrs. Elizabeth Comstock, a Quaker minister, paid a visit to Mother and me. She read from the 9th verse of Isaiah the words which she said are included in Handel's Messiah. They are, "For unto us a child is born, unto us a son is given; and the government shall be upon his shoulder: and his name shall be called Wonderful, Counsellor, The mighty God. The everlasting Father, The Prince of Peace." When she read those words, Mother began to cry. It was a moving experience. Mrs. Comstock told us that when King George II first heard those powerful words sung, he stood and everyone in the audience stood with him. Mother told her that she is going to ask that it be sung at the White House this Christmas season and that Mrs. Comstock will be invited to attend. Before taking her leave, Mrs. Comstock kneeled in prayer and Mother kneeled beside her.

Author's notes:

George Frideric Handel wrote the inspired piece in 26 days. At the end he wrote SDG, meaning Soli Deo Gloria, or Glory to God alone. In 1815 the Handel and Haydn Society was founded in Boston. On December 25, 1818, it debuted Handel's Messiah. On January 1, 1863, the society performed the piece to celebrate the Emancipation Proclamation. On June 1, 1865, the society performed the Messiah at a memorial service for Abraham Lincoln in Boston.

The White House – Election Day, Tuesday, November 8, 1864

Mother and I voted early, as we always do. People at the polls clapped when we entered and left. Results have been pouring in all day and night and appear to be very favorable. Initial reports suggest there will be a very large voter turnout. I believe that those troops who were able to vote were kind to me. Secretaries Stanton, Welles, Chase, Colonel John Eaton, Noah Brooks, J.G. Randal, Whitelaw Reid and a correspondent for the Cincinnati Gazette and many others came by during the day and evening to discuss returns being reported from the various states. All have been optimistic. Hay has been keeping count as the telegrams arrive. Everything is then written down on a big board for all to see. It is a slow process.

I received from presidential candidate George B. McClellan a telegram reading, "I have the honor to resign my commission as a Major General in the Army of the U.S.A., sir, very respectfully, George B. McClellan." I will send him my acceptance within the week.

Later in the day I was informed that an Illinois farmer by the name of Carlos Pierce had a "special gift" for me. When I went down to the front lawn, he presented me with a mammoth ox he named "General Grant." I thanked him for his generosity and two soldiers escorted it off the grounds. It is amazing the strange gifts that have been bestowed upon me.

Author's notes:

The November 9th edition of the Washington Star reported, "Abraham Lincoln has been elected by an overwhelming majority."

The White House – Wednesday, November 9, 1864

Between 1 A.M. and 2 A.M. a very large and enthusiastic crowd serenaded me. Many carried American flags and some carried Lincoln-Johnson banners and signs. Captain Thomas and a great many Pennsylvanians arrived with a good-sized band, which played the Battle Hymn and Dixie for me. I informed the crowd that it is no pleasure for me to triumph over anyone; but I do give thanks to the Almighty for this evidence of the people's resolution to stand by free government and the right of humanity.

I donated the large ox named "General Grant" that was given to me by Carlos Pierce, Esq., to the National Sailor's Fair where it is to be auctioned off, with the proceeds going to help sailors in need.

Author's notes:

On November 22nd Alexander H. Rice telegraphed President Lincoln that "The mammoth Ox, General Grant, which was presented to you by Carlos Pierce, Esq., of this city, and by you donated to the National Sailor's Fair, on the 9th inst. has yielded $3,200 to its treasury, and that sum is held as your contribution."

The White House – Thursday, November 10, 1864

The first person to call seeking employment after the election was the daughter of Jasper E. Brady, my good friend and former Pennsylvania congressman. I wrote to Postmaster General William Dennison asking him to try and oblige Miss Brady. Jasper served in the Congress from Chambersburg 1847 to 1849 and has been a clerk in the paymaster general's office from 1861 until today. Later I met with H.W. Hoffman, collector of Customs in Baltimore, and we discussed voter returns. He showed me that out of 1,428 Baltimore soldiers serving in the Army of the Potomac, 1,160 voted for your truly. A very impressive outcome!

This evening members of the Lincoln & Johnson Clubs of Washington, Georgetown and Giesboro Point, which is opposite of the arsenal, marched to the White House with torches and banners to serenade Mother and me. Tad was very excited by all the loud singing and band playing. They sang John Brown's song as well as Dixie, which I always ask to be played. My fondest hope is that one day soon Dixie will be reunited with the North for one United States again.

Author' notes:

On this date, Lincoln discussed with Secretary Seward and Welles the diplomatic implications of the seizing in Brazilian waters of the Confederate raider, "CSA Florida." Brazil had complained that the Rebel ship was illegally seized by the U.S. Navy.

On November 4th and 5th Confederate forces won a victory at the Battle of Johnsonville in Tennessee. The Southerners bombarded Union troops during the night after a fire started near Union positions.

The White House – Friday, November 11, 1864

Today Secretaries Stanton, Welles and General Halleck brought to the Cabinet's attention the results of the recent Battle of Johnsonville, fought in Benton County, Tennessee. Confederate cavalry and artillery under Major General Nathan Bedford Forrest did major damage. Our losses from this engagement were four gunboats, 14 transports, 20 barges, 26 cannon, 150 prisoners and property worth over $8,000,000.

On August 23rd I asked each member of the Cabinet to sign a document without reading it. Today, Hay read it to them. The contents pledged them to support the President-elect after the election regardless of who won the election. Later I met with J.W. Forney and F. Carroll Brewster, city solicitor of Philadelphia, to discuss the case of Cozzens, who is charged with supplying tents to the Army in violation of Army regulations. Aside from the gun, there is no piece of equipment as important as the tent, for it is the home to the men, and how it stands up in foul weather is vitally important to the well-being of them. With cold weather now upon us I do not want to hear complaints about tents that leak or tear apart. I have asked that several tents made by Cozzens be set up on the grounds so I can examine them after the next heavy rainfall to see how they perform.

Author's notes:

The Battle of Johnsonville is now the focus of two Tennessee state parks: Nathan Bedford Forrest State Park, which is located on the Benton County side of the Tennessee River, and Johnsonville State Historic Park, which is situated on the Humphreys County side of the river. The Civil War Trust has acquired and preserved 19 acres of the Johnsonville battlefield.

Lincoln was a hands-on president. He personally tested rifles, pistols and cannon, and when there were problems with tents, he tested them, too.

The White House – Saturday, November 12, 1864

At breakfast this day Tad asked me many questions about George Washington, who has been my lifelong model as the perfect statesman and soldier. Tad has been studying early American history. I told Tad that if Washington had not been able to flee from Brooklyn on Long Island into New York City on the rainy night of August 29, 1776, the Revolutionary War would probably have been lost at that very moment. He and his men were trapped by the British and greatly outnumbered by British and Hessian mercenary troops. General Howe had him bottled up. At that time the British had over 400 ships patrolling New York's harbors and surrounding waterways and an estimated 34,000 troops either encamped on Staten Island or on ships. On August 22nd the British sent their first troops from Staten Island to Long Island. On August 27th at the Battle of Brooklyn the British almost outflanked the Americans. Halleck told me that the Continental forces on Long Island probably never exceeded 9,000 when the were bottled up on the bluffs of Brooklyn Heights, along the East River. At that critical moment, Washington managed to get his Army onto a collection of small boats and cross from Brooklyn to Manhattan Island without being seen or heard in a massive downpour. The Army endured and the war for liberty took seven long years to win.

When things have gotten bad during the current difficulties, I have often reflected on how impossible things must have looked for Washington, yet he never lost hope. His calming exterior gave hope and strength to the Continental Congress and to the Army he commanded. It is the job of the chief executive to remain steady when events are at their worst. He must inspire those who need encouragement and hope. My sense is that our enemy is weakening, yet like a wounded bear, he is still a very dangerous foe. Jefferson Davis is still a dangerous man.

Author's notes:

Five days earlier, in Richmond, Jefferson Davis had said, "The delusion fondly cherished by the enemy is that the capture of Atlanta or Richmond would, if effected, end the war by the overthrow of our government and the submission of our people. If the campaign against Richmond had resulted in success instead of failure, if the valor of Lee's Army, under the leadership of this accomplished commander, had resisted in vain the overwhelming masses which were, on the contrary, decisively repulsed – if we had been compelled to evacuate Richmond as well as Atlanta – the Confederacy would have remained intact and defiant as ever. Nothing could have changed in the purpose of its government, in the indomitable valor of its troops, or in the unquenchable spirit of its people. The constant and exhaustive drain of blood and treasure must continue until he shall discover that no peace is attainable unless based upon the recognition of our indefeasible rights."

The White House – Monday, November 14, 1864

This weekend I spent a great deal of time reading congratulatory telegrams from across the country. I advised William H. Purnell of Baltimore that I will be pleased to meet with him and members of the Maryland State Central Committee of the Union Party on Thursday as he suggests. I accepted the resignation of General McClellan and appointed General Sheridan to the rank of major general. Illinois Senator Orville Browning came by in the evening and reminded me that it is time to prepare my Message to Congress. As always, he had several pertinent suggestions to offer which were appreciated by me.

I told visitors that he found consolation that the election contest had demonstrated to the world that "a people's government can sustain an election in the midst of a great civil war."

Mother reminded me of an event that occurred before I came to Washington. On election night 1860 I came home utterly worn out and decided to rest on a horsehair sofa in the parlor before going up to bed. When I happened to look in a mirror hung above a bureau, I saw myself reflected with two faces with one superimposed on the other. When I got up from the sofa to examine the mirror the illusion vanished. But when I lay down again it reappeared, plainer than before, and I could see that the image was paler than before. Again, I got up, but the double image disappeared never to return. I foolishly told Mary about what had happened and regretted doing so. She took it as a sign that I would be re-elected four years later, but the pallor of the second face meant that I would not live through the second term. I have not had the mirror experience since, and have attributed the phenomenon to being over-tired after a strenuous election day.

Author's notes:

Out of 4 million votes cast on election day, Lincoln received 2,203, 831, just over 55 percent – as compared to McClellan's 1,797,019. He received 212 electoral votes, including three from Nevada the newest state. McClellan won votes from Delaware, New Jersey and Kentucky totaling 21.

McClellan was soon off for a six-month European tour. Lincoln said, "I am like the starling in Sterne's story, "I can't get out."

The White House – Wednesday, November 16, 1864

Last evening Mother and I attended a grand performance of Hamlet at Grover's Theatre with E.L. Davenport in the leading role of the Prince of Denmark. I love the lines:

> "Neither a borrower, nor a lender be;
>
> For loan oft loses both itself and friend.
>
> And borrowing dulls the edge of husbandry.
>
> This above all: to thine own self be true.
>
> And it must follow, as the night the day,
>
> Thou canst not then be false to any man."

The audience was stunned by the brilliance of Davenport's words. How anyone can remember so much is beyond comprehension. The play ran over three hours.

Author's notes:

On November 16th General William T. Sherman begins his march from Atlanta to the sea. The president consulted with Thurlow Weed about the recent election in New York City and State.

The White House – Thursday, November 17, 1864

Secretary Stanton and General Halleck acquainted the Cabinet with the latest military actions in Hamblen and Greene Counties, Tennessee. As best we can learn this was a Confederate victory, but not much of one. The commanding officer of the Rebels at the Battle of Bull's Gap was General John C. Breckinridge, who apparently was given command of the Department of East Tennessee's forces after the death of General John Hunt Morgan. Breckinridge was vice-president under President James Buchanan and was on the ballot for president in 1860, coming in third in the popular vote in a four-way contest, but second in the electoral college, where the vote was 180 for me, 72 for Breckinridge, 39 for John Bell and 12 for Douglas. Curiously, it was Breckinridge's duty as vice-president to announce that I was the winner of the electoral college vote on February 13, 1861. He visited with me on February 14th at Willard's Hotel and often visited with Mary, his cousin. The war has separated so many people who normally would be united in friendly relationships. For Mary, this has occurred too often for her well-being. Too many of her kin and close family friends have been killed fighting for the Confederacy.

Author's notes:

On November 11th Confederate forces attacked Bull's Gap but were repulsed by artillery fire throughout the day. On the 12th both sides launched morning attacks. The Rebels gained little ground. On November 13, firing occurred throughout most of the day, but the Confederates did not assault Union lines. The federal soldiers, short of ammunition and rations, withdrew from Bull's Gap toward Russellville late in the evening. On the 14th Breckinridge pursued the federals, causing a rout.They fell back to Strawberry Plains outside of Knoxville. Breckinridge retired as Federal reinforcements arrived

When Secretary of War James A. Seddon resigned as Confederate secretary of war, Jefferson Davis named Breckinridge to fill the position on January 19, 1865. His first act as secretary was to appoint Robert E. Lee general-in-chief of all Confederate forces. Lee would surrender to Grant on April 9, 1865.

The White House – Friday, November 18, 1864

I deposited an April and July salary warrant at Riggs Bank. Tad came along with me. I asked the manager to show him into the bank's very large steel vault, and he was very impressed by it. I also gave him a brand new $10.00 greenback and that impressed him even more. My picture is on the bill. When I returned to the office, I sent a check for $260 to Martin B. Church, a former law student in the office of Lincoln and Herndon. It is a loan to be repaid in five months. Church is a promising prospect for a career in the law, and like many starting out, he is short of funds. I am pleased to be able to assist him. I am one who knows the meaning of being "short of funds"!

I conferred today with William P. Wood, superintendent of the Old Capitol Prison, regarding the fate of a Negro soldier sentenced to die. This is one of those cases where there seem to be no redeeming features to the matter. He will therefore be hung on the date set, November 25th.

The Reverend and Mrs. Phineas D. Gurley were our dinner guests this evening. They are good company and give Mother much pleasure.

Author's note:

The loan to M.B. Church was never repaid. After the president's death Mrs. Lincoln asked the administrator of his estate not to try to collect it from Mr. Church, who she considered a friend of the family. The April warrant was for $2,022.67 and the July warrant was for $1,981.67.

The White House – Saturday, November 19, 1864

Hay helped me put the finishing touches on a proclamation concerning the naval blockade. It modifies the government's earlier blockade order of April 1861. The new document allows commerce to again be transacted at Norfolk, Fernandina and Pensacola. The blockade the Union imposed at those ports is now officially ended. This is another strong indication that matters are normalizing as we continue to take mastery of areas formerly controlled by Confederate forces. That we can do this is due in large part to the achievements of the Navy in keeping these important ports closed to the enemy, thus denying the Rebels the ability to import goods of war and to export products like cotton that generated precious income for their cause. I thanked Secretaries Seward, Welles and Stanton for helping to achieve this important war goal.

I wrote to General Rosecrans in relation to Major Enoch O. Wolf, who is under sentence of execution for the murder of Major John Wilson. I stressed that I wish to do nothing for revenge in this case but that whatever Rosecrans decides to do be predicated upon the security of the future.

I issued another order to General Alfred Sully in Davenport, Iowa, calling for the immediate release from federal custody of Chief Big Eagle. Sometimes the wheels of progress grind slowly in a military bureaucracy.

Author's notes:

In the matter of Major Enoch Wolf, he was sent to City Point and exchanged for another prisoner rather than executed.

The White House – Monday, November 21, 1864

Today I wrote to Mrs. Lydia Bixby. It was a very difficult letter to compose for her loss has been so very great – five sons lost gloriously on the fields of battle. Mother and I discussed her sacrifices before I took pen to paper. This war has given us a harvest of grief never before seen. Those who began it still do not concede their errors and thus the slaughter continues to what is an inevitable end. Hopefully the day it ends will come sooner than later.

I wrote to John Phillips, age 104, thanking him for writing to me about my re-election. Every vote counts! Phillips is an amazing man. He rode two miles from his home to vote and advised me that he had first voted for George Washington! He says he is a Democrat of the Jeffersonian School. His son, Colonel Edward Phillips, aged 79, accompanied him to the Town Hall, where their votes were cast. He is the oldest citizen in the town of Sturbridge and may be the oldest one in the Commonwealth of Massachusetts. He wrote that he had "no desire to live but to see the conclusion of this wicked rebellion, and the power of God displayed in the conversion of the nation."

Author's notes:

On November 25th the Boston Transcript published a copy of Lincoln's letter to Mrs. Bixby. Later the Adjutant General's office revealed that only two of her sons had been killed: "Sergeant Charles N. Bixby, 58th Massachusetts Infantry, killed July 30, 1864, and Private Oliver Bixby, 58th Massachusetts Infantry, killed July 30, 1864."

The White House – Wednesday, November 23, 1864

I met yesterday with Albert G. Hodges, editor of the Commonwealth newspaper, published in Franklin, Kentucky, and General Samuel G. Suddarth of the Kentucky State Militia in hopes of devising strategies that may lead to creating a greater sense of harmony in the state following the election. I learned that the large ox that I donated to the Sailors' Fair brought $3,000.

Today I suspended the executions of Patrick Kelly, John Lennor, Joel Eastwood, Thomas Murray and Samuel Hoffman "until further order from here." I use that message often to save for future employment men who have done things that are improper or cowardly or both, but which in the great scheme of things are not disqualifying from future honorable and valuable service to the nation.

Author's notes:

On November 22, the Battle of Griswoldville was fought near Macon, Georgia. There, a Union Army brigade under Brigadier General Charles C. Walcutt fought three brigades of Georgia militia under Brigadier General Pleasant J. Philips at Griswoldville. This was the first battle of Sherman's March to the Sea. The day before, Union cavalry under Brigadier General Hugh Judson Kilpatrick had struck Griswoldville, capturing a train of 13 cars loaded with military supplies. His troops burned the station and factory buildings. On the 22nd Confederate cavalry attacked the 9th Pennsylvania Cavalry, which with the 5th Kentucky Cavalry made a saber charge that forced the Confederates to retire to their works. Walcutt's infantry and artillery battery drove the Confederate Army through Griswoldville, taking up a strong position with an open field in front and flanks protected by a swamp. At 2 P.M. three brigades of Georgia militia attacked in three compact lines but were met with a shower of cannister. They were repulsed with heavy losses. General Walcutt was wounded in the engagement and command fell to Colonel Robert F. Catterson of the 97th Indiana Regiment. Union losses were 13 killed, 79 wounded. Confederate losses were 51 dead, 472 wounded and 600 captured. General Sherman's March to the Sea continued.

The Georgia State Parks manage a 17-acre tract at the battlefield site.

The White House – Thursday, November 24, 1864

Yesterday, General Grant and six members of his staff met with me, Secretary Stanton, General Halleck and the Cabinet. He described for us the state of military affairs both outside of Richmond and in Georgia, where Sherman has begun his march to the sea. Grant speaks slowly but with conviction and offers us confidence in the inevitable outcome of victory and re-Union.

Today I received a letter of resignation from Attorney General Edward Bates to take effect on November 30th. He wishes to retire to private life. He has done a good job and has been a loyal Cabinet member. I know that he wished to be appointed to the Supreme Court upon the death of Chief Justice Taney and was disappointed when that did not happen. He is a remarkable man, having fathered 17 children. He has given the nation his best efforts, starting with service in the War of 1812. He was not sanguine about the Emancipation Proclamation but remained silent publicly about his opposition to it.

Author's notes:

Edward Bates was the 26th U.S. attorney general, serving from March 5, 1861, to November 30, 1864. He was a candidate for president at the 1860 Republican Convention, where Lincoln won the nomination. He was preceded in office by Edwin Stanton and succeeded by James Speed. He served in the U.S. House of Representatives and the Missouri House of Representatives and Senate, becoming a prominent member of the Whig Party. He was born September 4, 1793 and died March 25, 1869.

The White House – Friday, November 25, 1864

Yesterday we had an excellent traditional Thanksgiving dinner – Tad was especially enthusiastic about the pies: apple, cherry and mincemeat. He had a slice of each and then went back for another slice of the mincemeat. Charles François de Montholon Sémonville, the French ambassador, and his wife, Marie, joined us, along with Secretary Seward and his wife, Frances and their daughter, Fanny.

The French ambassador noted that Napoleon had wisely said, "An Army marches on its stomach." If so, the Confederate Armies are at increased risk every day as their access to rations diminishes. Seward mentioned that the duke of Wellington reportedly said of Napoleon that "His presence on the field made the difference of forty thousand men." I am afraid that the presence on the battlefield of General Robert E. Lee seems to have a similar effect on Confederate soldiers.

The ambassador mentioned to Mother a quotation of Georges Jacques Danton, a French legislator who was executed during the French Revolution. Danton had said, "Il nous faut de l'audace, encore de l'audace, toujours de l'audace," In English, it means, "Audacity, more audacity, always audacity."

Hay has heard from officials of the Union League in Philadelphia. They informed him that their drive to raise funds for Thanksgiving Day dinners for our troops and sailors in the east topped $56,000 and that 250,000 pounds of turkeys were provided to the Army and Navy so that traditional Thanksgiving holiday meals could be served to the men yesterday.

Grant told me yesterday that Confederate deserters from Petersburg and Richmond, Virginia, are reporting that their food situation is particularly dire, with starvation rations the diet of the day.

Author's notes:

Georges Jacques Danton's final words were, "Show my head to the people, it is worth seeing." During World War II General George S. Patton, Jr., who was fluent in French, often quoted Danton's line, "Audacity, more audacity, always audacity."

The White House – Saturday, November 26, 1864

Today I was surprised to receive a gift of an elkhorn chair sent to me by Seth Kinman, a hunter from California. It is a thing of beauty but not something of comfort for my particularly long frame. I have donated it to the Smithsonian Institution. President Andrew Jackson announced Smithson's generous bequest to Congress on July 1, 1836, which amounted to more than 100,000 gold sovereigns delivered to the U.S. Mint at Philadelphia. When made into U.S. currency, the gift amounted to more than $500,000. A remarkable present from an Englishman who never set foot on American soil. James Smithson was a scientist who left his money to fund an establishment to "Increase the diffusion of knowledge." Smithson never discussed his gift to friends or colleagues or relatives so no one knows what motivated him to do what he did. It has had great impact on the arts, humanities and the sciences in the United States.

Author's notes:

An Act of Congress signed by President James Polk on August 10, 1846, established the Smithsonian Institution as a trust to be administered by a Board of Regents and a Secretary of the Smithsonian. It is now the world's largest museum, education and research complex, with 19 museums, the National Zoo and nine research facilities.

The White House – Monday, November 28, 1864

Reports of the Battle of Columbia, Tennessee, keep coming in bit by bit. It now seems that the event was a Confederate victory. We will have to be patient to get a clearer picture of what is taking place. Grant has confidence in our forces there to prevail in what promises to be a major event with large numbers of men on both sides.

I am awaiting word from Judge Advocate General Joseph Holt as to whether he will accept the position of attorney general that he has been offered. He is currently doing a fine job in his present position.

I continue to receive gifts of the Thanksgiving season, mostly of foods, which Mother has given to the poor of Washington. Nine governors have been sent letters asking them to report the final votes in their states for president and vice president. I need the information in order to prepare a report for the Congress before it next meets.

Author's notes:

On this date the president wrote to Judge Andrew Wylie, associate justice of the Supreme Court, and Richard Wallach, mayor of Washington, asking them to find employment for two ladies in any department or bureau.

The White House – Tuesday, November 29, 1864

Mother has been wearing fashionable dresses made by Mrs. Elizabeth Keckley for several years that are especially attractive, and which always generate many flattering compliments from those who attend our various social events in the White House. A talented seamstress, before the war she made dresses for Mrs. Jefferson Davis and Mrs. Robert E. Lee. Mrs. Keckley founded the Contraband Relief Association, which just changed its name to the Ladies' Freedmen and Soldiers Relief Association. Her organization is helping recently freed slaves and sick and wounded Negro soldiers. Frederick Douglass has spoken at local black churches to help raise funds for her cause. After the war America will have to make greater efforts to care for Negro soldiers and their families. Men who fight and die for the Union must not be forgotten or their families neglected by the government.

Author's notes:

It is believed that at the time of Lincoln's second election the First Lady had incurred a personal debt of more than $27,000, (a quarter of a million in today's dollars), with much of the expenses attributable to her expenditures on fine clothing. When she died in 1882, she left behind 64 trunks filled with clothes. Mary Todd Lincoln was born December 13, 1818 and died July 16, 1882.

The White House – Thursday, December 1, 1864

Yesterday I had a long and profitable discussion with outgoing Attorney General Edward Bates. He told me that when he first joined the Cabinet, he often found my story telling a little off-putting. He said he was frequently annoyed by my seemingly endless store of humorous anecdotes. He admitted that over time he began to see that the introduction of levity helped matters and sometimes my stories made a point more forcefully than mere logic could. Bates is a stickler for facts and figures and takes the Constitution very, very seriously. He opposed the admission of West Virginia, believing it to be unconstitutional. He also objected to the enlistment of blacks into the Army and Navy, but later agreed it made good sense and argued in favor of the same pay for black men in the same positions as whites. Bates is not in good health and I can understand his wish to retire. He believes I have made a good choice in picking his successor.

Two ladies from Tennessee came by this afternoon asking that I release their husbands from Johnson's Island prison. I have asked Stanton to get me the facts in their cases.

Author's notes:

On December 1st, President Lincoln telegraphed James Speed, the brother of his close friend, Joshua Speed. The message: "I appoint you to be Attorney General. Please come at once." Speed was recommended for the post by Judge Advocate General Joseph Holt, who had declined to accept appointment as Bates' successor. Holt preferred to continue in his present position.

The White House – Friday, December 2, 1864

This afternoon I had a long and productive meeting with Indiana Congressman and Speaker of the House Schuyler Colfax. He came by specifically to recommend that former Secretary of the Treasury Salmon Chase be appointed to chief justice of the Supreme Court. I did not tell him that Chase is probably going to get the job, but right now I wish to keep my views on the subject private. He told me that his grandfather, William Colfax, was one of George Washington's Life Guards during the Revolutionary War. They were an important military unit that saw to the protection of the life of our first president. William became a general in the New Jersey Militia and married Hester Schuyler, a cousin of famed General Philip Schuyler. During the War of 1812 William was commander of troops stationed at Sandy Hook. Schuyler Colfax served in the Congress from Indiana's 9th District from 1855 to now. He has been speaker of the House since December 7, 1863. He has been very helpful in the efforts to pass the 13th Amendment. It reads simply, "Neither slavery nor involuntary servitude, except as a punishment for crime, whereof the past shall have been duly convicted, shall exist with the United States or any place subject to their jurisdiction." Short and sweet!

Author's notes:

Schuyler Colfax became the 25th speaker of the U.S. House of Representatives. He served in that role in the 38th, 39th and 40th Congresses. He served as the 17th vice president of the United States with President Ulysses S. Grant from March 4, 1869, to March 4, 1873. He was born in New York City on March 23, 1823. He died January 13, 1885, in Mankato, Minnesota.

The White House – Saturday, December 3, 1864

Seward and Welles came by the discuss the fate of the war steamer "Funayma Solace," which was built in the United States at the order of the government of Japan. Because of unrest in Japan, Seward has recommended that the ship not be delivered to the buyer. I have agreed, and the vessel will be purchased by the United States government, to be used for the war effort. Newspaper reporter and family friend Noah Brooks came by today to discuss the possible appointment of Salmon Chase to be chief justice to fill the seat vacated by the death of Justice Roger Taney. I did not tell him of my decision, but I do expect to see Chase appointed and confirmed sometime later this month. Two men could not be more different than Taney and Chase. I trust his judgment in legal matters and when the war is finally ended, I would expect Chase to be a strong friend of the Union and a just and lasting peace.

Author's notes:

On December 6, 1864, President Lincoln nominated Salmon P. Chase of Ohio to be chief justice of the Supreme Court of the United States. He was confirmed by the Senate on the same day. Chase had left the Treasury Department on June 30, 1864. He served on the Supreme Court from December 15, 1864, to May 7, 1873. In 1864 he placed on U.S. coins the words "In God We Trust."

The White House – Monday, December 5, 1864

Lord Lyons came by to say goodbye today; he is leaving Washington to go to New York where he will then sail for home for his health. He is a fine ambassador, representing his nation and queen with skill and dedication to peace between the U.S. and Great Britain. But he is a sick man and hopes to soon be in England to recuperate and regain his strength. He looks ravaged. He suffers from persistent headaches. I told him we expect to see him returning to our shores when he is in better health. He told me that the Emancipation Proclamation had done much in his country to win respect for the Union cause and to change attitudes about the South. Slavery is not popular in England and never will be. I hope Lyons will soon be back among us.

This evening Mother and I joined Secretary Seward at Grover's Theatre for a performance of Gounod's "Faust" by the Grand German Opera Company.

I sent several messages to Congress citing various naval officers for their recent victories against the Confederate warships Albemarle, Alabama and the capture of Plymouth, North Carolina.

Author's notes:

On this date the president sent to Congress his Annual Message. It is a positive report showing the Treasury in good shape, foreign affairs acceptable, including relations with Mexico, and relations with China and Japan improved. The public debt is $1,740,690,489. Money to pay for the war derived from taxes should be increased. The national banking system is operating in ways acceptable to capitalists and to the people. Organization and admission of Nevada is completed. Territories grow rapidly. Arkansas and Louisiana have organized loyal state governments. The president recommends passage of proposed amendment to the Constitution, abolishing slavery. The war will cease on the part of the government, whenever it shall have ceased on the part of those who started it.

The White House – Wednesday, December 7, 1864

Yesterday evening Mother and I were serenaded by citizens of Washington. I told them that General Sherman is doing a marvelous job beating the Confederates where he finds them on his way to Savannah. I told them that "I know where he went in, but I can't tell where he will come out!" I assured them that he will "come out all right!" They cheered and cheered when I called for three cheers for General Sherman and his Army.

In my annual report to Congress I noted that the present number of 16,770 invalid soldiers and 271 disabled seamen have been added to the pension rolls, making the total number of Army invalid pensioners 22,767 and Navy pensioners 712. Of widows, orphans and mothers, 22,198 have been placed on the Army pension rolls and 248 on the Navy rolls. $4,504,616 has been paid to pensioners of all classes, including 1,430 from the Revolutionary War.

Chief Justice Salmon Chase paid a personal visit. I wished him well in his new and important assignment on the court. I know he will do an excellent job there. I also know he'd rather be president, but I think I'll keep that job for a while.

Author's notes:

Chief Justice Chase wrote Lincoln on December 6th, "On reaching home tonight I was saluted with the intelligence that you this day nominated me to the Senate for the office of chief justice. I cannot sleep before I thank you for this mark of your confidence and especially for the manner in which the nomination was made. I shall never forget either and trust that you will never regret either. Be assured that I prize your confidence and goodwill more than nomination for office."

The White House – Thursday, December 8, 1864

I was joined for breakfast this morning by David McDonald of Indianapolis, who I am appointing to the District Court for the District of Indiana that was vacated by Judge Albert Smith White. I have known him over the years to be a sensible man. He will be a credit to the Federal bench.

The Cabinet attended a meeting with General Halleck and two of his aides in which recent battles were reviewed, including the Battle of Buck Head Creek in Georgia, which was a Union victory on November 28th; the Battle of Spring Hill in Tennessee on the same date; the Battle of Sand Creek on November 29th in the Colorado Territory against Cheyenne and Arapaho Indians; and the Battle of Honey Hill in South Carolina. The latter was a failed Union expedition under Major General John P. Hatch, which attempted to cut off the Charleston & Savannah Railroad in support of Sherman's projected arrival in Savannah. We were shown maps describing the Battle of Franklin, which occurred on the 30th of November in Tennessee. This was a huge Union victory in which Confederate General Hood had attacked General Schofield, suffering crushing losses.

Author's notes:

Judge McDonald served as a professor of law at Indiana University Bloomington from 1842 to 1852. He was a judge of the 10th Judicial Circuit of Indiana from 1839 to 1852. He was in private practice from 1853 to 1864. He was confirmed by the U.S. Senate on December 13, 1864, receiving his commission the same day, serving thereafter until his death on August 25, 1869 in Indianapolis.

The White House – Saturday, December 10, 1864

Last evening after a long Cabinet meeting I attended the theater with Senator Sumner and others. The performance was second rate, and I fell asleep during the second act. That is unusual for me, but of late I have been getting less sleep at night than I am accustomed to. At 10 A.M. today Dr. Robert K. Stone, my physician, examined me and found me "fit as a fiddle."

Today I created a special committee consisting of General William F. Smith and Henry Stanberg, former attorney general of Ohio, to investigate and report upon the civil and military administration in the military division bordering upon and west of the Mississippi River.

The highlight of the day was the visit by Thomas Nast, the famed illustrator for "Harper's Weekly." He is full of good humor and has been a strong supporter of the Union cause. I have called him our "best recruiting sergeant." His Christmas illustrations are particularly poignant. His 1862 Christmas Eve illustration for Harper's has a wreath framing a scene of a soldier's praying wife and sleeping children at home; a second wreath frames the soldier seated by a campfire gazing longingly at small pictures of his loved ones. In 1864, his cartoon "Compromise with the South" was directed against those in the North who opposed prosecution of the war. His drawings of battlefields in border and Southern states are marvelous to see. I thanked him profusely for his aid to our cause.

Author's notes:

On this date the president received a letter of resignation from Marshall Ward Hill Lamon because the president refused to take proper precautions against assassination. Ultimately Lamon did not resign. On the night of Lincoln's assassination, Lamon was in Richmond, Virginia. Ironically, before he left for Richmond, he implored Lincoln not to go out at night after he was gone, particularly to the theater.

The White House – Monday, December 12, 1864

Sunday evening, Mother and I discussed what we should give to Robert and Tad for Christmas. She believes Tad might like a folding pocketknife. Robert is never an easy one to pick a gift for. He seems to have everything he wants and needs. I think the best gift for the nation would be the continued successes of our arms, but in the spirit of the Holy holiday, one cannot but reflect that every victory celebrated is also accompanied by the grief felt by families whose loved ones have fallen in battle or been injured in the fight to bring a finish to the seemingly endless struggle. Robert has asked if he might be allowed to join the Army, which his mother strongly opposes. I told him that I will write to General Grant asking that he appoint Robert to the rank of captain, to serve on his staff. That may prove to be the gift he would like the most.

I have asked Secretary Seward to investigate an incident in which the Danish government has apparently seized a ship whose cargo contained 2,000 carbines belonging to American citizens.

This afternoon the Cabinet was given the details by General Halleck of the December 4th battle fought at Waynesboro, Georgia, which turned out to be a Union victory. Halleck believes we outnumbered the Rebels roughly 8,000 to 6,000. Union cavalry under Brigadier General Judson Kilpatrick faced Confederate cavalry under Major General Joseph Wheeler. The victory will help Sherman's Army as it now approaches Savannah.

Author's notes:

On January 19, 1864, President Lincoln wrote to General Grant requesting that Robert Lincoln be allowed to join the general's staff in some "nominal rank I, and not the public, furnishing his necessary means?" On January 21, Grant replied, "I will be most happy to have him in my military family in the manner you propose. The nominal rank given him is immaterial, but I would suggest that of captain as I have three staff officers now, of considerable service, in no higher grade. Indeed, I have one officer with only the rank of lieutenant who has been in the service from the beginning of the war. This however will make no difference and I would say give the rank of Captain." Robert Lincoln was appointed captain and assistant adjutant general of Volunteers, February 11, 1865, and resigned June 10, 1865.

The White House – Tuesday, December 13, 1865

After some polishing up of the language by Hay, I transmitted to the Senate treaties with the Republics of Haiti and Honduras. I issued orders at the request of Congressman William Randell of Kentucky that Thomas Rice, prisoner at Rock Island and Reuben Turner, prisoner at Johnson's Island, be discharged, on taking the oath on December 8, 1863.

I wrote to Cyrus Wick thanking him for sending me his poem, which was mailed to me by William Herndon, my law partner. Herndon told me that Wick's regiment, the 17th Indiana Volunteers, had been encamped for several weeks at Nolin Creek, one mile and a quarter from Hodgenville in La Rue County, Kentucky, in November of 1862. Wick wrote that his poem was inspired by a speech I had given early in 1861 and by the scenery where his childhood was passed. People must know that I love poetry because I often get poems in the mail. This one was particularly nice.

I sent a note to Captain Ira Goodnow, doorkeeper of the House of Representatives, asking him to try to find a suitable position for a fine little boy who I met today. He had been waiting in line to see me and looked cold and hungry. He told me that his older brother was a prisoner of war now being held by the Rebels somewhere in Georgia.

Author's notes:

The treaty of friendship, commerce and navigation between Honduras and the United States was signed by their respective plenipotentiaries at Comayagua, on the 4th of July 1864.

The White House – Thursday, December 15, 1864

Wednesday, I proclaimed ratification of a treaty with the Tabeguache Band of Utah Indians.

Late tonight I received a telegram sent from General George H. Thomas in Nashville to General Halleck. It confirmed that his forces have driven the enemy from the river, below the city, very nearly to the Franklin Turnpike, a distance of about 8 miles. He has captured General James Chalmers' headquarters and train, and a second train of about 20 wagons, and between 800 and 1,000 prisoners and 16 pieces of artillery. He says our troops behaved splendidly and that he will be attacking the enemy again tomorrow. Thomas plans to throw a heavy cavalry force in the enemy's rear to destroy his trains if possible. Curiously, it was only yesterday that I met with Grant, Halleck and Stanton to discuss the removal of General Thomas. I doubt Thomas will ever be threatened with removal again. I have telegraphed him expressing the nation's thanks for his good work

Author's notes:

On this date the Battle of Nashville, Tennessee, began. It was a great Union victory. General Thomas attacked and virtually destroyed General Hood's Confederate Army of Tennessee.

The White House – Friday, December 16, 1864

Secretaries Welles and Stanton came by late in the evening to bring me up-to-date on information received concerning the recent Battle of Fort McAllister, which is located near Savannah, in Bryan County, Georgia. This was the second battle fought to take this fortification. We employed troops from Illinois, Michigan, Ohio and Missouri and ships under the command of Admiral John A. Dahlgren. Sherman was on hand to observe the attack. Sherman wanted this fort taken because ships offshore had not been able to land needed supplies for his Army. Taking the fort meant the Union Army would control the Ogeechee River, providing an avenue to the sea and needed supplies. The fort fell in 15 minutes. With the supply line now open, Sherman advises that he will now prepare for the siege and capture of Savannah.

Author's notes:

The troops involved in the taking of Fort McAllister were the same troops Sherman had personally led as a division commander at Shiloh and a corps commander at Vicksburg. They were part of the 2nd Division, XV Corps, Army of the Tennessee.

The White House – Saturday, December 17, 1864

Yesterday I introduced new Attorney General James Speed to the Cabinet members. I received a delegation from the Freedmen's Aid Society of Baltimore. As more and more former slaves become freedmen, the need for aid to help them enter our society successfully becomes increasingly important. I promised them that I would do all in my power to help them and their families adjust to the new circumstances. I am particularly concerned that freedmen who have served in the Army and Navy will be recognized for the sacrifices they have made to save the Union.

This weekend Hay and Nicolay will be assisting me in the preparation of a proclamation calling for 300,000 volunteers, per the Act of July 1, 1864. This allows enlistments for one, two or three years. It also provides for a draft if our requirements are not met via volunteerism. The operative date is to be February 15, 1865, when a draft may commence should there be a shortfall in enlistments. I pray this may be our last such proclamation, and that no more soldiers and sailors will be needed to win the struggle.

Author's notes:

On this date the president decided to suspend the execution of James P. Boileau, until further order from the president. General Lew Wallace was sent a telegram to that effect on December 20, 1864.

The White House – Monday, December 19, 1864

Yesterday, Montgomery Blair and General Nathaniel Banks came by to discuss Ohio Congressman James Ashley's bill regarding states in rebellion. Blair was a very effective postmaster general and remains a close friend. I value his counsel in matters of law and politics. He was one of my earliest supporters and I trust his judgment totally. I miss him not being in our Cabinet meetings.

It seems that everyone has a "special event" to which I am invited. Just today I received an invitation to attend a soldiers' fair in Springfield, Massachusetts, a promenade at Ford's Theater to benefit some charity, and an invitation to be present at the annual festival of The New England Society to commemorate the landing of the Pilgrims. Maybe I should start going to these things and let the war run itself.

Mother has been away on a shopping trip, staying at the Continental Hotel in Philadelphia. She is due back in Washington on Thursday. The weather is colder than usual, so I have telegraphed that she does not take the night train but instead take the early morning train, when it should be a little warmer.

Author's notes:

On this date President Lincoln recognized Henri Enderis as consul of the Swiss Federation for the states of Michigan, Iowa, Wisconsin and Minnesota.

The White House – Tuesday, December 20, 1864

The Cabinet met at 11 A.M. We asked General Nathaniel Banks to review civic and military affairs in New Orleans and to describe his current duties there. Secretary Seward recommended that Dennis Donohue be recognized as consul of Great Britain for New Orleans.

General Halleck and two members of his staff presented a summary of events that took place on December 17 and 18 at Marion, Virginia. The Confederate forces there were under the command of General Breckinridge, including the 4th Kentucky Infantry Regiment. There was heavy fighting back and forth, with our side ultimately prevailing in large part because the Rebels reportedly ran short of ammunition. Prisoners revealed that the enemy had fired over 75 rounds per man in the engagement and typically were down to just 10 rounds when ordered to leave the field of battle. The results of our activities included the destruction of enemy supplies. Saltville fell on the night of December 20th and the salt works there were badly damaged. Additionally, the important lead mines near Wytheville were also damaged, with many railroad cars and engines destroyed along with bridges and depots in the vicinity. We captured 34 officers and 845 enlisted men during the attack on Marion. Salt and lead are both vitally important items to the Confederate war effort.

Author's notes:

On this date, President Lincoln recognized Moritz von Baumbach, as consul at Milwaukee for the Duchy of Saxe Meiningen.

The White House – Thursday, December 22, 1864

Yesterday, I received information that General Butler was holding elections on the Eastern shore of Virginia and notified him to cancel them.

Later today I received a remarkable telegraphic message from General Sherman. It reads, "I beg to present you as a Christmas gift the city of Savannah with 150 guns and plenty of ammunition and also about 25,000 bales of cotton." No message delivered since the war began was so pleasantly received by me as this one by the remarkable General Sherman.

Author's notes:

On this date, President Lincoln met with Secretary Seward, who had a letter from Senator Preston King of New York recommending that John Bigelow, author, editor and U.S. consul general in Paris, be named minister to France.

On December 27th General Benjamin B. Butler advised President Lincoln that no unauthorized elections would be forthcoming within his command in Virginia.

The White House – Friday, December 23, 1864

On Wednesday, I wrote a note to Dr. Robert K. Stone asking that he prescribe for me a medicine suitable for treating ringworm. He stopped by today and after examining me suggested that I drink strong tea three or four times a day. He also recommends that I wipe with cotton the affected area of my arms with apple cider vinegar. This is to be done for 10 or 15 minutes and then the liquid is to be removed and the arms rinsed with clear warm water and dried. He warns me that the condition may linger for two or three weeks. I have never had this before. It is annoying but not painful. I rarely ever get sick. I trust Dr. Stone's cures will be helpful.

The Cabinet met and Secretary Welles was late in arriving. Everyone and their families were invited to a reception at the White House to be held on Christmas Day. Mother is very excited about the entertainment and has asked that a military choir accompanied by a band provide Christmas carols for the occasion.

Author's notes:

On this date the president issued an order concerning James Harrison of St. Louis, who was to be provided protection and safe conduct for his boats and tows from New Orleans or Memphis to Red River and upon his return to places beyond federal lines.

The White House – Saturday, December 24, 1864

Eleven-year-old Tad has been very much in the holiday spirit. Today he brought to my office some very delicious Christmas Yule cake that was baked in the White House kitchen for tomorrow's reception. It was delicious. He told me it was made upon an ancient Swedish or Norwegian recipe.

Many months ago, I ordered a light brown leather English saddle to be made in London to his measurements as a surprise gift for Christmas morning. Lord Lyons kindly arranged the purchase for me through a saddle maker his family has been using for decades. Mother has asked the sergeant of the Guard to saddle up Tad's pony and bring it to the White House entrance tomorrow at 10 A.M. We can't wait to see the expression on Tad's face when he first sits upon that horse on his new saddle.

Secretary Welles called upon me and asked me to sign a commutation order, and to approve a pass to Richmond for Laura Jones. I was pleased to do so.

I recognized Robert Barth as consul of the Grand Dukedom of Baden at St. Louis.

Author's notes:

Thomas "Tad" Lincoln was born on April 4, 1853. He died July 15, 1871.

The White House – Monday, December 26, 1864

A Christmas reception was held at the White House and very well-attended. Mother looked her radiant best, as usual. I shook more hands than ever. The mood among our guests was one of joy and positive hope that the New Year will finally bring the victory all are praying for. I wrote to General Sherman thanking him for his gift of Savannah, Georgia. My belief is that his singular accomplishment will do much to convince European powers that the end is now in sight. It should also convince many Confederate sympathizers in the South that their cause is hopeless.

Author's notes:

President Lincoln wrote to General Sherman, "Many, many thanks for your Christmas gift – the capture of Savannah. When you were about leaving Atlanta for the Atlantic coast, I was anxious, if not fearful; but feeling that you were the better judge, and remembering, that 'nothing risked, nothing gained' I did not interfere. Now the undertaking being a success, the honor is all yours; for I believe none of us went farther than to acquiesce. And taking the work of Gen. Thomas into the count, as it should be taken, it is indeed a great success. Not only does it afford the obvious and immediate military advantages; but, in showing to the world that your army could be divided, putting the stronger part to an important new service, and yet leaving enough to vanquish the old opposing force of the whole – Hood's army – it brings those who sat in darkness to see a great light. But what next? I suppose it will be safer if I leave Gen. Grant and yourself to decide. Please make my grateful acknowledgement to your whole army, officers and men. Yours very truly. A. Lincoln."

The White House – Tuesday, December 27, 1864

Tad has been riding his pony more often now that he has his new English saddle. Mother and I are pleased that his new saddle is very much to his liking. He sits a horse nicely. I wrote to Lord Lyons thanking him for arranging for such a fine-looking saddle. Lyons has not been well. I wish him a rapid recovery from whatever is ailing him. Seward and I hope he may return to America one day.

Author's notes:

In December 1864, Lord Lyons left Washington, suffering poor health. Before he left, he had several amiable meetings with President Lincoln. When his health further deteriorated in the spring of 1865, he resigned his position of ambassador to the United States. Queen Victoria and Lord Palmerston attempted to persuade Lyons to return to the United States, but he would not. He nominated Sir Frederick Bruce as his successor; the queen and Palmerston immediately accepted his suggestion. Later he would serve as ambassador to the Ottoman Empire and in October of 1867, after the resignation of Lord Cowley, he was appointed British ambassador to France, in Paris, where he served with distinction for 20 years.

The White House – Thursday, December 29, 1864

Today I signed a letter to President John MacLean, thanking him for advising me that the trustees of the College of New Jersey in Princeton have conferred upon me the degree of Doctor of Laws. This is a singular honor of which I am greatly pleased. Hay reminded me that James Madison attended the College of New Jersey, receiving his degree in 1771. I am in very good company!

Secretary Welles and two naval officers on his staff presented information to me about failed attempts to take Fort Fisher, which is located in Wilmington, North Carolina.

Author's notes:

President Lincoln wrote to John MacLean in part, "Thoughtful men must feel that the fate of civilization upon this continent is involved in the issue of our contest. Among the most gratifying proofs of this conviction is the hearty devotion everywhere exhibited by our schools and colleges to the national cause. I am most thankful if my labors have seemed to conduce to the preservation of those institutions under which alone, we can expect good government and in its train sound learning and the progress of the liberal arts."

On February 10, 1865, President Lincoln wrote to Rear Admiral David D. Porter, Commanding North Atlantic Squadron, Hampton Roads, Virginia: "Sir, It is made my agreeable duty to enclose herewith the joint resolution approved 24th January 1865, tendering the joint Congress to yourself, the officers and men under your command, for their gallantry and good conduct in the capture of Fort Fisher, and through you to all who participated in that brilliant and decisive victory under your command, Very respectfully, Abraham Lincoln".

The White House – Friday, December 30, 1864

Mother and I spent a few hours yesterday evening talking about what we might do when this war is over and behind us. I told her that I had a recent dream in which the White House had burned down. Mary has great knowledge of human nature. She often reminds me that I can be a poor judge of men. I said to her that once the transcontinental railroad is completed, we should plan a trip to California and make it a point to see the gold fields. Mother is often upset by what the newspapers write about me. Occasionally, she gets to read a Southern paper and is doubly excited and aggravated by what she reads. I tell her that I care nothing about what they write about me, Northern or Southern newspapers. If I am right, I'll live and if I'm wrong, I'll die anyhow – so let them pass unnoticed. That's the way to learn; read both sides. My maxim is whatever is to be will be, and no cares of ours can arrest the decree. Mother is often concerned about those men she believes are out to harm me. I tell her that I like to do good to those who hate me and turn their ill will into friendship. I think Salmon Chase is a good example. We had our strong differences, but in the end, we have become friends who respect each other.

The Cabinet meeting today was longer than usual. We discussed the fact that General Butler and Admiral Porter are again at loggerheads. I have pretty much decided that Butler must be removed from command. I have been asked to do so by General Grant, who is convinced that Butler lacks the temperament and knowledge of arms to be a good military leader. I agree with Grant.

Author's notes:

In General Order Number 1 of 1865, President Lincoln relieved General Butler from command of the Department of North Carolina and Virginia and ordered him to report to Lowell, Massachusetts. He was replaced by General Edward O. Ord. Butler was retained by the Army until November 1865 with the idea that he might act as military prosecutor of Confederate President Jefferson Davis.

The White House – Saturday, December 31, 1864

The traditional New Year's Day reception has been postponed until January 2nd. At the event the diplomatic corps and cabinet officers and families will be attending. Mother is keeping Mrs. Elizabeth Keckley especially busy making her a gown of pale blue color. Tad asked me why it is that women must have so many new dresses, yet their husbands are content to wear the same old drab black suit? I assured Tad that I have no understanding of the matter, I merely pay the bills.

We established an office to receive subscriptions to capital stock in the Union Pacific Railroad.

Author's notes:

Mrs. Lincoln went to New York City after the president's election and purchased 300 pairs of gloves.

The Union Pacific Railroad was created and funded by the federal government by laws passed in 1862 and 1864. The laws were war measures to forge closer ties with California and Oregon, which otherwise took six months to reach. The railroad remained under partial federal control until the 1890s. The main line started in Council Bluffs, Iowa, and moved west to link up with the Central Pacific Railroad line, which was built eastward from Sacramento. Some 300 miles of track were built in 1865 to 1866 over flat prairies. The Rocky Mountains posed a much more dramatic challenge, but the crews had learned to work at a much faster pace, with 240 miles built in 1867, and 555 miles in 1868 to 1869. The two lines were joined in Utah on May 10, 1869. Interstate 80, built in the 1950s, parallels the main line.

The White House – Monday, January 2, 1865

Today, Mother and I hosted a large New Year's reception at the White House. It was a tedious affair, but she enjoyed it very much. The event began at noon for the diplomats and Cabinet members and families. At 12:30 military officers and the members of the Supreme Court came, followed by the public at 1 P.M. By half past two the jam was terrible.

At this year's event several members of the press from Washington, New York, Philadelphia and Baltimore were present. I asked them to come by tomorrow in the day after the crowds have left for an interview. I would like to inform them of recent events that they may deem to be newsworthy. The atmosphere at the reception was very positive, with many smiling and optimistic faces on hand. Mother is quite the diplomat, and she particularly liked the time spent with the international visitors, particularly the French members of the diplomatic corps.

Author's notes:

The White House received a complaint that members of Congress were not invited to the New Year's reception. A delegation from Kentucky asked the president to appoint General Benjamin Butler to a command that should embrace their state. Lincoln refused to do so. Lincoln wrote to the Kentuckians, "You howled when Butler went to New Orleans. Others howled when he was removed from that command. Somebody has been howling ever since at his assignment to military command. How long will it be before you, who are howling for his assignment to rule Kentucky, will be howling to me to remove him?"

The White House, Tuesday, January 3, 1865

It does seem a bit odd to now be writing "1865" in my new diary. Each year, my law partner and good friend William H. Herndon kindly sends me a leather-bound diary to write my confessions in, and you are the latest one I have received, with genuine appreciation. I frankly did not think I had the patience or discipline to keep a diary, but I am glad that I decided to do so. I find that by writing I can assemble my thoughts in a more organized and logical manner. Recording events also helps me to rethink some of my decisions. I pray that 1865 will be our year of military triumph and that our national energies can then be applied to reconciliation of our peoples and reconstruction of the war's damage. This will be especially important in the South, where destruction to the infrastructure has been devastating. I want to see the economy of the South quickly restored and its citizens again proud to be Americans who all salute the same flag.

At today's Cabinet meeting we discussed the fate of Southern leaders like Robert E. Lee and Jefferson Davis, once the war is ended. Attorney General Speed was sharp and hard on the leading Rebels and would hang them all for treason; so would many in the North. I told the Cabinet that I wish they could simply get away, yet if I let them get away the people will whip me for it. But I wish they would run away out of the land. Too many men have died to have the end result to be hatred and retribution. My natural instincts are to be kind, to show mercy and in that Christian manner inspire others to return to their homes in a positive frame of mind. We can never forget what the Rebels have done, but we can forgive.

Author's notes:

On this date, President Lincoln asked Secretary Seward to find a position for Colonel Philip Figelmessy, former aide-de-camp on the staff of General Julius H. Stahel. Lincoln appointed him consul at Demerara, British Guiana, which was confirmed by the Senate on January 30, 1865. The colonel was a Hungarian citizen who had joined the Union cause in 1861. He had political friends in Pennsylvania who wrote to the president requesting that a suitable position be found for Figelmessy.

The White House – Wednesday, January 4, 1865

Today, I brought into my office a Bible that was kindly presented to me by folks in Philadelphia, whom I visited during a charity affair that raised money for wounded soldiers. It is a very handsome edition. Its pages are edged in gilt and decorated with the words "Faith," "Hope" and "Charity," after I Corinthians 13:13. There the good book reads: "And now abideth faith, hope, charity, these three, but the greatest of these is charity." Hay brought a ruler to me and we measured the volume. It measures about 14.5 inches long by 11 5/8 inches wide. On the cover it says, "Presented to Abraham Lincoln, President of the United States, by the Ladies of the Citizens Volunteer Hospital of Philadelphia." This book has nice-sized letters, making it easier to read than the Bible used for my inauguration, which is only half as large. This is the sixth Bible I have owned and the finest in appearance.

I feel that the Bible passage encouraging "Charity" is the important one for me and the nation to heed. Those words remind me that when this war is ended, "Charity" must be the Christian behavior most needed to heal the wounds of war.

Author's notes:

Mary Lincoln gave the Bible to the Reverend Noyes W. Miner, who lived across the street from the Lincolns in Springfield, Illinois, and who spoke at Lincoln's funeral service. For the decades since, the Miner family kept the Bible in their home. It is engraved on the back, "Mrs. Abraham Lincoln to N.W. Miner, October 15, 1872," The family always displayed the book on a tall Victorian table in the corner of the sitting room in their house in Oyster Bay, New York. In 1994, the Bible was left to the son of Mrs. Sandra Wolcott Willingham (the great-great-great-granddaughter of Miner). William Prescott Wolcott, Jr. kept it on the mantel in his home. In 2018, Mrs. Willingham visited the Lincoln's home and the Lincoln Museum in Springfield, Illinois, and decided to donate the book to the museum. She said the election of President Barack Obama, the first African American president, had moved her to donate the book. She said, "It needs to go back to the country."

The White House – Thursday, January 5, 1865

Illinois Senator Orville Browning came by at my request to discuss the matter of Emily Todd Helm and Martha Todd White, who have cotton to sell. Both are Mary's half-sisters and love her dearly. One of my great regrets of the war is that Emily's husband, Ben Hardin Helm, refused my offer to join the Federal Army after Fort Sumter and joined the Confederate Army instead. The decision ultimately cost him his life. Three members of Mary's family have lost their lives in the Confederate cause. Ben was a marvelous man and was only 32 years of age when he fell at Chickamauga in 1863.

Author's notes:

Emily Todd Helm never remarried and wore widow's black for the rest of her life. She and Mary Lincoln were close friends and loved one another deeply. Supreme Court Justice David Davis said, "I never saw Mr. Lincoln more moved that when he heard of the death of his young brother-in-law, Ben Hardin Helm. I called to see him about 4 o'clock on the 22nd of September and found him in the greatest grief. Lincoln said, "I feel as David of old did when he was told of the death of Absalom". "I saw how grief-stricken he was, so I closed the door and left him alone."

The White House – Friday, January 6, 1865

The weather is colder than usual for this time of year, and all members of the staff and the Cabinet are wearing sweaters in the office today. I received my salary warrant today and put it in my desk drawer. I must remember to deposit it in the bank. The exact amount less taxes came to $1,981.66.

I telegraphed General Grant today, notifying him that Lieutenant Governor Richard T. Jacob of Kentucky, who is staying at the Spotswood House in Richmond under order of General Stephen Burbridge is not to return to Kentucky, but is to be granted leave to pass our lines and come directly here to the White House. Grant telegraphed me asking permission for him to relieve General Butler. This was agreed to. I will now ask General Butler to return directly to Washington to meet with the Committee on the Conduct of the War. It has many questions it wishes to ask the general about recent events within his command, including events at Fort Fisher.

Author's notes:

After President Lincoln's death, four undeposited pay warrants were found in his desk, along with several letters threatening his death.

The White House – Saturday, January 7, 1865

I had a long discussion about religion last evening with Senator Orville Browning and William N. Symington. Symington is convinced that God is on our side in this struggle, and I argued that I do not believe that God is for either side. It is my belief that men of good will, who believe in the same God that we do, are all praying for victory and God does not tip the scales in such matters. Browning and I have often talked about faith and religion. He asked me what I considered myself to be, and I told him that although I was raised a hard-shell or primitive Baptist and now go to a Presbyterian church here in Washington, I think I am more of a Deist than anything else. Many of the Founding Fathers were also Deists. The Bill of Rights shows that they strongly believed in freedom of religion. I have been a lifelong Bible reader and a believer in much of what the good book states, but I am also a born skeptic about religion, as about just about everything else in life. I seek answers to questions and find it much more difficult to ascertain truth about creation and the divinity than about almost anything else. That is the trouble with being a lawyer. You are trained to see two sides of every issue, and then you are required to defend one side against the other. Matters of religion are more than two-sided. I trust that God will be on our side at the end, and that he will understand what we have done was done to save the Union. I am convinced that the freeing of the slaves should be pleasing to a merciful God.

Author's notes:

President Lincoln, while in Washington, was a member of the First Presbyterian Church on 7th Street. He rented Pew Number Twenty each year for $50. It is still there in the seventh row on the left side from the front. It still has the original brass marker with Lincoln's name on it. In 1950, a Navy commodore donated a beautiful stained-glass window to the church. It depicts Lincoln with the pastor and a freed slave. Lincoln is flanked by Clara Barton, the founder of the American Red Cross, and Florence Nightingale, who advised Lincoln's government on the organization of the U.S. Sanitary Commission, which aided wounded soldiers and sailors. It can be seen today on the internet. I invite the reader to take a look.

The White House – Monday, January 9, 1865

Last week I neglected to put in my diary reference to the fact that Mother, Tad and I went to see Avonia Jones in a sold-out production of "Leah" at Grover's Theatre on Saturday evening. The actress is an American who has performed in London and in Australia. Her performance was outstanding. It is easy to see she has been well-trained. She has a commanding presence on the stage. I regret we will not be seeing her performing a Shakespearean role while she remains in America. The program notes that she will be returning to London later this year to perform in "East Lynne" at the new Surrey Theatre. When she played in "Romeo and Juliet" in Cincinnati, she played Juliet and her mother played Romeo. Tad said that he would have liked to see that performance.

Yesterday, by presidential telegram, General Butler was officially relieved from command of the Department of Virginia and North Carolina and was replaced by General Edward O.C. Ord.

Author's notes:

Avonia Stanhope Jones Brooke (born July 12, 1839, in New York City; died October 4, 1867, in New York City) came from a theatrical family. The New York Times reported in her obituary, "As an actress her chief excellence was in the force and fire of her personations; the representation of delicacy and girlishness was not so agreeable to her as that of a hardy and vehement nature. She was tall and robust in frame, with piercing black eyes and agreeable features. Her understanding of mimic character was quick and thorough, and her intellectual attainments of a high order. Few actresses at the present time have had so much experience and received so much praise at so early an age."

The White House – Tuesday, January 10, 1865

The first reception of the season took place Monday evening at the Executive Mansion. I was dressed in a new black suit and wore white kid gloves until I began shaking hands. Mother stood on my right and on my left stood Deputy Marshall Phillips. We stood just inside the door to the Blue or Oval Room. The affair lasted longer than we had anticipated. Mother was particularly pleased to spend time with the British and French ambassadors and their wives. About 11 P.M. I stopped receiving visitors.

At midnight I wrapped an old shawl around my shoulders and went to the War Department accompanied by a White House guard. There were important telegraphic messages to be reviewed and sent. I then retired and went to bed. It was a very long day. My right hand is still sore from shaking so many hands. It occurred to me that our vice presidents have very little to do other than preside over the Senate. Perhaps shaking hands at official receptions could be added to their list of obligations. I could have used some help in that department this evening!

Author's notes:

Earlier in the day, President Lincoln declared the port of St. Albans, Vermont, open to commerce.

The White House – Wednesday, January 11, 1865

At 9 A.M. this morning I had a short meeting with Senator O.M. Browning and W.N. Symington. Symington is being given a special pass allowing him to go to Richmond for exchange purposes.

Secretaries Welles and Stanton then arrived to bring me up-to-date on joint Navy-Army plans to again attack Fort Fisher at Wilmington, North Carolina. This is the last Confederate port needed to be taken by force. We will go into action within just a few days. The fort has proven to be very well-defended in the past. Both men have expressed high hopes that this time we will prevail. There will be soldiers, sailors and marines involved in the effort backed by powerful naval gunfire. Admiral David D. Porter will be commanding the fleet, and Major General Alfred Terry's amphibious assault will hopefully seize the fort. Wilmington has been a busy port for the rebels and if conquered will deprive the South of vital commerce once and for all. It has been a long struggle to implement General in Chief Winfield Scott's Anaconda Plan of choking off war supplies by boycott. Let's hope we succeed at Wilmington.

Author's notes:

The Second Battle of Fort Fisher was fought from January 13 to January 15. It was an important Union victory. Wilmington ceased to be of use to the Confederates as a port to receive military supplies from abroad. Confederate Admiral Raphael Semmes wrote after the war, "Our ports were now hermetically sealed. The Anaconda had, at last, wound his fatal folds around us."

The White House – Friday, January 13, 1865

Yesterday morning, Tad warned Mother and me that Friday the 13th is an unlucky day and that we should expect the worst on this day. I pointed out to our son that this is an unfounded superstition, but got little support from Mrs. Lincoln, who takes the 13th seriously. It is her strong belief that it is an unlucky day. I spoke to Hay and Nicolay today about the date and neither of them is superstitious.

For Mrs. Maria Davis, Friday the 13th is a lucky day, because on this day I granted a conditional pardon for her son.

Author's notes:

The 13th day occurs on a Friday in the Gregorian Calendar. It occurs during any month that begins on a Sunday. It happens at least once a year but can occur up to three times in the same year. The irrational fear of the number 13 has been given a scientific name: "Triskaidekaphobia." Fear of Friday the 13th is called Paraskevidekariaphobia, from the Greek words Paraskeví (meaning 'Friday") and Dekatreís, (meaning "thirteen.")

The superstition surrounding this day may have arisen in the Middle Ages, from the story of the Last Supper and crucifixion, in which there were 13 individuals present in the upper room on the 13th of Nisan or Maundy Thursday, the night before the death of Christ on Good Friday. Nisan in the Torah is called the month of the Aviv. It is the first month of the ecclesiastical year and the 7th month of the civil year. Maundy Thursday is the Christian holy day falling on the Thursday before Easter. It commemorates the washing of the feet and Last Supper of Jesus Christ with his apostles.

The White House – Saturday, January 14, 1865

Eight elderly Baptist preachers from the Baltimore area of Maryland stopped by this morning to wish me well. We spent quite a bit of time reminiscing about the songs I had sung as a lad in church. I told them that we had two song books: Dupuy's "Hymns and Spiritual Songs," and "Dr. Watt's Hymns." My voice was hardly the best among the church members, but I do recall our small choir singing "Am I a Soldier of the Cross, A follower of the Lamb," "Did my Savior Bleed" and "Alas." That particular song was composed by Isaac Watts. I recall singing it with Dennis Hanks, who had one of the world's least melodious voices. One song that used to be sung at the end of a service was "Oh to Grace how Great a Debtor." My father liked to hear a song with the lines, "There was a Romish lady, Brought up in Popery." It was never sung in church, but Dennis would sing it for my father at the drop of a hat. They both loved that odd tune.

Author's notes;

"The Romish Lady," a blatantly anti-Roman Catholic narrative, depicts a woman burned at the stake by the Church for secretly reading the Bible and renouncing the worship of idols. "Am I a Soldier of the Cross," "Alas" and "Did My Savior Bleed?" are songs by Isaac Watts that were sung by Lincoln in his youth. He also sang, "How Tedious and Tasteless the Hour," by John Newton.

Dupuy's Hymns and Spiritual Songs by Rev. Starke Dupey was published by John P. Morton & Company, Louisville, Kentucky, 1843.

Isaac Watts (July 17, 1674, to November 25, 1748) was a Congregational hymn writer, theologian and logician. He is credited with writing some 750 hymns. Many are still in use today and have been translated into numerous languages. He was born in Southampton, England. One of his first verses was, "A little mouse for want of stairs, ran up a rope to say his prayers." His most famous songs are "When I survey the Wondrous Cross," "Joy to the World," and "Our God, Our Help in Ages Past."

The White House – Monday, January 16, 1865

Congressman Samuel Hooper of Massachusetts kindly brought Professor Jean Louis Agassiz to visit Mary and me yesterday – a most remarkable man. Mother and he hit it off immediately. He kindly presented me with four volumes of his work, "Natural History of the United States," which I intend to donate to the Library of Congress. He told me that he has six or seven more volumes still to write on the subject. Mother was particularly interested in his descriptions of the last Ice Age on North America.

Later in the day Secretary Welles came by to announce that Fort Fisher has finally been conquered by our amphibious forces, according to a message received from Rear Admiral Porter. He message was short and sweet. It read, "Fort Fisher is ours!"

Today I learned that Edward Everett died Sunday morning. He was a good man and a good friend. He will be missed by all who knew him and whoever had heard him speak publicly. He was a man of wisdom and grace.

Author's notes:

Secretary of State Seward sent out a message to government offices that Edward Everett (April 11, 1794, to January 15, 1865) died at 4 A.M. on Sunday. Everett was the 20th U.S. secretary of state, a U.S. senator, the 15th governor of Massachusetts, a member of the U.S. House of Representatives and U.S. ambassador to the United Kingdom. He was considered the greatest orator of the antebellum and Civil War eras. At Gettysburg cemetery he spoke for over two hours before President Lincoln delivered his famous two-minute Gettysburg Address.

The White House – Tuesday, January 17, 1865

Yesterday afternoon, Mrs. Albert T. Bledsoe, the wife of Confederate Colonel Bledsoe, came by to see me. She is a former neighbor from Springfield, Illinois. Albert attended the U.S. Military Academy with both Robert E. Lee and Jefferson Davis. He has taught college and practiced law, including before the Supreme Court. Before the war he authored "Liberty and Slavery," making a case for the righteousness of slavery. Albert believes that slavery laws ensure proper social order. He must have choked when he read the Emancipation Proclamation.

After serving as a colonel in the Confederate Army, and then as assistant secretary of war, Davis sent him to London to help influence British public opinion in favor of the Southern cause. She asked for a pass to be allowed South to visit her family living there. I granted it to her and we both prayed that peace will come soon to the nation.

Author's notes:

After the Civil War Albert Bledsoe moved back to the United States and published the "Southern Review." He remained the epitome of an unreconstructed Southerner. He argued that secession was a constitutional right before the War of 1861. He died on December 8, 1877, in Alexandria, Virginia, at the age of 68. His daughter was the well-known author Sophia Bledsoe Herrick.

The White House – Wednesday, January 18, 1865

Yesterday I laid before the Senate a treaty with the Chippewa Indians of Michigan as signed by the chiefs and headmen of the Chippewas of Saginaw, Swan Creek and Black River. It was signed by H.J Alvord, special commissioner, and D.C. Leach, U.S. Indian agent.

Secretary Welles and two members of the Navy Department presented to the Cabinet a comprehensive review of the second Battle of Fort Fisher. It had a very well-organized plan of action which resulted in a solid victory. Wilmington was an important port for the Rebels, and the loss of it will make their cause ever more hopeless.

I wrote to Francis P. Blair, Sr, Esq., advising him that he may say to Jefferson Davis that I have "constantly been, am now, and shall continue, ready to receive any agent whom he, or any other influential person, now resisting the national authority, may informally send to me, with the view of securing peace to the people of our one common country."

Author's notes:

On this date the Lincoln wrote to George C. Miller, Esq., a manufacturer of agricultural instruments at Cincinnati, to thank him for a cane he sent to the president on December 30, 1864. Miller wrote, "The cane is composed of many sections and pieces as there were states and of a very beautiful Curled White Oak. Not of the kind that could be split into rails and wedge conveniently. The sections are not bound together by a rope of sand but with a rod of iron. It is a measure emblematical of what I hope our nation will be before your second term expires."

The White House – Thursday, January 19, 1865

I instructed Benjamin Franklin Irwin to deposit in the Springfield Marine Bank $182.83, the balance of principal plus interest on my Springfield bond, and to withdraw $50.88 to pay my local property taxes. Irwin handles all of my financial affairs in Illinois and is one of my closest friends.

Today I asked General Grant "if our son, Robert, without embarrassment to you, or detriment to the service, go into your military family with some nominal rank, with me, and not the public furnishing his necessary needs." Mother is against Robert serving for fear of his death. I believe he will be relatively safe in a headquarters position.

Author's notes:

On January 19th, President Lincoln received Baron Nicholas G. de Wetterstedt, as minister plenipotentiary from Sweden.

On January 21, General Grant telegraphed President Lincoln suggesting that Robert Lincoln join his headquarters staff with rank of captain.

The White House – Friday, January 20, 1865

Today I interviewed Mrs. Mary E. Morton regarding the seizure of her home and furnishings by the provost marshal. I wrote to General Joseph Reynolds to handle the matter. It is a case of a Northern woman whose husband left her to join the Rebels and who has not returned. I question whether the property, which may belong to the wife, should be seized and used for military purposes. If she is a traitor, she should be arrested, and the matter left to the courts and not the military. My sense is that she has been wronged by the husband and need not be also wronged by the government. I rely upon Reynolds to solve the problem.

At the Cabinet meeting, Secretary Stanton gave the members a summary of his recent trip to visit the liberated city of Savannah, Georgia.

I attended ceremonies of the U.S. Christian Commission in the House of Representatives.

Author's notes:

The U.S. Christian Commission was an organization that furnished supplies, medical services and religious literature to Union troops during the Civil War. It distributed more than $6 million worth of goods and supplies in hospitals, camps, prisons and battlefields.

The White House – Saturday, January 21, 1865

I informed Robert that General Grant has agreed that he shall be serving as a captain in his headquarters company. Next week he will be visiting a Georgetown tailor, who was recommended by General Halleck, to be fitted for his uniforms. Secretary Welles on behalf of all the members of the Cabinet kindly purchased a Model 1860 staff officer's sword with scabbard as their thoughtful gift for Robert. It is marked "Emerson and Silver, Trenton, N.J. - 1864." The 35-inch blade is of high-quality Solingen German steel. I know that he will be pleasantly surprised and honored to receive it from them.

Seward brought me the documents to sign that we shall release certifying the appointment of C.F. Mebius as consul at San Francisco for the Electorate of Hesse Cassel.

Mother wore a heavy black corded silk dress, elaborately trimmed with a shawl of white point lace, and a large hat composed of black velvet and lace for her afternoon reception.

Author's notes:

On the afternoon of Sunday, January 22, 1865, President Lincoln conferred with Governor Reuben E. Fenton of New York about filling troop quotas for the state. Fenton was the 22nd governor of the state. He was a U.S. Senator from 1869 to 1875. He had previously served as a member of the U.S. House of Representative. He was known as the "Soldier's Friend" for his efforts to help returning Civil War veterans. He worked to removed tuition charges for public education, helped to establish six schools for training teachers, and signed the charter for Cornell University. He was a Democrat who helped found the Republican Party.

The White House – Monday, January 23, 1865

Today I spent much of the day reviewing 45 courts-martial cases. It is tedious and depressing work, but only I can do it. Andrew Johnson asked that he be allowed to continue in Tennessee until its state government is re-inaugurated. The Cabinet suggested that Johnson return to Washington to take his vice-presidential oath on the same day as I do. I have ordered him to be here on March 4th to be sworn in. I regret that I never fully utilized the talents of Vice-President Hamlin. He is a fine man who never complains and when asked always gives me sound advice. I must do a better job employing the time and talents of Andrew Johnson once he has taken Hamlin's place.

Author's notes:

In just a few days before he had been in office for three years, President Andrew Johnson was impeached by the House of Representatives, on February 24, 1868. There were 11 articles of impeachment. The primary charge was violation of the Tenure in Office Act passed in March 1867, over his veto. Specifically, he had removed Edwin Stanton, the secretary of war – whom the act was largely designed to protect. Earlier, Johnson had suspended Stanton and appointed General Ulysses Grant as secretary of war ad interim. The U.S. Senate failed to convict him on the articles. Johnson then served out the remainder of his term of office. He was elected to the U.S. Senate from Tennessee and served from March 4, 1875, until July 31, 1875, when he died at age 65.

The White House – Wednesday, January 25, 1865

I wrote to the president of the Burns Club of Washington, D.C., on the occasion of the anniversary of the poet's 106th birth date. Willie and Tad's tutor, Alexander Williamson, a clerk in the Second Auditor's Office, asked me to attend the group's annual dinner. I wrote this to the members, "I cannot frame a toast to Burns. I can say nothing worthy of his generous heart and transcending genius. Thinking of what he has said, I cannot say anything which seems worth saying." Burns is my favorite poet, and I never tire of reading his words or reciting some of them from memory. I am now thinking of these words of his: "Man's inhumanity to man. Makes countless thousands mourn." No truer words can describe how I feel about our present civil strife. I love the lines, "Princes and lords are but the breath of kings, An honest man's the noblest work of God." But the words most dear to my heart are these:

"But to see her was to love her, Love but her, and love forever. Had we never loved sae kindly, had we never loved, sae blindly, never met – or never parted – We had ne'er been brokenhearted. "

Mother likes these lines from Auld Lang Syne: "For auld lang syne, my dear, For auld lang syne, We'll take a cup o' kindness yet, For auld lang syne."

I regret not being able to join the Burns lovers at their meeting. Maybe next year I'll be able to attend.

Author's notes:

On this date President Lincoln wrote to Secretary of War Stanton regarding Major Leopold Blumenberg of Baltimore, "He should not be dismissed in a way that disgraces and ruins him without a hearing." On this day he reviewed 30 courts-martial cases.

The White House – Thursday, January 26, 1865

I interviewed a committee representing working women who are stationed at the Philadelphia Arsenal. They had many serious complaints about working conditions and are fearful for their lives because they believe there could be explosions within the buildings where they work. They said that repeated complaints have not been taken seriously by the managers there. I've asked Secretary Stanton to get personally involved in this matter. I instructed him to establish a committee to visit the arsenal and to report back to me within 30 days with their recommendations. I thanked the ladies for all they have done to bring victory. I admire their spirit and appreciate their contributions to the war effort. I am concerned for their safety and am counting on Stanton to protect them from harm.

Author's notes:

At the start of the Civil War the U.S. Army had 2,283 guns on hand, but only about 10% of these were field artillery pieces. By the end of the war, the Army had 3,325 guns of which 53% were field pieces. The Army reported as "supplied to the Army during the war" the following quantities: 7,892 guns, 6,335,295 artillery projectiles, 2,862,177 rounds of fixed artillery ammunition, 45,258 tons of lead metal, and 13,320 tons of gunpowder.

The White House – Friday, January 27, 1865

This morning about 300 members of the U.S. Christian Commission, who are attending an annual meeting of their fine organization, came to the White House. I responded to a speech given by the Reverend George H. Stuart, chairman of the group. On Monday of this week I had responded to remarks by the Reverend William Studdards of the Philadelphia Sanitary Fair. It is remarkable to consider how many noble men and women are doing important voluntary work to help the war effort. Studdards presented me with a beautiful vase which held skeleton leaves from the Gettysburg cemetery battlefield. I was reminded by them that it was at Gettysburg that I was joined by the late Edward Everett to speak of the brave men who fell and were wounded in that great battle. Everette was what I call a truly great American patriot.

I wrote to Secretary Stanton about the case of Captain Gilbert E. Winters, who was ordered dismissed from the Army for inefficiency in handling commissary accounts under his jurisdiction. I personally know the captain and believe the man should be given another chance. I asked that the court martial decision against him be set aside upon him making good upon the accounts. I consider him an honorable man who made some mistakes. He should be allowed to serve the nation. I expect him to do a good job upon his return to duty.

Author's notes:

Lincoln said to the members of the U.S. Christian Commission, "We have been only doing our duty my friends, whatever we have been able to do together. You owe me no thanks for what I have done for the country, whatever that may be - and I owe none, to you. We cannot repay the soldiers."

The White House – Saturday, January 28, 1865

I spent several hours with Francis P. Blair, Sr. discussing possible future peace negotiations with Confederate President Jefferson Davis. Blair and Davis have known each other for years and trust one another. When they recently met, Blair gave Davis a letter from me in which I refer to "our common country." I used the words because Davis' recent letter referred to "the two countries." I have endeavored over the past years to favor negotiation rather than continuing the bloodletting, but to date, all my efforts have been in vain. My sense of the matter is that Davis now surely knows he cannot sustain the war effort indefinitely and is being pressured from all sides within his government to end the fighting. Yet while talks may come to fruition, my fear is that they may again lead to nothing but bitter disappointment for both parties. On Monday I will send a letter to General Grant titled "Peace Mission," in which I will invite Southern representatives of Davis to come within our lines for purposes of an informal peace discussion.

Official duties precluded my attending Mother's reception in the White House this afternoon.

Author's notes:

The president sent Major Eckert to the Headquarters of the Army of the James to begin arrangements for Confederate Vice President A.H. Stephens, former Justice of the U.S. Supreme Court John A. Campbell, and former U.S. Senator Robert M.T. Hunter of Virginia to pass through military lines for the purpose of an informal conference on the basis of terms outlined by President Lincoln.

The White House – Monday, January 30, 1865

Last evening Mother and I went to the House of Representatives to attend the third anniversary meeting of the U.S. Sanitary Commission. I asked George H. Stuart, chairman of the Commission, to request that the famed Cincinnati soloist, Philip Phillips, sing "Your Mission" for a second time. I asked George not to say that I called for it. Mother loves that song. Today a messenger brought to Mother in the White House a small singing book, autographed by Phillips in which he wrote, "A Little Singing Book for your little boy. It contains the song, 'Your Mission.'He added,"I have given two hearty votes for the president during the past five years."

Author's notes:

On this date, Lincoln telegraphed Major General Edward O.C. Ord to "pass through the lines Mssrs. Stevens, Hunter and Campbell to Fortress Monroe under military precautions as you may deem prudent, giving them protection and comfortable quarters while there. Let none of this have any effect upon your military movement or plans."

The White House – Tuesday, January 31, 1865

At a meeting of the full Cabinet, I asked Secretary of State Seward to arrange to meet with three Confederate peace commissioners at Fortress Monroe and to confer informally with them. He personally knows each of the men. The Cabinet has been sworn to secrecy about the meeting. I do not want the press to be aware of it as it could only raise "false hopes" if we cannot get an agreement that meets our requirements for peace. I remain skeptical but feel obligated to give peace a chance.

I sent to Seward copies of the documents that have gone back and forth between me and Davis on the matter. No meeting is to begin until Major Eckert receives a signed document from the commissioners stipulating that the meetings are to be informal.

Author's notes:

On this date, President Lincoln thanked Congressman Samuel Cox of Ohio for a copy of his recent speech. Lincoln wrote, "I sought it for humor, said to be in it; but while it meets expectations in that respect, it has a far higher merit."

The White House – Wednesday, February 1, 1865

Today was a red-letter day. I approved the resolution submitting the 13th Amendment to the states for ratification. I could only do so because yesterday 13 House Democrats switched sides and voted to approve the measure. It is a much more important document than the Emancipation Proclamation because that only freed slaves in the disloyal states. As a war measure it might have been revoked in times of peace or by a future president for any reason. The amendment is a King's cure for all the evils of slavery. My home state of Illinois was the first to ratify the amendment.

Author's notes:

The XIII Amendment reads: "Section I. Neither slavery nor involuntary servitude, except as a punishment for crime whereof the party shall have been duly convicted, shall exist within the United States or any place subject to its jurisdiction." Section II reads, "Congress shall have power to enforce this article by appropriate legislation." Ten months later the needed 27th state ratified the amendment.
Ironically, it was Georgia.

The White House – Friday, Feb 3, 1865

Yesterday, I took the train to Annapolis, Maryland, and from there sailed on the Thomas Collyer to Hampton Roads and then landed at Fortress Monroe. Before leaving Washington, I telegraphed General Grant to let nothing transpiring vis-à-vis possible peace discussions to change, hinder or delay his military movements.I asked Secretary Seward to join us in our meeting. Today I met with the Confederate commissioners for four hours aboard the U.S Steam Transport River Queen. No papers were exchanged or produced. The conference was friendly and informal and useful. They were not willing to admit that they would never consent to reunion, and yet they equally omitted to declare that they would never so consent. They seemed to desire a postponement of that question, and the adoption first, which might or might not lead to reunion. We believed that could only lead to an indefinite postponement. We viewed their suggestions as leading to an armistice or truce, and we advised that we cannot agree to a cessation or suspension of hostilities, except upon the disbanding of the insurgent forces and the restoration of the national authority. Thus, the conference ended without result. I plan within a few days to render a report to the Congress so it may understand what was and was not accomplished by our brief meeting.

Vice President Alexander Stephens, who is president pro tempore of the Confederate Senate, had a personal favor to ask of me. His nephew, Lieutenant John Stephens is a federal prisoner being held on Johnson Island, Ohio. He asked if he could be sent home. I ordered his release today.

Author's notes:

On February 10, Lincoln wrote to Hon. Alexander Stephens: "According to our agreement, your nephew, Lieut. Stephens, goes to you bearing this note. Please in return, to select and to send to me, that officer of the same rank, imprisoned at Richmond, whose physical condition most urgently requires his release. Respectfully, A. Lincoln."

The White House – Saturday, February 4, 1865

At 7:30 A.M. I left Annapolis, Maryland, for the White House and a Cabinet meeting to discuss the recent conference with Confederate commissioners, following an overnight trip from Hampton Roads, Virginia, on the River Queen. I ordered that Lieutenant John Stephens (CSA) be sent from Johnson's Island military prison to the White House, where I will give him a letter allowing him to return to his home as an exchange prisoner. I was pleased that I could accommodate the wishes of his uncle, who is trying hard to arrange terms of peace on behalf of the Rebels. Unfortunately, Jefferson Davis believes in miracles, and none are going to happen to change the outcome of the struggle!

The full Cabinet met to learn about our recent meeting with the three Confederate commissioners. I told them that I was dubious about ever getting a fruitful outcome. The meeting however, did convince me that the Confederates are at the end of their rope and must soon realize that further combat and death can earn them nothing but ruination. Secretary Seward gave his view on the matter to the Cabinet and echoed my thinking that the fact that they came to Hampton Roads demonstrates that they are at their wit's end yet are unable to accept defeat.

Stanton was asked to telegraph General Grant, informing him that "Nothing transpired, or transpiring with the three gentlemen from Richmond is to cause any change, hinderance or delay of your military plans or operations."

Author's notes:

From 1 to 3 P.M. Mary Lincoln held a reception in the White House.
The president arrived late but did get to shake as many hands as possible.

The White House – Monday, February 6, 1865

Last evening, I read to the Cabinet a proposal for a joint resolution of Congress, whereby a payment of $400 million would be distributed among the 16 states pro rata upon their slave populations in return for cessation if all resistance to national authority by April 1, 1865. No decisions were reached, but each man was asked to give my suggestion due consideration before I bring it to the Congress.

Today, Stanton and General Halleck and two staff members reviewed with us the happenings in Bamberg County, South Carolina, where on the 3rd of February Federal troops under the command of Major General Francis Preston Blair, Jr. defeated the forces of Major General Lafayette McLaws at the Salkehatchie River. The engagement delayed Sherman's forces for just one day as it continued its march toward the state capital of Columbia. The North had roughly 5,000 men involved to the Rebels' 1,200. Halleck noted that this battle involved men from Missouri, Ohio, New Jersey, Wisconsin, Illinois and Indiana. It demonstrates how many states are serving in Sherman's victorious Army. The Rebel brigades came from Georgia, North and South Carolina.

Author's notes:

In 1876, men from nearby communities reburied the Confederate dead from Rivers Bridge in a mass grave about a mile from the battlefield and began an annual tradition commemorating the battle. The Rivers Bridge Memorial Association eventually obtained the battlefield and in 1945 turned the site over to South Carolina for a state park.

The White House – Tuesday, February 7, 1865

Yesterday I interviewed the Committee of the Board of Supervisors of New York regarding troop quotas. The board is to examine into proper quotas and credits for the various states.

At 3 P.M. a good-sized reception was held at the White House, including many foreign diplomats. During the reception I unveiled an oil painting by William Tolman Carlton that was sent to Mother and me by William Lloyd Garrison. It is called "Waiting for the Hour" and shows a large gathering of slaves, waiting for midnight on December 31, 1862, for New Year's Day of 1863 – the date when the Emancipation Proclamation went into effect. Garrison thoughtfully noted in his letter, which came with the painting, that I was "the most fitting person in the world to receive it." Mother wishes that it be hung in my office, the room where I signed the proclamation. I must remember to send a suitably appreciative letter to Mr. Garrison, who has done so much to call attention to the evils of slavery during his lifetime.

Author's notes:

After the assassination, the painting disappeared from the White House. An earlier version of the painting was purchased and has hung in the Lincoln Bedroom for many years. To this day, many black churches celebrate Watch Night on New Year's Eve with praise music.

The White House – Wednesday, February 8, 1865

Today I transmitted to Congress a copy of a note of the 4th instant addressed by J. Hume Burnley, Esq., her Britannic Majesty's chargé d' affaires to the secretary of state, relative to a sword which it is proposed to present to Captain Henry S. Stellwagen, Commanding the United States frigate Constellation, as a mark of gratitude for his services to the British brigantine Mersey. The expediency of sanctioning the acceptance of the gift, I submitted to Congress' consideration.

The note we received from Burnley reads, "Her majesty's consul at St. Thomas has reported the friendly and efficient assistance given by Captain Stellwagen to the brigantine Mersey, which he fell in with in a state of imminent peril from the effects of a severe hurricane. Stellwagen went on board and most liberally supplied the wants of ship and crew, thus enabling her master to bring her in safety to St. Thomas." With the note came a sword of honor as a mark of their gratitude with a request that the captain may be permitted to accept it. I have asked that Stellwagen be asked to come to the White House for a presentation here with Navy Secretary Welles asked to attend, along with the British representative.

Late this afternoon a telegram confirmed a Federal victory in Dinwiddie Country, Virginia, where from February 5 to 7 an estimated 35,000 Union forces defeated about one-third that number of Rebels. The U.S. forces were led by Brigadier General David Gregg's cavalry.

Author's notes:

Confederate Brigadier General John Pegam was killed in the action on February 6th. Union troops extended their siege works to the Vaughn Road crossing of Hatcher's Run. The Confederates kept the Boydton Plank Road open but were forced to extend their thinning lines. The Civil War Trust has acquired and preserved 387 acres of the battlefield in four different transactions dating back to 1990.

The White House – Thursday, February 9, 1865

My good friend and law partner William Herndon sent me a checkerboard and a small box of checkers. I plan to play tonight with Tad. He had a set but lost some of the pieces. My expectation is that he may become a good player. He is not a fast player but is a steady and thoughtful one. My father was a good player in his day. The best player I ever challenged was probably Joshua Speed. He had a quick mind and seemed to always be two moves ahead of me in his thinking. I once had a client who owed me ten dollars and admitted to me that he could not pay me right away. He made checkerboards using two colors of wood, a light brown and a dark brown. We negotiated and I came home with five dollars and one of his checkerboards as payment for the balance due. I always thought that I'd made a fair bargain. That checkerboard lasted for years, whereas five dollars would only last a few days at most. I wonder whatever became of it. All the checkers that came with it were made of a rose-colored wood. The set that Herndon gave me reminds me of it, because its checkers are almost the very same color. Herndon is a very thoughtful man. I miss his company and his fine sense of humor. A rare commodity, particularly in times of war.

I received a delegation today from the New York Young Men's Republican Union. Their obvious enthusiasm attests to the strength of the party in their state.

Author's notes:

On this date John Hay helped the president prepare copies of all documents related to the recent meeting of the president with Southern commissioners at Hampton Roads, Virginia. They were sent to the Congress on February 10, 1865.

The White House – Friday, February 10, 1865

A long Cabinet meeting and a very good one. I like it when we get differing opinions on a subject and good argumentation on the various points of disagreement. When lawyers disagree it can be troubling; however, when doctors disagree, it may prove fatal! After the meeting, Senator Garrett Davis of Kentucky came by to discuss the release of certain prisoners of war with whom he is acquainted, or whose cases he has become familiar with. In the border states, like Kentucky, it is common to have men in the same families serving on both sides of the conflict. Davis is a very serious man and I respect his views. Garrett opposed secession before the war and has been helpful in convincing Kentuckians to stand by the Union.

Author's notes:

On this date the president sent to Rear Admiral Porter copies of a joint resolution of Congress thanking him and the officers and men under his command for their gallantry and good conduct in the capture of Fort Fisher.

The White House – Saturday, February 11, 1865

The day began with a long walk after breakfast with Mother and Tad. We discussed the fact that tomorrow I will be a year older. But am I a year wiser? That is the important question. I was born on February 12th in Hardin County, Kentucky, and was therefore the first United States president born outside of the 13 original colonies. Mother asked me what I wanted for my birthday and I told her that it would please me greatly if the White House baker could make me a chocolate cake with vanilla icing on it. Tad agreed that such a gift would suit him, too.

Later, I interviewed George T. Hammond, the editor of the Newport Daily News. I gave him a card addressed "To the head of any department," which will allow him quick access to any official of the government for purpose of gathering information for his writings. I have read some of his reports and they are thorough and highly interesting. He does not pull his punches and is fair in his news making. I wish more reporters were like him.

Author's notes:

Later in the afternoon the President joined Mrs. Lincoln in hosting a reception honoring General and Mrs. Ulysses S. Grant. Lincoln's law partner sent him a check for $133 drawn on the First National Bank of Springfield, Illinois, as Lincoln's half of current collections from their law firm.

The White House – Monday, February 13, 1865

I don't feel a year older, but I surely am. Sunday we all enjoyed the baker's delicious chocolate cake with the thick white icing, especially Tad, whose appetite for cake is prodigious. Mother asked Secretary Stanton if she could arrange for a military choir to come over to the White House on Sunday to serenade the family, which he did. They sang Dixie for us and some other tunes that we enjoyed very much. The short concert ended with a powerful rendition of the Battle Hymn of the Republic. I particularly like the verse that goes, "In the beauty of the lilies, Christ was born across the sea, With a glory in his bosom that transfigures you and me: As he died to make men holy, let us die to make men free, While God is marching on." The chorus included three Irish tenors whose voices when singing those lines brought tears to my eyes. How remarkable it is that Julia Ward Howe was sufficiently inspired to compose those stirring words in just one evening, as I seem to recall. Remarkable! And God bless her. The song inspires the men probably more than any they hear. It is particularly powerful when trumpets and bugles are introduced as happened yesterday.

Author's notes:

Julia Ward Howe's poem appeared in the February 1, 1862 edition of The Atlantic Monthly magazine on the front cover. The lyrics Lincoln admired the most are from the fourth verse. The tune used for her poem is from "John Brown's Body," which was first written by a South Carolinian by the name of William Steffe before the war. Julia Ward Howe and her husband, Samuel Howe, a Boston political activist, were friends of John Brown and supported him financially. The name of Steffe's original music was "Say, Brothers," published by Steffe in 1853. It was a popular tune sung at revival meetings. It was a Camp Meeting Song of Invitation, later published in the Hymn and Tune Book of the Methodist Episcopal Church South, Nashville, Tennessee, in 1889.

The White House – Tuesday, February 14, 1865

Last evening Michigan's Senator Zachariah Chandler and his wife, Letitia, were our dinner guests. He is a self-made man, who has been a strong supporter as well as a powerful political leader in his state. He has been a helpful member of the Committee on the Conduct of the War. He was one of the founders of the Republican Party, whose radical wing he has long dominated as a lifelong abolitionist. Letitia is a very smart woman, a native of Baltimore.

Today I sent communications to the Senate and House of Representatives relating to international exhibitions to be held in Bergen, Norway, during the summer and in Oporto, Portugal next August. Each invites American manufacturers to display their merchandise and industrial products. These are events requiring no governmental expenditures, which can benefit American businesses. The invitations are positive signs that foreign governments consider the United States capable of trade considerations while being engaged in a civil conflict. I hope that some U.S. companies send representatives to call attention to their products and services.

Author's notes:

Senator Chandler was mayor of Detroit. He served as a four-term U.S. senator from Michigan and served as secretary of state under President Ulysses S. Grant. As secretary of the interior he reformed the Bureau of Indian Affairs, the Pension Bureau and the Land Office, the Patent Office and banned Indian attorneys.

The White House – Wednesday, February 15, 1865

Mrs. Elizabeth Hutter of Philadelphia and a committee of like-minded women met with me to discuss the vitally important matter of providing care for the war's widows and orphans, who are numerous, and many are now in desperate need. When the war finally ends there will be thousands of impoverished mothers and children requiring succor. I believe a separate department of government will need to be established just for the purpose of extending just such aid.

I suspended at least 20 executions ordered by courts-martial and will continue to do so. As the war nears its bitter end it is better that men who have sinned be forgiven than killed. There has been no shortage of killing by the enemy; let's not have more of it by our own men killing fellow soldiers and sailors.

Author's notes:

In Lincoln's Second Inaugural Address of March 4, 1865, he said in closing, "To care for him who shall have borne the battle, and for his widow and his orphan – to do all which may achieve a just, and a lasting peace, among ourselves, and with all nations."

The White House – Thursday, February 16, 1865

I released a Proclamation Convening the Senate to Extra Session to take place on the 4th of March.

Today I issued a pardon for Edwin Sprague, a young man who had deserted the 30th Maine Army Volunteers and immediately enlisted in the Navy, where he has served honorably ever since. I asked that upon his completion of naval service that he be pardoned for his earlier offense. His reputation is vouched for by U.S. Senator Farwell of Maine, who took office in October last upon my naming Senator William Fessenden to become secretary of the treasury. He has told me that he will soon resign from the Senate and return to running his successful insurance company.

Author's notes:

On March 3, 1865, Senator Nathan A. Farwell resigned his U.S. Senate seat and returned to his lucrative insurance business in Maine.

The White House – Friday, February 17, 1865

This was an especially proud day for me because at noon I signed my son Robert's commission as a captain in the U.S. Army. He is now officially assigned to serve as an aide on General Grant's staff and will commence his duties tomorrow. He looked splendid in his new uniform. Mother is apprehensive but seems convinced that he will be safe in a headquarters assignment rather than with the troops in action.

I received Washington McLean, the publisher of the Cincinnati Enquirer. I gave him a card which he is to give to Secretary Stanton, who is to authorize the release of General Roger Pryor (CSA), a former U.S. Congressman from Virginia. McLean is an impressive man. He has been the chairman of the Ohio Democratic Party and has been a stalwart defender of the Union cause. His newspaper has been supportive of our war efforts in every possible way, for which I am grateful.

Author's notes:

Washington McLean and his brother, S.B.W. McLean, acquired a share in the Cincinnati Enquirer and became partners with editor James J. Faran. In the 1860s McLean bought out Faran's share and in 1872 sold a half interest in the newspaper to his son, John. In 1881 John bought out his father's share and in 1905 purchased the Washington Post. In 1882 Washington McLean moved to Washington, D.C., but kept a legal residence in Cincinnati. He made large investments in Washington real estate and greatly expanded his wealth. He died on December 8, 1890, in Washington. His wife, Mary McLean died on December 9, 1900, in her 72nd year and was interred with him in a mausoleum in Washington's Rock Creek Cemetery.

Roger Atkinson Pryor left the House of Representatives when the Civil War began and received a colonel's commission in the 3rd Virginia Regiment of the Confederate Army. He was promoted to brigadier general on April 16, 1862. He fought in the Peninsula Campaign and at Second Manassas, when he temporarily served under Stonewall Jackson. In 1863 he resigned his commission and enlisted as a private and scout under General Fitzhugh Lee. He was captured and confined to Fort Lafayette in New York as a suspected spy. He was later released on parole by President Lincoln and returned to Virginia, where he abandoned the Confederate cause. He moved to New York City and established a law firm with Benjamin Butler of Boston. Pryor became active in Democratic politics in New York and was appointed a judge of the New York Court of Common Pleas, where he served until 1894. In 1912 he was appointed as official referee by the appellate division of the New York State Supreme Court and served until his death on March 14, 1919.

The White House – Saturday, February 18, 1865

Yesterday I conferred with Senator O.H. Browning concerning the case of John Y. Beall, who has been charged with violating rules of war and sentenced to death as a spy. This is a complicated legal matter and once the press learned of Beall's impending execution, I have received many letters and telegrams asking for leniency in his case. Browning was strong in his arguments for a pardon. A legitimate military tribunal tried him and found him guilty, with telling testimony from a co-conspirator, George S. Anderson. Beall was represented at his trial by James T. Brady. Six senators and 91 members of Congress have asked that he be spared. I have decided not to interfere in the court's decision, but to let it stand. I do not wish to undermine General Dix and the court's authority. Secretary Seward has argued strenuously for the execution because many of Beall's crimes occurred in New York State.

Author's notes:

John Y. Beall was wounded in the lungs while serving in the Confederate Army, which left him incapable of active military service. Inspired by John Hunt Morgan, he conceived a plan to launch privateers on the Great Lakes. Confederate authorities declined to act since the plan might endanger relations with Canada. However, Beall was commissioned an acting master in the Confederate Navy, though not given a command. He then became active in the Chesapeake Bay and Potomac River area, commanding a crew of 18 men and two boats, The Raven and The Swan. He was captured in 1863 and exchanged in May of 1864. Upon his release he returned to the north shore of Lake Erie to Canada in order to free Confederate prisoners on Johnson's Island. The plan failed and Beall then decided to free some captured prisoners by derailing a passenger train. He and George Anderson were arrested in Niagara, New York, and imprisoned in Fort Lafayette on December 16, 1864. Anderson agreed to testify against Beall in return for leniency. General John Adams Dix ordered a military trial, and on February 8, 1865, Beall was found guilty on all charges and sentenced to death. He was executed on February 24th on Governor's Island in New York Harbor at Fort Columbus.

Beall's attorney, James Topham Brady (April 9, 1815 – February 8, 1869,) was born in New York City, the son of a prominent lawyer. He tried 52 criminal cases and lost only one, that of John Y. Beall. Brady was admitted to the bar at age 20. He defended Daniel Sickles during his trial for the murder of Philip Barton Key, the then-attorney general of the District of Columbia. Brady was on John C. Breckinridge and Joseph Lane's 1860 Democratic ticket for governor of New York. When the Civil War began, Brady became an ardent supporter of Abraham Lincoln and his Republican Party.

The White House – Monday, February 20, 1865

I sent a letter to James Gordon Bennett, publisher of the New York Tribune, offering to appoint him ambassador to France. Bennett did not endorse me for president but has been supportive of the Union cause throughout the war. His son James G. Bennett, Jr. volunteered his yacht, Henrietta, for naval service and was commissioned a third lieutenant in the Navy. His ship was assigned to the U.S. Marine Revenue service and was part of the fleet which captured Fernandina, Florida, in 1862. He and his yacht returned to civilian life later that year, and he joined his father's newspaper.

I have written to Governor Thomas Fletcher of Missouri asking him to encourage public meetings in his state, which would be called to ask citizens to obey the laws at a time when laws are being broken by disreputable people. There are no Confederate forces in the state and the people there are entitled to live in peace and security.

Author's notes:

James Gordon Bennett advised the president on March 6, 1865 that he must decline the honor offered to him by the president by writing, "At my age I am afraid of assuming the labors and responsibility of such an important position. Besides, in the present relations of France and the United States, I am of the decided opinion that I can be of more service to the country in the present position I occupy."

The White House – Wednesday, February 22, 1865

Yesterday I held a long meeting with Attorney General Speed and Secretary Welles related to an anticipated decision of Chief Justice Salmon Chase. I also discussed with Speed the case of William Rogerson and Asa Marvin for counterfeiting. General Grant confirmed that my son Captain Robert Lincoln arrived and is now serving at his headquarters.

Today, Mrs. Jane Lurton of Tennessee visited me to discuss the matter of her son, Sergeant Horace H. Lurton of the Confederate Army, who is ill and being held in prison. She is very well-spoken and feels concern for the well-being of her sick son, who was captured and is being held at Johnson's Island Prison Camp at Sandusky Bay, Ohio. I made his release subject to his taking the oath of allegiance, which his mother says he is willing to take.

Author's notes:

Horace Harmon Lurton was captured twice during the Civil War. He served with the 5th Tennessee Infantry, the 2nd Kentucky Cavalry and the 3rd Kentucky Cavalry. He attended the Old University of Chicago and then received a Bachelor of Law degree from Cumberland Law School, now part of Sanford University. He entered private practice in Clarksville, Tennessee from 1867 to 1875. He was chancellor for the Tennessee Chancery Court for the Sixth Judicial District from 1875 to 1878. He resumed private practice until 1886 and was a justice of the Tennessee Supreme Court from 1886 to 1893. President Grover Cleveland appointed him to the U.S. Circuit Court for the sixth Circuit in 1893. He was elevated to the U.S. Supreme Court by William Howard Taft on December 20, 1909. Appointed at age 65, he was the oldest justice to be appointed to the Supreme Court. He served until his death on July 12, 1914.

The White House – Thursday, February 23, 1865

Late yesterday evening, Secretary Stanton and Welles, accompanied by Lieutenant Commander William B. Cushing, came by to bring me and the rest of the Cabinet up-to-date on the surrender of Fort Anderson on February 20th following a successful combined land and sea attack. The enemy fort was pounded continuously for three days and nights, and our soldiers then occupied the fort after Rebel forces retreated to Town Creek. We understand that the Confederates under General Johnson Hagood have now left the important City of Wilmington, North Carolina undefended and it is now being occupied. This means the South will no longer have access to the port or to the Cape Fear River.

Author's notes:

Before leaving Wilmington, General Braxton Bragg ordered bales of cotton and tobacco burned so they would not fall into Federal hands, along with storehouses, shipyards and ships. Bragg retreated from Wilmington with Union prisoners located there at 1 A.M. on the 22nd, with General Terry's forces entering one hour later. Wilmington was the last major port of the Confederate States on the Atlantic Coast. It had served as an important port for blockade-runners, carrying tobacco, cotton and other goods to Great Britain, the Bahamas and Bermuda; much of the supplies for the Army of Northern Virginia came through Wilmington. With the port closed the Union blockade was complete. Bragg came under severe criticism from the press for the Confederate defeat in the Wilmington campaign. Bragg's forces retreated toward Goldsboro, North Carolina, where it united with forces commanded by General Joseph E. Johnston.

The White House – Friday, February 24, 1865

I met first thing this morning with Hiram Hibbard, who has been serving with Company A in the 50th New York Engineers. He came to me voluntarily expressing concern that he might be punished as a deserter; which he swears he is not. I admire his candor and have asked the War Department to pardon him for any supposed desertion and to put him back into his regiment on the condition that he serves out his term honorably.

A delegation from Congress arrived determined to appeal to me in the matter of a pardon for J.Y. Beall. I informed Montgomery Blair and friends that I do not wish to discuss this unpleasant matter. There is much sympathy for Beall, which is understandable, but my decision is correct, and he is to be executed as ordered.

Author's notes:

Special Orders No. 114, March 8, 1865, promulgated the pardon of Private Hiram Hibbard.

The White House – Saturday, February 25, 1865

I started the morning off with pancakes, bacon, butter and maple syrup. Tad seems to grow a little each day and I noticed that for each pancake I ate, he devoured two. He likes Saturdays because he has no tutoring on Saturdays. I have offered to pay him fifty cents for every book he reads in order to stimulate an interest in more book reading. So far, the offer has met with enthusiasm. I noticed that he had a copy of Aesop's Fables with him. This morning he wore an Army uniform to breakfast. He is very proud of it and looks smart in it. I now have two sons in uniform, Tad and Robert.

I issued a pass for Roger Pryor to report to General Grant for exchange. Grant believes that Pryor can do us no harm, and I agree with him. Tribune editor Horace Greeley wrote urging Pryor's exchange and will be pleased to learn that it has been accomplished.

At a reception in the White House, Charles Adolphe de Pineton, Marquis de Chambrun, a visiting French diplomat, dominates everyone present and maintains his exalted position without the slightest effort. Mother was especially pleased to have a good opportunity to converse again in French with him. The diplomat is a good friend of Senator Sumner and was optimistic that our war will soon be ended. I told him that it was my wish one day to visit Paris. Mother said to him in French that when my term ends, she wishes to spend time in the City of Light.

Author's notes:

Mary Lincoln sailed for Europe on the City of Baltimore in October of 1868. She and Tad stayed in Frankfort, Germany, then visited Nice, France, before returning to Germany, where Tad attended school in Frankfort. They spent seven weeks in 1869 touring Scotland. They returned to the United States in May of 1871 on board the S.S. Russia, a Cunard liner, which sailed from Liverpool to New York in 11 days. General Philip Sheridan also happened to be aboard ship. On Saturday, July 15, 1871, Tad died at age 18 in Chicago. Mary made a second voyage to Europe in 1876 sailing from New York on the S.S. Labrador, arriving in Le Havre, France. She traveled to Bordeaux and then to Pau in the Pyrenees, where she stayed at the Grand Hotel and later at the Henri Quatre. She visited Marseilles, Avignon, Naples, Rome and Sorrento. In 1879 Ulysses and Julia Grant visited Pau but did not call upon Mary. She returned to the United States on the S.S. Amerique, arriving back on October 27, 1880. She was slowly going blind. On July 16, 1882, she died at age 63.

The White House – Monday, February 27, 1865

Francis B. Carpenter, the gifted artist, and some friends came by yesterday and I asked their opinion of the draft my second inaugural address, which will soon be given. It is brief and to the point and after they listened to the words they clapped just after I spoke the last word. I was embarrassed but pleased by their reaction to it. It needs a bit more "pruning," as my law partner Herndon often said as I read to him a proposed address to be delivered to a jury. Herndon has an ear for such things. Francis commented that he particularly liked the very last sentence that reads, "With malice towards none, charity for all, with firmness in the right, as God gives us the right, let us strive to finish the work we are in; to bind the nation's wounds; to care for him who shall have borne the battle, and for his widow and orphan to do all we can which may achieve and cherish a just and lasting peace among ourselves, and with all nations." I hope and pray those words are well-received.

Author's notes:

Lincoln's Second Inaugural Address was only 703 words long. It mentions God 14 times, gives four Biblical allusions and three invocations to prayer. Ron White, the author of "A. Lincoln: A Biography," writes that Lincoln's God mentions are not "ornamental but part and parcel of the strength of his argument." White believed that Lincoln was "a theological but not a religious man."

On April 22, 1864, President Lincoln signed the Mint Act, which authorized the U.S. Mint to imprint the words "In God We Trust" for the first time on U.S. coins. The two-cent coin was the first to display the motto.

The White House – Tuesday, February 28, 1865

The last day of February, hurrah! While the weather in the north has been cold and rainy, the weather in the South has favored the men in Sherman's Army as it strides forward to victorious destinations. I issued a pass to Dr. Frederick Tompkins to visit Norfolk, Charleston, Savannah and return. He is from England, where he serves as the secretary of the National Freedmen's Society of London. He has come to America to gather facts about the status of freedmen in our country, particularly in the South. He comes highly recommended by the Rev. Henry Ward Beecher.

I forwarded to the Senate a treaty made and concluded with the Klamath and Modoc Tribes of Oregon, at Fort Klamath on the 5th of October 1864. The treaty was ratified by the Senate on July 2, 1866 with amendments.

Author's notes:

On this date, President Lincoln wrote to Thomas D. Eliot, "If a majority of the Massachusetts delegation in Congress will, in writing on this sheet, request the pardon of this man, it shall be granted." The petition was for a pardon for Zeno Kelly of New Bedford, Massachusetts, who was convicted on charges of fitting out a vessel to be engaged in the slave trade. Eliot and nine other members of Congress signed the request, which Lincoln required. On March 2, 1865, Lincoln advised the attorney general to make out a pardon in this case.

The White House – Wednesday, March 1, 1865

I reviewed my second Inaugural Address with Frederick Douglass and later with Thurlow Weed. Douglass actually called the words "a sacred effort," for which I am humbled and very grateful. My intent is to stress "malice toward none, with charity for all," in the hope that when peace is restored the theme of renewed friendships and trust will ultimately prevail. Weed said that he thinks the speech will wear well and be perhaps better than any speech I have ever delivered. I hope he is right. There is too much hatred and anger in the nation, which is understandable but also which threatens any peace achieved by arms. We must have reconciliation between North and South, and it must be accomplished as rapidly as is humanly possible.

At noon Illinois Senator LymanTrumbull, Iowa Representative James F. Wilson and Pennsylvania Representative John L. Dawson, as a committee from Congress, notified me that I am officially elected president. I told them that I accept the people's renewed trust, with its yet onerous and perplexing duties and responsibilities. Later I met with Thomas Conway, general superintendent of Freedmen, Department of the Gulf, and thanked him for the success in the work of their moral and physical elevation.

Author's notes:

On this busy day President Lincoln wrote to General Winfield Scott, Howard Potter, William E. Dodge Jr. and Theodore Roosevelt Sr., members of the Protective War Claim Association of Sanitary Commission: "I shall at all times be ready to recognize the paramount claims of the soldiers of the nation, in the disposition of public trusts. I shall be glad also to make these suggestions to the several Heads of Departments." Lincoln pardoned Christian Emerick and recommended that he be discharged from Albany Penitentiary upon his taking the oath of allegiance. Emerick had been found guilty of recruiting for the Rebel service.

The White House – Thursday, March 2, 1865

I requested that Provost Marshall General James B. Fry not draft William H. Crook and Alexander Smith, members of my bodyguard as I cannot spare them. Crook has already served in the Army and has a young wife and baby who need him, and he cannot afford to pay a substitute. Crook asked me to also request that Smith be spared, and I agreed to do so. I like both men and know that they do a good job in protecting me from harm.

General Grant notified me today that all is well with General Sherman and his Army. I was worried when no word from Sherman had come to me lately.

I sent a note to Postmaster General William Dennison asking that he consider the request of the widow of Lt. Colonel Edward F.W. Ellis, late of the 15th Illinois Volunteers who was killed at Shiloh. Mrs. Ellis seeks the position of Postmaster of Rockford, Illinois.

Author's notes:

Records show that Annie M. Smith served as postmaster of Rockford, Illinois until May 10, 1865, and that Anson S. Miller succeeded her.

The White House – Friday, March 3, 1865

Early this evening Mother and I were serenaded by a large delegation of citizens from New York City and Poughkeepsie who were accompanied by Eastman's Business College Band. I was asked to address the crowd and told them that "Sherman went in at Atlanta and now comes out right. He has gone in again at Savannah, and I propose three cheers for his coming out gloriously!" Many shouted that they were here for tomorrow's inauguration ceremonies, and they all wished me well. The event ended when a chorus of Army soldiers from a nearby fort joined the Eastman Band and the public in the singing of the Star-Spangled Banner. Someone had thoughtfully printed up sheet music so that everyone would know the words to the song.

Later I went to the Capitol to sign final bills approved by Congress and approved an act establishing a bureau for relief of Freedmen and refugees.

Secretary of War Stanton interrupted me to bring to my attention a message from General Grant notifying that General Lee has proposed a meeting to end hostilities. I directed Stanton to reply to Grant that a conference with Lee may only be held based on Lee's surrender. Grant is not to decide, discuss or confer upon any political question. Such questions the president holds in his own hands and will submit them to no military conferences or conventions. Meanwhile, Grant is told to press Lee's Army to the utmost.

Mother remained in the Diplomatic Gallery with friends until 9 P.M.

Author's notes:

The 38th Congress remained in session until 8 A.M. on March 4.

The White House – Sunday, March 5, 1865

March 4th, Inaugural Day, was a time to remember. Vice President Hannibal Hamlin escorted me to the Senate Chamber to witness the swearing in of Vice President Andrew Johnson. From there I proceeded to a platform in front of the central portico of the Capitol. The sun came out just as I took the oath of office. Mother was given the Bible by Chief Justice Chase, who said to us that he regarded the sun's arrival as a positive sign that the war will be ending soon. I delivered my address just after noon. It was a very brief message but one that made all the important points on my mind. Frequent applause broke out during my reading. Tad joined Mother, Senator Lafayette Foster of Connecticut and me in the carriage in the procession back to the White House. On the way we stopped at Willard's Hotel so Mother might visit a friend. At 8 P.M. we had a public reception, where I shook hands with an estimated 6,000 people.

At 9 P.M. I excused myself and met with Secretary of War Stanton and several Army officers. We discussed the recently fought battle of Waynesboro in Virginia, which was an impressive victory for our side and a disaster for troops under the command of Confederate General Jubal Early. Reports state that we have captured as many as 1,500 to 1,800 men, 14 pieces of artillery, 150 to 200 wagons, hundreds of horses, many ambulances and 16 stands of colors.

Author's notes:

Early himself, with about 15 of his staff, escaped through Rockfish Gap. His entire army was captured or scattered across the countryside, never to form an effective fighting force. Fifteen Medal of Honor citations for the capture of flags were issued to Union soldiers. Captain Christopher C. Bruton of the 22nd New York received the Medal of Honor for the capture of Early's headquarters flag during the battle. Commanding General Sheridan crossed the Blue Ridge Mountains to Charlottesville destroying the James River Canal locks near Goochland Court House. He joined forces with the Army of the Potomac near Petersburg on March 26th for the opening of the Appomattox Campaign. Early never received another field assignment for the rest of the war.

The White House –Tuesday, March 7, 1865

Last evening Mother and I attended the Inaugural Ball with Senator Charles Sumner and his wife, Alice. It was held in the Patent Office. Our son Robert attended with Mary Harlan, the Iowa senator's daughter. Dinner was served at midnight, and we left around 1 A.M.

Earlier in the day I appointed Comptroller of the Treasury Hugh McCulloch to be the new secretary of the Treasury, replacing Secretary Fessenden, who has resigned.

I asked Mother to join me when I was interviewed by Henri de Mareil, editor of the prominent French newspaper, Messager-Franco-Americain, published in New York City. They had a pleasant conversation in his language. His English is excellent, and we had a profitable exchange. He delivered a message for me from the emperor of France, who congratulated me upon my re-election. I have asked Secretary Gideon Welles to place government advertising in his newspaper if it can legally and appropriately be given to his paper.

The Cabinet met at 3 P.M. Later I wrote to General Grant. I did so in accordance with a Joint Resolution of Congress, which approved on December 17, 1863 that a gold medal be ordered and directed to the general in thanks for the arduous and well-performed public service of him and all under his command. The medal and a copy of the Congressional Resolution engrossed on parchment was sent to Grant today. No American general in this war was ever more deserving.

Author's notes:

On this day President Lincoln spent much time endorsing applications for jobs and issuing orders for persons who owned products within insurrectionary states to bring such products within military lines for sale to agents of the government.

The White House – Wednesday, March 8, 1865

I received the resignation of Secretary of the Interior John Usher today. He has done a fine job and will be missed. I met with Secretary Seward today to consider an appropriate ambassadorial appointment for Montgomery Blair. I have been thinking of appointing him to represent the United States in either Spain or Austria. Mother said that before I do so I had better speak with Montgomery's wife, Mary, and get her views on the subject. Mother is usually right in such matters. She asked me why some important appointments are not given to women. Only postmaster positions seem to be awarded to women. It is a good question. Women deserve the vote and deserve to serve in high posts, but by custom they have been discriminated against in our society. I personally believe that the right to vote should not be denied on account of sex. Perhaps a future amendment to the Constitution shall agree with my thinking on this matter. I have favored the idea since before I served in the Congress.

Author's notes:

On June 13, 1836, Abraham Lincoln wrote to the New Salem Journal, "I go for all sharing of the government who assist in bearing its burdens. Consequently, I go for admitting all whites to the right to suffrage who pay taxes or bear arms (by no means excluding females)."

The 19th Amendment granting women the right to vote was passed in 1920 following years of struggle to grant women suffrage.

The White House – Thursday, March 9, 1865

I sent a letter to John Usher accepting his resignation and agreeing that it is to take effect on May 15, 1865. I have suggested to Hannibal Hamlin that the post of collector of the Port of Boston is a suitable assignment for him following the vice-presidency and am expecting to hear from him shortly as to whether he would like to fill the post. If not, I might consider a Cabinet position for him.

The Senate is set to adjourn on the 11th of March. I have not been able to ask it to confirm James Gordon Bennet's appointment to the French court because I have not received word from Bennet that he wishes to assume the post.

Author's notes:

Hamlin resigned as collector because of his disagreement with President Andrew Johnson over reconstruction of the former Confederacy. In 1869 he was again elected to the U.S. Senate, and served two terms. He served briefly as ambassador to Spain in 1882. He died July 4, 1891, in Bangor, Maine.

The White House – Friday, March 10, 1865

At 9:30 A.M. I discussed with John A. Poor, a member of the committee from Maine, the possibility of asking Hannibal Hamlin to join the Cabinet rather than offer him the post of Collector of the Port of Boston. Poor thinks Hamlin would be happier with the Boston assignment and I will heed his advice in the matter.

Author's notes:

On March 6, 1865, the Battle of Natural Bridge was waged in Leon County, Florida, in Woodville, near Tallahassee. A small band of Confederate troops and teenagers from the Florida Military and Collegiate Institute (later Florida State University) prevented a detachment of U.S. Colored Troops from crossing the Natural Bridge on the St. Marks River. Sailors from the U.S.S. Hendrick Hudson also participated and two were awarded the Medal of Honor: Seaman John Mack and Coxswain George Shutt. Confederate forces under Brigadier General William Miller defended the bridge for most of the day before Union troops retreated to the protection of the fleet. A monument at the battle site was erected in 1921 by the Florida legislature to commemorate the victory saving their capital from the invaders. Tallahassee was the only Southern capital not captured during the Civil War. 110 acres of the battlefield have been preserved and are managed by the state park service.

The White House – Saturday, March 11, 1865

Tad's tutor has been introducing him to the Latin language. I deeply regret that in all of my very limited schooling I was never taught a single word of this marvelous language. Today he read me some words from ancient Rome. I particularly liked this line from Julius Caesar, "Fere libenter homines id quod volunt credunt." In English, "Men willingly believe what they wish." How very true.

Today Hay helped me prepare a proclamation offering pardon to deserters who return to service and inflicting loss of citizenship on those who do not. I expect to soon appoint Hay to become secretary of our legation in Paris. He will probably reach there within the next month or six weeks and serve under John Bigelow, a fine man for whom I have great admiration. I will miss Hay but realize that he has worked long and hard and desires to see much of the world. This appointment will suit him admirably. Secretary Seward is sanguine about Hay and Nicolay joining the State Department in France. He has high hopes for both men in the diplomatic service.

From 1 P.M. to 5 P.M. today Mother, assisted by me, held our last reception of the season. John Nicolay, who has served me loyally since the very beginning of my presidency, was confirmed by the Senate as American consul in Paris, France. The salary will be $5,000. I envy his assignment. I have never seen any of Europe and from what I've heard, one must see Paris before all other cities on the continent. Mother has been listening to some of his French and has been giving him suggestions on pronunciation.

Author's notes:

On Sunday, March 12, Lincoln conferred with former Congressman Isaac Arnold of Illinois and offered him the position of auditor of the Treasury Department.

John Bigelow, a respected newspaperman with close ties to Secretary Seward and Thurlow Weed, was appointed by Lincoln to succeed William Dayton as the U.S. minister to France. When Dayton passed away in late 1864, Lincoln appointed Bigelow to the ministerial post and he thus became Nicolay and John Hay's boss. Long after they left Paris, Hay and Nicolay would remain close friends and frequent correspondents.

The White House – Monday, March 13, 1865

Today I was feeling feeble and sickly and denied all visitors access to me. Mother has been serving me beef tea, which she considers a cure-all. I have sent word to the Cabinet that I will expect them here tomorrow afternoon for a short meeting to take place in my bedroom.

Secretary Stanton forwarded to me a written report concerning the recent battle of Wyse Fork, which took place between March 7 and 10 in Lenoir County, near Kinston, North Carolina. I read it today and found it very enlightening. It is estimated that we outnumbered the foe 12,000 to 8,500. The enemy probably had 1,500 casualties to our 1,000. General Braxton Bragg commanded the Rebels; our men were under Major Generals John M. Schofield and Jacob Cox. Bragg moved against our forces near Kinston. Initially Bragg captured a New England brigade, the 15th Connecticut Volunteers. The fighting went on for three days. Confederate General D.H. Hill moved against the Federal center, but Union artillery proved decisive and the attackers were repulsed. Elements of the Federal XXIII Corps which had just arrived in New Bern from Tennessee, moved on Kinston. Realizing he was now facing five Union divisions, Bragg withdrew.

Author's notes;

Bragg had only momentarily been able to check Cox's advance. Schofield's forces reached two full corps and were organized into the Army of the Ohio. Sherman's armies, which had just defeated Johnston's army at Bentonville, joined with Schofield at Goldsboro, North Carolina, on March 23rd. Facing three Union armies, Johnston retreated to the north, and on April 26th Johnston surrendered to Sherman.

The Civil War Trust has acquired and preserved 115 acres of the Wyse Fork battlefield. It is listed on the National Register of Historic Places in Lenoir County, North Carolina.

The White House – Tuesday, March 14, 1865

I remained in bed until noon, when the Cabinet met with me here. Everyone except Seward attended. We began by listening to a report from General Halleck concerning a recent battle fought at Monroe's Crossroads near Fayetteville, North Carolina. Inconclusive fighting took place on March 10th involving almost 5,000 troops on both sides. While initially routed, our men soon counter-attacked, pressuring the Rebels to withdraw from the Union camp they had occupied. We were outnumbered and sustained 183 casualties. Four Confederate commanders were wounded in the action. Halleck indicated that the fighting resulted in delaying our reaching the Cape Fear River bridges when planned. We are now in possession of the town of Fayetteville.

I am feeling much better and hope after a good night's sleep I'll be in my office tomorrow. I plan to limit visitors to just Cabinet members and others on urgent business. I will not meet with the public until I feel 100% fit.

Author's notes:

The Battle of Monroe's Crossroads gained time for the Confederates to conduct an organized crossing of the Cape Fear River unmolested by Federal troops. With their troops and equipment east of the river, the Confederates burned the bridges as Union forces entered the city of Fayetteville. The battle occurred on land now within the property of Fort Bragg, North Carolina.

The White House – Wednesday, March 15, 1865

I was much stronger today; it must be Mother's beef tea that was the magic cure for what ailed me. I was in my office all day.

I received the credentials of Count Wydenbruck, the Austrian minister, who was joined by Secretary Seward, who introduced us. The count had only good words from Emperor Francis Joseph I, and was encouraging in his outlook for peace soon in our nation. I was also interviewed by Reverend Samuel Roberts, who is writing articles about America for newspapers in England and Wales. He had kind things to say about the Emancipation Proclamation and claims it is popular with the people of the United Kingdom and especially with the queen.

I wrote to Thurlow Weed and confessed that I felt that my Inaugural Address may have offended some listeners and readers. I wrote to him that "Some men are not flattered by being shown that there has been a difference of purpose between the Almighty and them."

Mother and I went to see the Magic Flute at Grover's Theatre. Joining us were Clara Harris, the daughter of Senator Harris, and General James G. Wilson. We have seen it several times before, but considered this performance particularly first rate.

Author's notes:

In his comments to Count Wydenbruck, the president said, "Your sovereign has been discreet, frank, and friendly, and has thus won the confidence and good will of the American people."

The White House – Thursday, March 16, 1865

I wrote to General O.C. Ord suspending the execution of Lieutenant Henry A. Mecker of the 1st U.S. Colored Cavalry, until further order from here. He was accused of murder and breach of arrest for participating in the shooting of a sutler in Norfolk, Virginia. Unfortunately, Mecker was drunk at the time and troops under his command attacked a sutler's store in Norfolk. When the sutler drew his pistol to defend himself he shot Mecker, and Mecker then ordered a soldier to return fire, which was done. The sutler soon died. I am told by I.N. Baylor of Norfolk that Mecker "shows a very contrite heart." I have concluded that this event would not have happened but for the use of spiritous liquors. I do not wish to see the lieutenant hung and therefore have ordered the execution suspended.

Later I took Tad for a ride in my carriage. I am still not feeling quite right. I did not return to the office but retired early. I am still feeble.

Author's notes:

According to Webster's Encyclopedic Unabridged Dictionary, a sutler is a person who follows an army and sells provisions to the soldiers.

The White House – Friday, March 17, 1865

Mother reminded Tad and me this morning that today is St. Patrick's Day in Ireland and in America, and wherever an Irishman or woman is to be found around the world. Archbishop John Hughes of New York City kindly sent me a telegraphic message which reads, "Erin Go Bragh" - meaning "Ireland Forever," I believe. The bishop is a good friend of mine and of the Union. In his telegraphic note he writes, "A pleasant surprise is coming your way today!" Indeed, at noon a dozen or so bagpipers came to the White House lawn along with about 50 soldiers from New York's famed 69th Regiment, who serenaded Mother, Tad and me with some sentimental Irish ballads. Stanton informed me recently that out of over 2,000 regiments, the 69th has had more casualties than all but five regiments in the entire Union Army.

I issued a proclamation concerning illegal trade with Indians. It calls for the arrest and trial by court-martial of any person furnishing arms to hostile Indians.

At 4 P.M. I addressed soldiers from the 140th Indiana Regiment who presented me with a Rebel flag captured recently at Fort Anderson, North Carolina. I reminded the men that although I was born in Kentucky and have lived in Illinois, I spent much of my childhood in their state, Indiana.

Author's notes:

The date March 17th is St. Patrick's Day, or the Feast of St. Patrick, and is believed to be the date of St. Patrick's death in 461 A.D. St. Patrick's Day became an official Christian feast day in the early 17th century and is observed by the Catholic Church, the Anglican Communion (especially the Church of Ireland), the Eastern Orthodox Church, and the Lutheran Church.

The White House – Saturday, March 18, 1865

My first order of business today was to authorize General Edward Canby to give the Reverend Thomas C. Teasdale assistance in his efforts to open an Orphan's Home in the state of Mississippi. Teasdale is a highly regarded Baptist minister who lives in Springfield, Illinois. I know of his good works and have sent him a contribution to aid him in his efforts. Unfortunately, wars create orphans and this one has created vast numbers of them. I admire what Teasdale is doing, as does Mother.

Author's notes:

Edward R.S. Canby (November 9, 1817 – April 11, 1873) was born in Kentucky. He graduated from West Point in 1839. He helped defeat Confederate forces during the New Mexico campaign. In 1864, he became commander of Union forces along the Gulf of Mexico. In 1865 he captured the city of Mobile, Alabama. During Reconstruction he commanded U.S. forces in the South. In 1872 he was sent to the Pacific Northwest to fight Indian tribes. In 1873 he was killed while trying to make a peace treaty with the Modoc Tribe in Northern California.

The White House – Monday, March 20, 1865

Yesterday, after church, I approved Major General John Pope's plan of action for Missouri. The idea is to suspend martial law by private instructions to commanding officers to withdraw their provost marshals and to refrain from any interference with citizens. Thus slowly, county by county, the military forces of the United States can be withdrawn from all connections with the civil affairs of the state. If afterward troops are required, let the governor declare martial law and enforce it by the state militia. I trust the loyal state executive and civil officers to settle all controversies between citizens without referring to the administration in Washington. This plan has been approved by Governor Thomas C. Fletcher.

General Halleck explained recent events in North Carolina to the Cabinet. He explained that four days ago, in Harnett and Cumberland county, North Carolina, our forces under the command of General Sherman engaged the troops of Confederate General William Hardee. The Rebels were probably outnumbered by at least 5,000 men. Sherman's right column was led by Major General Oliver O. Howard and the left by Major General Henry W. Slocum, who encountered the enemy at Averasborough, and who drove our side back. Soon Federal reinforcements arrived, and we drove back two lines of Confederates but were soon halted by a third line. At that moment, Major General Jefferson C. Davis's XIV Corps began to arrive on the field. Badly outnumbered, the Confederates, in danger of being outflanked, withdrew. Each side suffered casualties of about 500 to 700 men.

Author's notes

The Averasborough Battlefield Historic District was listed on the National Register of Historic Places in 2001. The Civil War Trust has acquired and preserved 520 acres. The battle was fought on the grounds of Oak Grove, near Erwin, North Carolina. The battle was a prelude to the climactic Battle of Bentonville, which began three days later.

The White House – Tuesday, March 21, 1865

Yesterday I appointed Joseph M. Patterson, a one-armed soldier, to be a postmaster in his hometown. How I regret that we do not have hundreds more vacant postmaster jobs to give to men who gave so much for their country. Patterson lost his arm at Gettysburg.

Yesterday we dined with Russian Ambassador Baron Eduard de Stoeckl and his American wife, Elisa. Her maiden name is Howard. He expressed the belief that the war will be over much sooner than we all expect. Stoeckl has often suggested to Secretary Seward that the vast territory of Alaska, known as Russian America, should be purchased by the United States. Seward also favors the idea, but to date the Russian government has shown no interest in such an acquisition.

I have agreed to meet Grant at City Point, Virginia. Mrs. Lincoln will join me. We are anxious to see Robert, who will be at Grant's headquarters. The date is expected to be March 24, and we will go by the River Queen.

Author's notes:

Baron Stoeckl believed that the Alaska purchase would prevent the United Kingdom from seizing the territory in case of war between the two countries and would allow Russia to concentrate its resources on the vast area of Eastern Siberia, particularly the Amur River area. He also insisted that by doing so, Russia would avoid any future conflict with the United States. He considered further U.S. expansion in North America as inevitable. Stoeckl signed the Alaska Treaty in March of 1867. Tsar Alexander II rewarded him with $25,000 and an annual pension of $6,000. He died in Paris on January 26, 1892.

The White House – Wednesday, March 22, 1865

Senator Sumner visited Mother and me for about an hour. It was mostly quiet conversation. He showed us a letter that he had received from Elizabeth Georgiana Granville, the duchess of Argyll, dated March 2nd, who wrote kind things about the Gettysburg Address.

John Hay has been officially appointed secretary of the Legation at Paris, France, and is expected to arrive there within a month to six weeks. I shall miss John; he has been an excellent aide, and more than that, a good and trusted loyal friend. I predict a fine public career for him in the nation's service.

Author's notes:

The duchess of Argyll wrote to Senator Sumner, "We feel great confidence in the President. It is sad to hear of the Abolition Party so much divided since his nomination. I think the speech at Gettysburg Cemetery must live."

John Hay served as ambassador to Great Britain in 1897 and 1898. He was U.S. secretary of State from 1898 to 1905.

En route to Virginia – Thursday, March 23, 1865

Mother, Tad and I traveled this date to City Point, Virginia, on the River Queen to visit with General Grant and his staff. We departed from Arsenal dock, 6th Street wharf at 1 P.M. We were in torrential rain and experienced rough water on the Potomac, so the trip was not an enjoyable one, except for Tad, who got to know the crew and visited the engine room several times. He has an inquisitive mind and makes friends easily. The crew enjoyed his company. When we reach Grant's headquarters, we will have an opportunity to be united with son Robert.

I mentioned to Mother that I had a dream last evening in which the White House caught fire and burned to the ground. It was particularly vivid and woke me up. Ever since she has been worrying about the house's safety.

Author's notes:

On this day Lincoln's banker in Springfield, Illinois, Robert Irwin, paid $4.23 taxes on Lincoln's property on Council Bluffs land. Irwin drew a draft on the Springfield Marine Bank.

Mrs. Lincoln was accompanied by her maid. W.H. Crook and Captain Charles B. Penrose were also in the president's party.

En route to Virginia – Friday, March 24, 1865

I have been feeling unwell on the trip. It is partly due to the weather and waves and perhaps due to the quality of the drinking water. We are taking on a fresh supply of water when we arrive at the first stop, which is Fortress Monroe, at noon. The plan is to anchor off City Point at 8 or 9 P.M.

Author's notes:

Captain Penrose telegraphed Secretary Stanton, "The President desires me to say he has just arrived at this point safely, and both he and family are well, having entirely recovered from their indisposition of this morning."

Anchored off City Point, Virginia, Saturday, March 25, 1865

I got up early and was not feeling well. Yesterday and the day before the water may have been bad. I attempted to eat some breakfast but did so without enthusiasm for food. A cup of coffee tasted good. Robert came aboard the River Queen and joined Mother, Tad and me. He described some of the fighting that is going on at the front. Several officers came aboard to escort me to General Grant's headquarters. About noon we left by special train to visit General Meade's troops. I mounted an officer's horse and rode for a short distance to view evidence of recent fighting and to see burial details attending to the dead. On the return to City Point by a slow-moving train I noticed that the passenger cars attached to our train were filled with wounded soldiers. Weary and still not feeling fit, I advised Grant that I would not be joining him and his staff for dinner. My impressions so far are that our troops are in good physical shape, and they believe it is just a matter of time before the enemy must concede defeat. General Grant is inspiring to watch and listen to. He has solid command of matters and has an intensity of energy that is inspiring to those under his command.

Author's notes:

President Lincoln traveled to the battle front. At 1:25 P.M. he telegraphed Secretary Stanton, "I am here within five miles of the scene of this morning's action. I have nothing to add to what General Meade reports, except that I have seen the prisoners myself and they look like there might be the number he states – 1,600."

On the River Queen at City Point, Virginia
– Sunday, March 26, 1865

This was a very busy Sunday with the troops. We watched Sheridan's cavalry cross the river at Harrison's Landing, Virginia, and later, reviewed a sizable naval flotilla on the James River. Our party had lunch aboard Rear Admiral Potter's flagship and then we went ashore to watch General Ord's division march in review near Malvern Hill. I was on horseback, as were General Ord and his wife. Unfortunately, Mother was not feeling well from a bump on the head and was out of sorts. She had hit her head on an iron rib on the side of a covered ambulance and was not herself. I believe she will be feeling much better tomorrow after a good night's rest.

Plans are being made that will include General Sherman returning to Charleston for a ceremony to be held there on April 14th to celebrate the recapture of Fort Sumpter four years after it was seized by the Confederates. General Robert Anderson, who pulled down the American flag on that memorable occasion, will be there to run the original flag up the flagpole to be saluted by Federal cannons.

Author's notes:

At the review of General Ord's troops, Mary Lincoln objected loudly to the presence of Mrs. Ord riding next to the president. She continued to complain about Mrs. Ord during the day and at dinner. She demanded that the president fire General Ord immediately. The tirade lasted long into the night, much to Lincoln's embarrassment.

At 9 A.M. on Sunday, March 26th, President Lincoln telegraphed Secretary Stanton, "I approve your Fort Sumpter programme." Stanton's program included Reverend Henry Ward Beecher delivering an address on raising the American flag upon Fort Sumter and the firing of a 500-gun salute. The flag was to be raised by Major General Robert Anderson. (Throughout the war Lincoln misspelled the name, Sumter, preferring to spell it Sumpter.) The event was scheduled to occur on the 14th day of April 1865 in Charleston Harbor upon the ruins of Fort Sumter. The same U.S. flag that flew over the battlements during the Rebel assault was to be lowered and saluted by General Anderson and the small force in his command when the works were evacuated on April 14, 1861. The flag was to be saluted by 100 guns from Fort Sumter, and by a national salute from every fort and Rebel battery that fired upon Fort Sumter. The salute ceremonies were to be under the direction of Major General William T. Sherman, whose military operations compelled the Rebels to evacuate Charleston, or in his absence under the charge of Major General Q.A. Gillmore, commanding the department. The naval forces at Charleston took part in the ceremonies.

City Point, Virginia – Monday, March 27, 1865

I have been informed that General Sherman will be joining General Grant, Admiral Porter and me tomorrow on the River Queen. He will be arriving from Goldsboro, North Carolina, where his army is still fighting and on the move. I look forward to a good discussion with Sherman, whose accomplishments in the war are beyond description. In the beginning of the war, critics called Sherman "crazy" and Grant "a drunk." I can only imagine they have eaten their words.

Today I visited Grant's headquarters for a very good discussion with the general and his staff about the overall military picture. We reviewed the recent action in North Carolina, where a battle was fought at Bentonville. It was another victory for Sherman's troops. Grant also described the battle at Fort Stedman in Virginia. After lunch, I sailed up the Appomattox River to the Point of Rocks. With our party were men from Grant's staff, Lieutenant Commander Barnes and my son, Captain Robert Lincoln.

Stanton telegraphed me about finding a suitable head for the Freedmen's Bureau, which is to be reorganized under the Act of March 3, 1865. He has suggested James B. Yeatman for the post. I know Yeatman very well; he has done fine work in helping soldiers by the work of the Western Sanitary Commission. He was the founder of the Merchant Bank and the Mercantile Library in St. Louis. He is a very wealthy man and a generous philanthropist. I have spoken to Grant about him and have recommended that Stanton ask Yeatman to take the job.

Author's notes:

James E. Yeatman moved to St. Louis in 1842. He founded the Missouri Institute for Education of the Blind, and Washington University in St. Louis. He was also a founder of the St. Louis Philharmonic Society, founded the Provident Association of St. Louis and the Western Sanitary Commission. He advocated for and ran the Missouri Pacific Railroad. He served on the board of the St. Louis Children's Hospital. He consulted with Lincoln during the war but turned down the position offered with the Freedmen's Bureau. He died in 1901 at the age of 83.

The Battle of Fort Stedman was a four-hour action. Union casualties were 1,044. Confederate casualties were 4,000 (600 killed, 2,400 wounded and 1,000 missing or captured). This was Lee's last opportunity to break the Union lines and regain momentum. It was the final offensive action of the Army of Northern Virginia. Immediately following was the Appomattox Campaign and the final surrender of Lee on April 9, 1865.

City Point, Virginia – Tuesday, March 28, 1865

During my meeting with General Sherman he confirmed that, in his opinion, James Yeatman is the "best man in the country for anything he will undertake." The general gave him the highest praise. Sherman is in fine physical condition for a general who has been on such an arduous campaign through a vast part of the Confederacy. His famed March to the Sea has made military history. He has a strong handshake and an indominable spirit. I told him I was pleased that he was on our side in the conflict!

Author's notes:

Sherman's March to the Sea was catastrophic to the Confederacy. Sherman estimated that he had inflicted $100,000,000 in destruction, about one fifth "inured to our advantage, while the remainder is simple waste and destruction." His Army wrecked 300 miles of railroad and numerous bridges and miles of telegraph lines. It seized 5,000 horses and 4,000 mules. It confiscated 9.5 million pounds of corn and 10.5 million pounds of fodder and destroyed uncounted cotton gins and mills. 10,000 liberated slaves followed his Army. He defied military traditions by operating deep within enemy territory without lines of supply or communication. Elements of the decline in agricultural investment, farming asset prices and manufacturing in affected areas of the South persisted until the 1920s.

City Point, Virginia – Wednesday, March 29, 1865

For the third day the issue of the expected surrender of General Johnston's Army and the fate of its surrendered soldiers and even that of Jefferson Davis came up. My viewpoint has been to encourage surrender with submission but not retaliation. I want them to be allowed to go back to their homes peacefully with no more needless bloodshed. As to Davis, he may quietly leave the country. I cannot make that Federal policy, but I think it would be the best result for the nation. I fear that punitive peace terms could encourage some die-hard Rebels to resort to guerrilla warfare rather than disarm. That would be disastrous for both the North and the South. The large number of deserters and prisoners taken each day signifies that Lee must soon concede to Grant.

Just before retiring I heard large booming noises coming from Union cannonading of Rebel positions as well as intense musket fire from the direction of Petersburg. It must have lasted a full two hours. I have spoken to Mother and suggested that she plan to take Tad and return to Washington on the 1st of April. She is looking forward to being back at the White House. She has not been the same since she injured herself in her ambulance accident. Tad is all for staying, but I do not want him to be away from his tutor and books any longer.

Author's notes:

Mary Lincoln returned to Washington on April 1st escorted by Secretary Seward. Tad was permitted to remain with his father.

City Point, Virginia, – Thursday, March 30, 1865

Secretary Seward and Secretary Welles arrived today, and we made a trip up the James River to confer and lunch with Admiral David Porter. Seward has offered to accompany Mother back to Washington tomorrow afternoon. She is anxious to return and appreciates the secretary's kind offer.

Seward raised the question of what our policy should be if Jefferson Davis were to leave the country and escape to Cuba, Mexico or somewhere else. It was doubted that he could manage to get to Canada. The possibility was also raised that he might sail to Bermuda and then on to either Britain or France. I instructed Seward that if any nation receives him, we are not to make a fuss. It is my preference that he leave America and act not as a president in exile, but as a private citizen, and hopefully one who would be willing to accept the inevitable surrender of the various Confederate armies. The attorney general has suggested that he be given a presidential pardon for all acts of rebellion. It would create an obvious public outcry, but in time such an act might make sense. I understand he lost a son last year in a household accident. I can sympathize with any man who loses a son. I would not be averse to such a pardon if asked for by Davis. He is a very proud man and might deem asking to be demeaning. My hunch is he would consider a pardon a confession of guilt, and I know he does not feel guilty of a crime. His view has always been that secession is legal. Time will tell. In my mind, Davis has done much for his country and before the war opposed slavery. I think a pardon might do much to heal the nation's wounds, which are deep and many. I must discuss this with Grant and the members of the Cabinet and get their thinking on the matter.

Author's notes:

Jefferson Davis' son, Joseph Evan Davis, was born April 18, 1859, and died tragically in an accidental fall on April 30, 1864.

City Point, Virginia - Friday, March 31, 1865

I was in a depressed mood much of the day. Mother has tried to cheer me up without much success. Victories do not come without deaths and there have been far too many of late. General Sherman joined Mother, Tad and me for a late dinner. Stanton telegraphed me today urging that I remain here. He feels that my presence affects the generals and the troops in a positive way. He tends to think that if I am present there is less likelihood that the Army will order any pause in the fighting. Heavy rain and muddy roads have made things difficult for everyone. We have successfully driven the enemy from the Boydton Plank Road and in turn have taken the White Oak Road. This gives us all the ground the enemy occupied this morning. I will miss Tad and Mother when they leave tomorrow for home.

Author's notes:

Grant telegraphed Lincoln that he was being sent a battle flag taken from a Virginia Regiment of Hunter's Brigade. It was one of four Confederate battle flags won on this date at Petersburg.

City Point, Virginia – Saturday, April 1, 1865

Robert and I had a good long man-to-man talk about all sorts of things. It was a wholesome time together. We rarely in our lives have done just that: talk openly about what is on our minds. I am very proud of his growth in judgment and character. He has become a fine young man of great promise. He speaks highly of Grant and Sherman and the officers with whom he is working. I expect that one day he will prove to be an able attorney.

After he left for headquarters, I spent much of the night pacing the deck of the River Queen. I like the fresh air, and walking is good for one's health. Tad will be with me today. Grant has told me that if we had not had heavy rain, we would have taken Petersburg earlier. Heavy rains make swift movement impossible for an army.

Author's notes:

On this date President Lincoln telegraphed Secretary of War Edwin Stanton: "Sheridan had pretty hot work yesterday, that infantry was sent to his support during the night, and that he, Grant, has not heard from Sheridan. Mrs. L. has started home; and I will thank you to see that our coachman is at the Arsenal wharf at Eight (8) o'clock tomorrow morning, there wait until she arrives." Lincoln's coachman was Alfonso Donn.

City Point, Virginia – Sunday, April 2, 1865

Mother arrived home safely today, having sailed from here on the steamer Monohasset. I went ashore in a barge provided by Rear Admiral David Porter. I met with General Grant for an hour and a half and then returned to City Point. Grant has confirmed that Petersburg is now evacuated by the Rebels and that our troops are trying to cut off his retreating army.

At 8:15 P.M. I telegraphed General Grant congratulations for his victory at Petersburg and tendered to him, and all of his men, the nation's grateful thanks for this additional and magnificent success. I advised him that I plan to visit him tomorrow.

Author's notes:

On this date the president telegraphed Mary Lincoln, "At 4:30 P.M. today General Grant telegraphs that he has Petersburg completely enveloped from river below to river above, and has captured, since he started last Wednesday, about 12,000 prisoners and 50 guns. He suggests that I shall go out and see him in the morning, which I think I will do. Tad and I are both well and will be glad to see you and your party here at the time you name." (Apparently Mrs. Lincoln had telegraphed that she was returning to City Point, but her telegram has not been found.)

City Point, Virginia – Monday, April 3, 1865

Last night Tad and I slept aboard the admiral's ship, the Malvern. I discovered that my bunk was about four inches shorter than I am. Today when the admiral inquired how I slept, I told him that "You can't put a long blade in a short scabbard." He agreed! I was up early and started for Grant's headquarters at 8 A.M. A train was made up which took me to Patrick Station, which is located about one mile from Petersburg.

Grant and I ultimately caught up with each other, and we met in a small house in Petersburg for about 90 minutes. He has confirmed that Robert E. Lee has abandoned Petersburg with his army and believes that Jefferson Davis has evacuated his government from Richmond. If that is confirmed, I shall go there tomorrow.

It seems that Jeff Davis and Bobby Lee have given my son Tad a marvelous birthday present. Tomorrow he will be 12 years old. I am writing this diary entry from my cabin aboard the U.S.S. Malvern.

Author's notes:

When President Lincoln returned to the Malvern, he discovered that Admiral Porter had enlarged his cabin and installed a bunk that was twice as wide and a half-foot longer than before. Lincoln suggested to the admiral that overnight he must have "shrunk six inches in length and about a foot sideways!"

City Point and Richmond, Virginia – Tuesday, April 4, 1865

A full and satisfactory day. With Admiral Porter, Tad, Captain Penrose and W.H. Crook, my White House guard, we went ashore from the Malvern in the admiral's gig manned by 12 sailors. We found ourselves about 100 yards from Libby Prison in Richmond, where so many of our men were held captive. We were taken to a large house now occupied by General Godfrey Weitzel. Its last occupant was Jefferson Davis. Tad and I lunched with General Weitzel after inspecting the house and the room from which Davis ran the Confederate government. I sat in his chair, as did Tad.

After lunch we rode around town in an ambulance to see the condition of the Rebel capital. Crowds surrounded us wherever we went. Former slaves were particularly enthusiastic to see me there.

Duff Green visited with me. He was the former editor of The Reformation, a newspaper devoted to free trade, states' rights and Manifest Destiny. Later he published the Pilot in Baltimore. He had harsh words for me and refused to shake my hand when I offered it to him in friendship. Instead he called me a murderer and a tyrant. I listened to him and then condemned him as a traitor to the United States. I ordered him off the Malvern.

I visited briefly with former U.S. Supreme Court Associate Justice John Campbell and agreed to meet with him again tomorrow.

Author's notes:

When seen by several black workmen as he entered Richmond, one cried out, "Bless the Lord, there is the Great Messiah!" The man fell on his knees and sought to kiss Lincoln's feet. Lincoln said to him, "You must kneel to God only and thank Him for the liberty you will hereafter enjoy."

After the Mexican War, Duff Green was engaged in railroad building in Georgia and Alabama and was one of the founders of the New Mexican Railroad Company. He profited greatly from strategic land purchases. As his wealth grew, he donated land for many public projects in Dalton, Georgia. After the Civil War, Green was pardoned by President Andrew Johnson for his support of the Confederacy and paid a $20,000 fine.

Richmond and City Point, Virginia – Wednesday, April 5, 1865

At Army headquarters I met again with former Associate Justice John Campbell, a man who has endeavored to use his energies to facilitate peace between the Union and the Confederate forces as best he has been able. His life story is remarkable. A prodigy, he graduated from the University of Georgia at age 14 and attended the U.S. Military Academy for three years. He read law with an uncle and was admitted to the bar at age 18 by a special act of the Georgia legislature. John was appointed to the court by President Franklin Pierce, and some of the opinions he has written were especially well thought out. I personally admire John. I know he wants military matters in Virginia and the rest of the defeated Confederacy to be quickly resolved as peacefully as possible. He and I both want to see Virginia brought back into the Union as fast as possible.

At 6 P.M. a telegraphic message told that Secretary Seward was thrown from his carriage and was dangerously injured. I am anxious to learn of his condition.

Author's notes:

In March and April of 1861, at the outbreak of the Civil War, Associate Justice John Campbell tried to serve as mediator between those commissioners representing the Confederacy (Martin Crawford, Andre Roman and John Forsyth, Jr.) and the Lincoln administration. After the bombardment of Fort Sumter, Campbell resigned from the U.S. Supreme Court on April 30, 1861, and returned South. He was appointed assistant secretary of war by President Jefferson Davis in October of 1862 and held that position through the end of the war. In early 1865 Campbell, with Alexander H. Stephens and Robert M.T. Hunter, met with President Lincoln at the Hampton Roads Conference in an unsuccessful attempt to negotiate an end to the Civil War. After the fall of Richmond, Campbell was arrested and imprisoned at Fort Pulaski, in Georgia, for six months. He later resumed his law practice in New Orleans, Louisiana. He argued a number of cases before the U.S. Supreme Court, including cases designed to obstruct radical reconstruction in the South. Campbell died in 1889. During World War II the Liberty ship SS John A. Campbell was built in Brunswick, Georgia, in his honor.

Richmond and City Point, Virginia – Thursday, April 6, 1865

Mother and Senator Sumner arrived today having sailed down here on the steamer Monohasset along with Senator Harlan, the marquis de Chambrun and Mrs. Keckley. They left Washington at 11 A.M. yesterday, making good time in fine weather. Mother seems refreshed and in fine form. Her head injury is fully healed. Tad is happy to be with his Mom! They will spend the day and this evening aboard the River Queen.

I notified General Weitzel to give permission to gentlemen who have acted as the Legislature of Virginia, in support of the rebellion, to assemble at Richmond and take measures to withdraw Virginia troops.

I discussed with General Grant the accident of Secretary Seward and of my meeting with Judge Campbell. I have also informed him of my message to General Weitzel authorizing the Virginia legislature to meet for limited purposes. A telegram from Secretary Stanton confirmed that Seward, although seriously injured, is not in danger. The surgeon general sees no cause for alarm. Seward continues to be doing as well as could be expected from the nature of his injuries. His spirits are good.

Army headquarters has reported that Confederate generals Ewell, Kershaw, Burton, Corse, DuBose and C.W. Custis Lee have been captured. At a fight at Sailors Creek we won two guns, 3 flags, a considerable number of prisoners, 70 ambulances with mules and horses, 30 to 50 wagons abandoned. The enemy seems to be collapsing everywhere we meet them.

Author's notes:

Late in the evening the president visited Army headquarters to await the latest news from General Grant in the field.

City Point, Virginia – Friday, April 7, 1865

I forwarded detailed telegrams from Generals Humhreys, Meade and Wright to Secretary Stanton so he may be kept fully up to date on all military matters at the front. After receiving an encouraging message from General Sheridan, who said, "If the thing is pressed, I think Lee will surrender," I advised Grant, "Let the thing be pressed."

Later in the day I reviewed troops who were stationed nearby. I believe I may have shaken a hundred hands or more. Congressmen Washburne and James Blaine came to the River Queen this evening to pay a visit and learn what is transpiring here at the front. Washburn is planning to meet with important congressional leaders upon his return to Washington to acquaint them with what he has seen on his visit here. At the pace our attacks have sustained, Grant anticipates that the enemy's ability to continue fighting should soon cease. I trust he is right and tend to agree with his reasoning. The time is ripe!

Author's notes:

President Lincoln interviewed Assistant Secretary of War Charles A. Dana and remarked that, "Sheridan seemed to be getting Virginia soldiers out of the war faster than this legislature could think."

City Point, Virginia, and en route to Washington – Saturday, April 8, 1865

I met with my good friend Congressman Elihu Washburne on the shore early this morning and gave him a letter to bring to Robert when he is at Army headquarters later today. On the River Queen I showed the marquis de Chambrun and Senator Sumner the seating arrangements for the Hampton Roads Conference, which like so many well-intended meetings came to nothing. Mother and I with companions, then traveled to Petersburg by special train to inspect hospital camps and meet with generals at headquarters on the far side of town. The damage to Petersburg from artillery shelling that we observed has been extensive. The South has paid a terribly high price for insurrection!

As we walked over a recently fought battlefield, the marquis quoted the Duke of Wellington to me. He told me that Wellington wrote in a dispatch from the fields of Waterloo in June of 1815 that, "Nothing except a battle lost can be half so melancholy as a battle won." I agreed with him. The terrible scene of carnage here over many weeks of fighting does tear at the heart. It makes one realize how many young men, on both sides of the contest, were alive just weeks and days ago and are now dead and gone forever.

After dinner and before we embarked, a military band serenaded our party and crew with joyful music, including Dixie, which I personally requested. We will now steam back to Washington starting around 11 P.M. The captain has told me to expect to land in Washington tomorrow at around 6 P.M. if the fair weather holds and the Potomac River behaves itself.

Before retiring after a long day, I read from Shakespeare to our guests. I selected lines from Macbeth. The last lines I read were, "Duncan is in his grave, after life's fitful fever he sleeps well, Treason has done his worst; not steel, nor poison, Malice domestic, foreign levy, nothing can touch him further." At that point Mother burst into tears, Tad clapped loudly, and I deemed it time to end the reading.

Author's notes:

On this day, General Robert E. Lee met with General Ulysses Grant at Appomattox Court House, Virginia, at about 1 P.M., when Grant would accept the surrender of the Army of Northern Virginia.

En route and at the White House – Sunday, April 9, 1865

The voyage was uneventful. Much of the day turned to literary subjects including Shakespeare. I am feeling stronger than before I left. Much was seen and done during the many days spent in Virginia with the Army and Navy. Upon our arrival at sundown we saw that the streets were filled with people. Flags were being waved and crowds were singing and cheering. While we were on board ship, messages had been received in the nation's capital from Grant's headquarters that Lee had surrendered. Bonfires were lit everywhere. I went immediately to Secretary Seward's house to see how he is feeling after being severely injured by a fall from his carriage. The secretary looked battered and bruised but is in good spirits, which were only heightened by news of Lee's surrender. Before retiring I gave brief remarks to a large crowd on the White House lawn.

Author's notes:

The terms of surrender offered to Lee were as generous as Lee could have hoped for. His men would not be imprisoned or prosecuted for treason. Officers were allowed to keep their sidearms, horses and personal baggage. Grant allowed the defeated men to take home their horses and mules to carry out the spring planting and provided Lee with a supply of food rations for his starving army. The terms of surrender were completed around 4 P.M., April 9, 1865, in the McLean House. On April 10, Lee gave his farewell address to his army. The Confederate forces then marched out in a formal ceremony of surrender of their arms and colors. Brigadier General Joshua L. Chamberlain was the Union officer selected to lead the ceremony. Chamberlain saluted the surrendered army. The veterans in blue gave a soldierly salute to the vanquished heroes of the South. About 28,000 Confederate soldiers passed by and stacked their arms. The surrendered soldiers were paroled. General Joseph E. Johnston's army in North Carolina surrendered to General Sherman in Durham, North Carolina on April 26, 1865. Jefferson Davis met with his Confederate Cabinet for the last time on May 5, 1865, in Washington, Georgia, and officially dissolved the Confederate government. Davis and his wife, Varina Davis, along with their escort, were captured by Union forces on May 10 at Irwinville, Georgia.

Commander James Iredell Waddell of the CSS Shenandoah, a commerce raider, surrendered his vessel to the British government on November 6, 1865. Confederate General John Brown Gordon cherished Chamberlain's simple act of saluting his surrendered army, calling Chamberlain "one of the knightliest soldiers of the Federal Army." The Federal government issued a commemorative stamp in 1965 that read, "Civil War Centennial APPOMATTOX With Malice Toward None…" 1865 – 1965 to celebrate the surrender at Appomattox Court House, Virginia.

The White House – Monday, April 10, 1865

My good friend Noah Brooks came by for breakfast this morning. He is a remarkable news writer who know how to keep a confidence. He reminded me that we first met in 1856 when he was in Illinois working on John Fremont's first Republican campaign for president. He is a close friend of mine and of Mother, who finds him full of news whenever they meet and talk. When he was in Chicago covering the 1864 Democratic Convention, he kept me posted on events there.

I went to the Navy Yard and made a short but sweet speech, thanking all who work there for their important contributions to the war effort. The Cabinet met and all were in a victorious mood. We agreed that it can only be a matter of days when the remaining Rebel forces surrender and disband. Mother asked that I have my photograph taken, so Tad and I went to the studio of Alexander and James Gardner. Outside the studio a crowd gathered to cheer us. Washington is in a celebratory attitude today. Yes, we have much to be happy about. When historians write of this war, I am sure many will question how it could have ever happened. Many will also wonder why it took so very long to bring to and end. I place the blame solely upon the South. It started the struggle and of that there is no doubt in my mind. It could have ended it at any time but refused to do so.

At 5 P.M. a large crowd gathered at the White House with bands playing to celebrate Lee's surrender and Grant's victory. I made some brief remarks and enjoyed it when the band played Yankee Doodle and Dixie at my request. Later a delegation of 15 gentlemen from the Senate and House of Representatives came by at 6 P.M. to present me with a large photograph of me in a handsome silver frame.

After dinner I dropped a note to War Secretary Stanton thanking him for his prodigious efforts to achieve victory. At Tad's request I asked him to send some captured enemy flags, which Tad will treasure. I also asked Navy Secretary Welles to send Tad a captured Navy sword.

Author's notes:

Lincoln told the crowd, "I have always thought Dixie one of the best tunes I have ever heard. Our adversaries over the way attempted to appropriate it, but I insisted yesterday that we fairly captured it. (Applause). I presented the question to the Attorney General, and he gave it as his legal opinion that it is our lawful prize. (Laughter and applause. I now request the band to favor me with its performance." After the performance, howitzer cannons belched forth their thunder and the people cheered. The president then asked the crowd to give three cheers for General Grant and all under his command. He then asked for three cheers for our gallant Navy.

The White House – Tuesday, April 11, 1865

Noah Brooks interviewed me briefly this morning before I left to attend a Cabinet meeting. He asked me questions about the reconstruction of the South, and I told him that it is my goal that unity and reconstruction must be our first order of business, right after we have begun to reduce the size and expenses of the military and naval forces. Meanwhile, we have certain Rebel armies in the field that need to formally surrender to Federal forces, and that effort is now underway. Noah was with me tonight when I gave a speech from the White House.

The Cabinet meeting considered the subject of cotton and the need to allow the South's cotton to again be traded here and internationally. It is the South's main source of revenue, and the South is badly in need of cash. European mills are also in dire need of American cotton.

I spoke to General Butler about the many vexing problems related to freed Negroes. Many are destitute and are sorely in need of food, clothing and employment. He has been asked to work with Secretary Stanton and staff members in the War Department to come up with plans for immediate relief where possible.

In the evening I addressed a large and rather boisterous crowd from open windows at the North Portico. Mother and Tad were at one while I spoke from the other. Noah held a candle as I read my words. My general theme was the imminent status of the Southern states and my plans for restoring them to their traditional places in the Union as quickly as possible. I want to see unity and not retribution.

Author's notes:

Noah Brooks, (October 25, 1830 to August 16, 1903) was born in Castine, Maine. He was a journalist, author and editor. He wrote "Washington in Lincoln's Time" and also wrote for the Sacramento Daily Union from Washington, D.C. during the war. He authored the first book exclusively about baseball, "Our Base Ball Club and How It Won the Championship" (New York: E.P. Dutton, 1884). 258 Washington dispatches for the Sacramento newspaper were published under his pen name, "Castine." In 1901 Brooks published "The Story of the Lewis and Clark Expedition." During his lifetime, Brooks wrote for newspapers in Sacramento, San Francisco, Newark and New York City.

The White House – Wednesday, April 12, 1865

I met at breakfast with my friend Orville Browning and W.J. Bibb, a prominent Unionist from Montgomery, Alabama. I agreed to issue passes to Bibb so that he and his family may quickly and safely return to their home. I spoke at length with the marquis de Chambrun about our re-united nation's problems and stressed that I view clemency as the principal policy of our government. I asked him to communicate my views to the French emperor. I also requested that he inform the French leader that I personally appreciate the fact that during our conflict his government remained neutral as regards the North and South. It is my hope that French policy vis-à-vis Mexico will soon honor the Monroe Doctrine as it has in past. I reiterated that our government cannot consider the rule in Mexico of Emperor Maximillian to be legitimate. The United States government believes that Mexico is a democracy and not a kingdom.

I advised General Weitzel that on this coming Sunday I have taken no official position on the matter of prayers in Richmond churches to be ordered for either Jefferson Davis or for me. My belief has always been that we need to maintain a strict separation between Church and State. Let people pray as they wish with no suggestion coming from me on the matter. However, any prayers that are said for me would be greatly appreciated. I need all that I can get.

I issued a pass last night for Ward Hill Lamon and friend with ordinary baggage to pass from Washington to Richmond and return. Lamon has done a fine job protecting me and my family since the day we arrived here. He will be in Richmond for only a few days and then return to the White House with a report on conditions he finds in the captured Rebel capital. Now that the longed-for peace is at hand, I anticipate that my old and trusted friend will return to the practice of law in Illinois.

Author's notes:

Ward Hill Lamon was not in Washington on the night Lincoln was assassinated. Before he left for Richmond, he implored the president not to go out at night after he was gone, particularly to the theater. After the assassination, Lamon accompanied the funeral procession to Springfield, Illinois. He authored "The Life of Abraham Lincoln from his birth to his Inauguration as President." He practiced law until 1879. His home in Danville, Virginia, is a museum. He was born January 6, 1828 and died May 7, 1893.

The White House – Thursday, April 13, 1865

I was at the telegraph office early this morning and thanked operator Charles Tinker for his steadfast devotion to duty throughout the conflict. He has not only great skills at the keys, but has a fine sense of humor, an attribute to be highly prized in times of stress and strain. One of our most important weapons of war has been the telegraph. I did not fully realize its value early in the war, but I have become dependent upon its many services over the years. We have had significant advantage over the South in telegraphic messaging and in railroad expansion. The industrial power of the North was one of the key factors in achieving victory.

General Grant and Secretary Stanton met with me to review many military matters. Navy Secretary Welles joined us to talk about the re-establishment of federal authority in the defeated states. Later I rode horseback to the Soldiers' Home accompanied by an escort of six cavalrymen and assistant secretary of the Treasury, Maunsell B. Field, who came out by carriage. I issued passes to Field allowing him to visit Mobile, Alabama, and Richmond, Virginia. Field and I have spoken recently of our future relations with France. He represented the United States as president of the Board of U.S. Commissioners to the French Universal Exposition before the war and was made a knight of the Legion of Honor by the late Emperor, Napoleon III.

Author's notes:

Maunsell Bradhurst Field was born in New York City on March 26, 1822, and died in the same city, after a lingering illness, on January 24, 1875. He graduated from Yale College in 1841 and studied law in New York and Connecticut. He served as secretary of the U.S. Legation at Paris in 1848 and later served in the U.S. mission to Spain. He joined the Lincoln administration as deputy sub-treasurer of the U.S. in New York City and in 1863 was appointed assistant secretary of the Treasury in Washington, which office he resigned June 15, 1865, on failure of his health. He then was appointed collector of internal revenue for the 6th District of New York, which position he held until 1870, when he resumed the practice of law. In December 1873, Governor John Adams Dix appointed him judge of the 2nd District Court in New York City. He was present when Lincoln died after being shot. Field wrote in a letter to The New York Times, "There was no apparent suffering, no convulsive action, not rattling of the throat...only a mere cessation of breathing...I had never seen upon the president's face an expression more genial and pleasing."

This was Lincoln's last diary entry. He was assassinated the next evening at Ford's Theatre at 13 minutes past 10 P.M. by John Wilkes Booth while watching a performance of "Our American Cousin" featuring Laura Keene. He had been accompanied to the theater by Mary Lincoln, Clara Harris and Major Henry R. Rathbone.

On April 14, surgeons maintained constant observation of the president. About 2 A.M. on April 15 the vice president paid a call to the house of William Petersen, where the president had been placed on a small bed in a small room at the rear on the ground floor. The president stopped breathing at 7:21 and 55 seconds on the morning of April 15th, and at 7:22 A.M. his pulse ceased to beat. Silence followed, and then the voice of Secretary of War Stanton said, "Now he belongs to the ages."

Epilogue

Volume IV is the final book in the series: The Secret War Diaries of Abraham Lincoln – Including His Recurring Dreams. Volume I begins on November 9, 1860 and ends December 30, 1861. Volume II begins on January 1, 1862 and ends on December 31, 1862. Volume III begins on January 1, 1863 and ends on December 31, 1863. Volume IV continues the narrative from January 1, 1864 until April 13, 1865, the evening when Lincoln penned his last thoughts.

The books are a work of "faction" – part fact and part fiction. Abraham Lincoln died intestate and never kept a diary, so I decided five years ago to write one for him. I have endeavored to put down on paper what he might have written based upon the events of the time. Almost every military and naval engagement has been referenced. I have also included some of his dreams. He was a melancholy man who used humor to deal with the difficult times in which he lived. He literally never took a day off, working seven days a week, including holidays. The Cabinet met constantly. To my mind he is American's greatest president, except perhaps for Washington, whose life Lincoln greatly admired from when he was a boy.

Autographed copies of all volumes are available at the Country Bookshop, 140 N.W. Broad Street, Southern Pines, North Carolina 28387.

Copies may also be ordered from Amazon.com and Kindle.

Paul R. Dunn, Author, 125 Lake Shore Drive, Pinehurst, North Carolina 28374

www.abrahamlincolndiary.com

paulandbj@nc.rr.com

DATE DUE

DISCARDED

PRINTED IN U.S.A.

GIVEN MEMORIAL LIBRARY
150 Cherokee Rd PO Box 159
Pinehurst, NC 28370
910-295-6022